# The Graphic Art of Federico Barocci

## SELECTED DRAWINGS AND PRINTS

EDMUND P. PILLSBURY

LOUISE S. RICHARDS

The exhibition and this catalogue
have been aided by a grant
from the National Endowment for the Arts,
a Federal Agency.
The exhibition in Cleveland is also supported
by a grant from the Ohio Arts Council.

THE CLEVELAND MUSEUM OF ART    February 15–March 26, 1978

YALE UNIVERSITY ART GALLERY    April 11–June 4, 1978

FRONT COVER ILLUSTRATION
Federico Barocci,
*Flowering Bush above an Eroded Bank,*
black chalk, brown wash,
heightened with white and pink.
(Cat. 33)

# Contents

Copyright (C) 1978
by the Yale University Art Gallery.
All rights reserved.

Library of Congress Catalogue Card Number: 77-94097

International Standard Book Number:
ISBN 0-89467-004-2

# Preface

Federico Barocci (ca. 1535-1612) was one of the most important Italian painters of the second half of the 16th century, but his work has only recently come under serious scholarly scrutiny. Although the state of our knowledge of Barocci was greatly enhanced by major exhibitions of his work in Florence and Bologna in 1975, those exhibitions did not include any drawings from American collections and also left open numerous questions about Barocci's working method and the sources and development of his style. The present exhibition includes all known Barocci drawings in America; the drawings borrowed from European museums and private collections have been carefully selected because of their relation to drawings owned in America or because of their crucial importance to the understanding of how Barocci worked or developed his major compositions.

The research for this catalogue grew out of Edmund Pillsbury's work on Barocci drawings and was the subject of a graduate seminar Dr. Pillsbury gave at Yale in 1973-74. Graduate students assisted in the selection of drawings and in the preliminary research. The section on Barocci's prints, the first serious analysis of the artist's achievements as a printmaker, was written by Louise Richards of the Cleveland Museum of Art. Thus, the exhibition and the accompanying catalogue are a collaborative effort of our two institutions in every respect. We are grateful to the two authors for making this — the first exhibition of Barocci's work ever to take place in the United States — a major contribution to the study of 16th-century Italian art.

This publication was seen through press by Greer Allen of the Yale Printing Service. Pierson College Press undergraduates assisted in its layout. The burden of arranging for the shipping and insurance of the exhibition was shared by our two registrars, Nan Ross of the Yale Art Gallery and Delbert Gutridge of Cleveland. Mary Ann Nelson of the Yale Art Gallery took care of much of the lengthy correspondence. Like so many other exhibitions in the United States in recent years, this one was supported by a generous grant from the National Endowment for the Arts, a federal agency.

Alan Shestack, Director
*Yale University Art Gallery*

Sherman E. Lee, Director
*Cleveland Museum of Art*

# Foreword

Although Federico Barocci (ca. 1535–1612) may have enjoyed a greater popularity and exerted a more profound influence on the art of his time than any other artist of the second half of the sixteenth century in Italy—his patrons included the Pope, Emperor, King of Spain, and Grand Duke of Tuscany and his admirers, Cigoli and Annibale Carracci, Rubens and Guido Reni—his work has never achieved the widespread recognition and acclaim accorded that of some of his contemporaries, like Tintoretto and El Greco. Several factors have contributed to the demise of his reputation. One has been the relative inaccessibility and scarcity of his painted works, the bulk of which were done on commission for specific locations in remote parts of Italy where they have remained to this day, and the type of painting he produced, which was almost exclusively devoted to religious subjects, except for a few portraits and one secular painting executed expressly for the collection of Emperor Rudolf II of Prague (*Aeneas' Flight from Troy*). Barocci's easel paintings were likewise very few in number, and not a single autograph example of the artist's painted work has ever reached this continent; the *Fischieri Portrait* in Washington and pair of *Prince Ubaldo Portraits* in Detroit being the work of studio assistants rather than of the master. Scholarship on the work of the artist has also failed to keep pace with that undertaken and completed over the last thirty years on the artists working in the preceding and succeeding generations. Pontormo, Andrea del Sarto, and even Taddeo Zuccaro on the one hand and Annibale Carracci, Guercino, and Pier Francesco Mola on the other are better known to us today as painters than Federico Barocci. While the comprehensive exhibition of the artist's work held in Bologna and Florence in 1975, and their accompanying publications, have done much to redress this situation, awakening a new popular as well as scholarly interest in the artist, several aspects of the artist's work require further study. Documentary evidence is lacking on several of the important commissions. In addition, the artist's large (nearly 2000), and beautiful, oeuvre of drawings has neither been catalogued systematically nor discussed critically in terms of function, technique, and history; since the documents for such a study are available and since Barocci's drawings not only occupy a significant place in sixteenth-century draughtsmanship, with their pivotal position between Raphael, Titian, and Correggio, but they also shed light on the creative process in general and the development of individual compositions in particular, such a task is long overdue. A third area of Barocci's work which has been left virtually unexplored, except for one or two incomplete studies on his technique and an occasional mention in surveys of the prints of the period, is the artist's contribution to the development of etching in the sixteenth and seventeenth centuries.

The aim of the present exhibition has been twofold: to suggest avenues and methods for possible further research in several of the abovementioned areas and to introduce this important, but still relatively little known, artist to the American museum public. For this purpose an extensive selection of paintings and drawings was both impractical and unnecessary. Instead an attempt has been made to gather together all the drawings ascribed to the artist in American collections, supplemented by a small group of loans from various private, and a few public, sources in Europe; for obvious reasons nothing was requested from the large repositories of Barocci's drawings in Berlin, Florence, Paris, and Vienna, which were already heavily taxed in 1975.

The first criterion in the selection of drawings was to exhibit little-known, overlooked, or problematic works. The Bologna exhibition failed to include the newly discovered, and very significant, pen modello in Stuttgart for the artist's first documented painting, the *Ecstasy of Saint Cecilia*, which is a critical document for the understanding of Barocci's training and development as an artist (Cat. 1). Conversely, drawings like the chalk sketch for the *Madonna della Gatta* (Cat. 58) were included because they raised questions of authenticity or identification which required discussion. Although it was regrettable to have to request the loans of certain well-known examples of Barocci's drawing which had already been seen in Bologna—in particular, the *Two Trees* and doublesided *Visitation* sketch in the Lugt Collection and the modello for the *Madonna del Popolo* from

Chatsworth—their inclusion not only gives the exhibition greater representation and scope but also provided the opportunity to reconsider a number of important questions which these works raise. In the case of the *Madonna del Popolo* drawing (Cat. 35) it was possible to establish the work's correct place in the sequence of preparatory studies by drawing attention to a hitherto unnoted pentimento (or correction) pasted to one corner. The exhibition has also brought to light a number of unpublished works: among them an important figure study for the Perugia *Deposition* (Cat. 20), compositional models for the *St. Vitalis, Entombment,* and *Presentation* altarpieces (Cats. 45, 40, 67), a pastel study for the *Visitation* (Cat. 52), and an oil study for the Allendale *Noli me tangere* (Cat. 44). Finally, the exhibition has afforded the opportunity to suggest new identifications for certain works, for example the pen sketch for the Casino of Pius IV decorations in Chatsworth (Cat. 6) and the donkey study for the *Madonna della Gatta* in a Swiss private collection (Cat. 59).

There are many paintings by Barocci for which less than complete documentation has survived. While both Olsen and Emiliani have been content to rely upon the abundant amount of information discovered by Gronau and a group of local historians working during the first quarter of the century, valuable archival material still can be found in quite predictable places. One example of this is the *ricordo* of the commission of the Louvre *Circumcision* found, in the sacristy of the church in Pesaro for which the painting was done, soon after the Bologna exhibition opened (see Cat. 57). Another is the contract and two unpublished letters—one by Barocci himself—for the *Madonna del Popolo* which we publish here. Overlooked by Gualandi when he selected his anthology of artists' letters in the nineteenth century, these documents were readily available in the archive of the commissioning body, the Fraternità dei Laici in Arezzo, and help to answer various questions about the commission (see Cat. 35).

We are also not the first to include an annotated edition of Bellori's seventeenth-century biography of the artist in an exhibition catalogue devoted to the artist's drawings. The same was done by Giovanni Poggi for the catalogue introduction to the large exhibition of Barocci's drawings and cartoons held in the Uffizi in 1912–1913. Since Bellori's biography is a fundamental source of information about the artist's paintings and his use of drawings, having it available when one is viewing the artist's preparatory studies is of particular value. In addition, Bellori's *Vita* has so much to say about Barocci's character and how he expressed himself in his paintings that the text serves as a natural introduction to the subject. Our translation, the first ever in English, will, we hope, make the biography more widely read and appreciated by students of the period.

Finally, we have placed special emphasis, in both the catalogue and exhibition, upon Barocci's role as a printmaker. Although Barocci produced only four prints, he approached the medium with the same degree of inventiveness and originality as he had shown in painting and drawing. In the catalogue we attempt to establish the correct chronology and development of the prints in terms of Barocci's own work and in terms of the history of sixteenth and seventeenth century printmaking. Unlike the Bologna exhibition, the selection includes impressions of the highest quality, and in one case more than one impression is shown in order to demonstrate the changes made by the printer in the inking and wiping of the plate to compensate for technical flaws in the print. A few prints after Barocci's works by the most important and influential contemporary printmakers, Cort and Agostino Carracci, provide an idea of the quality and character of reproductive printmaking at the time.

An exhibition of this kind would not have been possible without the cooperation and support of many individuals and institutions. The organizers are particularly indebted to those European owners of Barocci's works who consented to lend drawings and prints to the exhibition despite the risks of overseas shipment. We also wish to acknowledge the help that we have received, in numerous scholarly as well as practical ways, from the following individuals: J. Q. van Regteren Altena; Keith Andrews; Jacob Bean; Egbert Haverkamp Begemann; Suzanne Boorsch; James Burke; Hans Calmann; H. Carroll Cassill; Jean Kubota Cassill; Geraldine Cohen; Cara D. Denison; John Gere; Walter Gibson; Antony Griffiths; Carlos van

Hasselt; Harold Joachim; Ursula Korneitchouk; Trude Krautheimer; Suzanne Folds McCullagh; Edward Olszewski; Armide Oppé; Hannelore Osborne; Ann Percy; Vincent Price; Elio Rambaldi; Vidal R. Rivera; Elizabeth Roth; Charles Ryskamp; Eckhard Schaar; Frederick G. Schab; Ellen Sharp; John Shearman; Esther Sparks; Felice Stampfle; Mary Cazort Taylor; Christel Thiem; Gunther Thiem; Richard West; Christopher White; and Thomas Wragg. In the early stages of the planning of the exhibition Lora Palladino, an advanced graduate student in the Art History program at Yale, gave valuable assistance in the selection and cataloguing of works and in the preparation of the Bellori translation for printing. The translation was subsequently edited and revised under the direction of Professor Alfonso Procaccini of the Italian Department of Yale University and Mrs. Emily Procaccini. Dr. Gino Corti of Florence generously contributed his expertise to the task of correcting and editing the transcriptions of the *Madonna del Popolo* documents. And the following individuals were indispensable for their help in preparing and editing the final manuscript of the catalogue: Sally W. Goodfellow; Lawrene Groobert; and Josephine Poda. To all of these persons as well as the directors and staffs of the Cleveland Museum of Art and Yale University Art Gallery, we owe our sincere thanks.

E.P.P. *and* L.S.R.

# The Creative Process

*I know that some persons will ridicule these studies and efforts as useless and superfluous, but there are even others who will mock their ignorance, vainly persuading themselves that they can create a fine composition with a simple sketch or with a couple of strokes of the chalk on the canvas. This explains why in so many paintings one sees not only no well-ordered scenes, but not even a beautiful drapery fold, a good outline, a fine head, or a natural and real gesture. For the most part, such preliminary studies were carried out by all the great masters, who were never satisfied with only a caricature of the right color and contour.* [1]

With these words of approbation Giovanni Pietro Bellori, the seventeenth-century champion of Poussin and the classicizing school of painting established in Rome by Annibale Carracci and Domenichino, concluded his long biography of the Marchigian painter of the sixteenth century, Federico Barocci. These words not only serve to justify the inclusion of the older Barocci in the select group of twelve younger artists discussed in Bellori's *Vite* published in 1672—which was made up of architects and sculptors as well as painters, and foreigners like Poussin and Rubens as well as native Italians—but also explain Bellori's general characterization of the artist as a diligent and serious craftsman whose working methods elevated his art, morally as well as aesthetically, above that of those, like Cavaliere d'Arpino, who practiced in the so-called *maniera* style or those who followed the example of Caravaggio's tenebrist realism.

In his discourse on the *Idea del pittore* of 1664 and again in his *Vite* of 1672, Bellori expounded the classicistic theory of painting which became the cornerstone of the academic theories of the eighteenth and nineteenth centuries. [2] This theory consisted essentially of an empirical idealism compatible with the method of study and with the

classical tradition of the High Renaissance. According to Bellori, nature as we see it is imperfect, and the artist formulates his ideal of superior beauty by selecting the best parts of what he sees and transforming them with his imagination. In Bellori's opinion the perfect combination of art and nature was to be found in the remains of Classical art and in the paintings of Raphael and his contemporaries. The writer exhorted artists to study the works of the High Renaissance painters, especially Raphael and Titian, and the works of Antique sculpture, not as models to imitate literally but as masters to follow in order to discover the essence, or idea, of perfect beauty. In selecting the artists for his *Vite*, therefore, Bellori made no attempt to chronicle the period as writers like Vasari and Baglione had tried to do before him, but followed a criterion of choice based upon excellence and importance measured against Raphael and the Antique.

Barocci's art possessed several qualities that commended themselves to Bellori. First and foremost, his art was based upon an arduous method of preparation employing protracted study from nature. Secondly, his work formed itself not only upon observation of nature but a thorough knowledge of High Renaissance and Antique art: Bellori relates that as a youth the artist copied plaster casts and reliefs of Classical art under the guidance of his first teacher, Battista Franco, and that he made the obligatory trip to Rome where he copied the works of Raphael, Michelangelo, and Polidoro, and at other times studied the works of Titian and Correggio. Thirdly, Barocci's art possessed the rare quality of decorum: that is to say the gestures and actions of the figures in his paintings expressed the most elevated human emotions and evoked an appropriate response from the viewer; for example, his religious subjects inspired feelings of piety and devotion. And finally, Bellori praised Barocci for excelling in the difficult task of creating draperies which were both beautiful in their own right and corresponded to the movements of the figures. In sum, Barocci's paintings achieved what Bellori called (in reference to the *Perdono*) "reasoned artistry" ("ragionevole artificio"), which neither imitated the appearance of nature, the alleged shortcoming of the naturalists (the followers of Caravaggio, the

---

1. *Sò che alcuni si burleranno di questi studi, e diligenze, come inutili, e super-flue, ma altri ancora deriderà la loro ignoranza, persuadendosi essa vanamente di formare un componimento con uno schizzo ò con trè colpi di gesso sù la tela. Questa ambitione è causa che non si vegga, non dirò bene ordinate historie ma ne meno una bella piega, un bel dintorno ò una bella testa, e ne meno un moto vivo, e naturale. Con simili studij, chi più chi meno, hanno caminato li gran maestri, senza insuperbirsi d'una caricatura di colore, e di contorno; . . .* (Bellori, 1672, pp. 240–241).
2. See K. Donahue, "Bellori, Giovanni Pietro," in: *Dizionario biografico degli italiani*, VII, 1965, pp. 781–789, which provides an excellent summary of Bellori's life and theoretical writing.

Bambocianti, and others), nor indulged in imaginary fantasy, the supposed fault of the mannerist and high baroque artists.

While Bellori deserves credit for recognizing Barocci's role as a forerunner of aspects of seventeenth-century art, his account of the artist's life betrays a critical bias which not only misrepresents but in some cases even distorts the artist's temperament and career to suit the writer's classicizing theories of art. According to Bellori, there were several distinct stages in Barocci's creative process, each one of which led logically and rationally to the next, until the artist was ready to paint the final work. If we try to chart these stages described by Bellori, however, we soon discover that the writer's knowledge of the artist's drawings was limited and that his intention was to demonstrate similarities of approach and method between Barocci and certain artists of the High Renaissance rather than to see his art as an individual response to particular problems of representation and interpretation. One apparent example of Bellori's bias—and one that continues to confound students of the period—is the analogy which he draws between the working method of Barocci and that of Correggio. Bellori maintains that Barocci emulated Correggio in both theory and means of conception and that he actually adopted the use of pastels—artificially produced colored chalks—after studying examples of the Lombard artist's drawings. Although one cannot deny the influence of Correggio on certain works by the younger artist, the relationship between the actual working procedures of the two artists is difficult to establish, especially since the "pastel" drawings by Correggio to which Bellori refers have failed to come to light and, for that matter, may never have existed.

An examination of the various assumptions made by Bellori in regard to Barocci's working method not only brings into focus the seventeenth-century writer's critical position vis-à-vis Barocci's art but also dispels some of the more common misunderstandings that have arisen about the function, and even authenticity, of his large (nearly 2000) oeuvre of drawings.

The first, and most general, observation which Bellori makes about Barocci's procedure is that he always worked from life, ". . . not allowing himself to paint even a small part without first having observed it."[3] From this statement writers have tended to believe that almost everything the artist ever drew, save a few compositional studies and cartoons, should be classified as life studies. It is indeed true that the artist made numerous sketches and studies from life to establish the poses of individual figures and to refine the draperies and particular parts of the figures—he left 800 such drawings in his studio at his death—but it is also a fact that a great many of the studies the artist executed did not depend upon an observed model but derive from an internal process of copying, transfer, and elaboration independent of observation; squaring and incising were the artist's favored means of transfer. The artist was also quite content to re-use a figure or motif, without making any preparatory drawings, if the design permitted. Barocci also copied the work of other artists on occasion rather than use a life study. For example, he began his studies for the heroic figure of Saint Sebastian in the Genoa *Crucifixion* by making a *ricordo* of a figure in the famous *Laöcoon* sculpture group (see Cat. 62) and executed a drapery study for the figure of Christ in the *Perdono* over the traced contours of a copy taken from Raphael's *Mercury* in the Villa Farnesina loggia.[4]

Bellori also suggests that Barocci developed his multi-figured compositions by making *garzone*-studies—that is to say life studies of groups of figures. In this case Bellori would seem to be imposing upon Barocci a common practice of Raphael rather than describing a procedure regularly employed by the painter. Barocci often sketched more than one figure on a single sheet but rarely made drawings from nude models posed according to a preconceived plan of the composition, which was Raphael's habit. In the case of Barocci his nude studies are invariably of individual figures, and his compositional studies are of two kinds: purely imaginary pen or chalk sketches done in the early planning, which are referred to in a seventeenth-century document as *scarpigni*,[5] and

---

3. *Egli operando ricorreva sempre al naturale, nè permetteva un minimo segno, senza vederlo; . . .* (Bellori, 1672, p. 239).
4. Uffizi 11374F, repr. Olsen 1962, fig. 38b.
5. In a letter dated 27 October 1658 Giovanni Battista Staccoli, one of Cardinal Leopoldo de' Medici's agents in Urbino, describes a collection of Barocci drawings belonging to Padre Giovanni Antonio Vagnarelli, former brother-in-law of the artist's nephew, which included the following: *Un libro di carte sedici, nel quale vi sono varij dissegni, e schizzi, o scarpigni, come soleva dire il Barocci* (see Baldinucci-Barocchi, VI, pp. 77–78).

more developed compositional studies, such as the *disegno compito*, from which the artist developed the full-scale cartoon.

Bellori would also have us believe that the artist concerned himself with the matter of lighting and color only at an advanced stage in the development of the composition. He states that Barocci, after executing his first sketches and life studies, undertook a small cartoon in oil or gouache, in chiaroscuro, to work out the lighting in the composition. This, in turn, he says, was followed by another small cartoon in which he experimented with the tones of each color he planned to use in the painting to achieve balance and harmony in the modeling. In actuality Barocci concerned himself with local color, lighting, and even texture, as early as his first life studies. In fact, one of the most reliable yardsticks to use in establishing the relationship of any particular sketch or life study with an individual painting is the correspondence of the lighting, an element of the painting that was usually fixed in the early stages and remained relatively constant throughout the development of the composition. As Marilyn Lavin has demonstrated, the artist's choice of medium and support in his drawings often reflected the coloristic and lighting effects he sought to create in the final painting.[6] The natural blue paper or beige-tinted paper used in his life studies serves as a middle tone between the highlights and shadows, the light and dark chalks, shortening the tonal range and unifying the lighting. This ground color in his studies may also be compared with the gray and brownish priming of the final painting, on which the artist sketched the design in chiaroscuro tones of black and yellow. Likewise, the artist was extremely disciplined and careful in his use of local colors in his drawings, limiting himself to the precise effects he sought in the final work: for example light-pink pastels served for the flesh tones, a yellowish ochre for the hair, and red chalk for the eyelids, ridge of the nose, ears, and other critical facial features—all applied over a soft black outline and lit with white chalk and smoothed and blended with the stump to create the proper texture and continuity of surface. The artist even studied certain individual figures and heads in oil (Cats. 43, 44, and 53) and on more than one occasion corrected an aspect of a painting by doing a separate study in oil on a piece of paper which was then applied to the surface of the final painting.[7] In this way the entire preparation and execution became one single, continuous process, and it is impossible to think of the artist studying the sculptural masses of the composition apart from the pictorial problems of light and color. In fact, no more than one of the so-called *cartoncini per i colori* described by Bellori can be identified with any degree of certainty—the bozzetto for the Senigallia *Entombment* in Urbino[8]—which suggests that the artist may have found it necessary to make an independent modello to study the colors only in the cases of certain works. Although there are more surviving chiaroscuro studies, or *cartoncini per i lumi*—the best known of which are the ones for the *Madonna of the Rosary* in Oxford and for the *Last Supper* in the Uffizi—these drawings appear to have been done at a stage in the creative process earlier than Bellori believed and in all likelihood before the bulk of the large pastel head and other detail life studies.

By the same token Bellori creates the impression that all of Barocci's life studies and preliminary sketches found their final resolution and statement in the full-scale cartoon. An examination of Barocci's surviving cartoons in relation to the other studies and finished paintings suggests, however, that the cartoons preceded rather than followed the bulk of large-scale life studies and that the artist made numerous changes after the cartoon. This is documented particularly well in the case of *Aeneas' Flight from Troy* where the artist revised the entire background after executing the full-scale cartoon in the Louvre and considered making other changes in the composition as well (see Cat. 54). If one examines closely the artist's finished paintings, one invariably encounters changes in the design between the incised outlines of the cartoon and the finished design of the painting—changes that were not merely made *alla prima* as

6. M. Aronberg Lavin, "Colour Study in Barocci's Drawing," *Burlington Magazine*, LXLVIII, 1956, pp. 435–439.

7. Barocci did this for the head of the female donor in the *Madonna di S. Simone* and for the head of St. Francis in the *Perdono*.
8. Repr. Emiliani, 1975, fig. 117. For Barocci's use of color *bozzetti* see Pillsbury, *M.D.*, 1976, pp. 58–59.

the artist was painting, but changes that were carefully thought out in separate chalk studies.[9]

Like all great artists of his period—from Raphael to Tintoretto—Barocci's approach to drawing was flexible and inventive, and his working methods evolved as he developed and as he faced new and more challenging artistic problems. While it is tempting to codify or lay down a system to explain all his procedures, such an endeavor requires making assumptions which, like those of Bellori, run the risk of reflecting the views of the writer rather than illuminating real aspects of the artist's creative approach. This catalogue by no means pretends to offer a final explanation or definition of Barocci's various drawings. That, it would seem, is impossible. It does attempt to present a small group of works, done in various media and at various times in the artist's career, from the point of view of the position they occupy in the overall sequence of preparatory drawings and from the point of view of their aesthetic function in relation to the final work. In undertaking this task, however, one is aware of certain hazards. And a recent remark made in regard to the study of Raphael's drawings applies equally to that of Barocci's: "The creative [mind] does not aspire to the same virtues as the historical—that is to say, reconstructive—mind, and the latter usually operates most erroneously, and most ahistorically, when it fails to observe the distinction."[10]

With this caveat the reader is invited to explore the intricate fabric of the artist's creative process as revealed in the selection of works that follows.

9. An example of this is the painting of the *Calling of Saint Andrew* where the hands of the kneeling Andrew are re-arranged between the incised cartoon and the finished version of the painting.
10. J. Shearman, *Raphael's Cartoons in the Collection of Her Majesty the Queen and the Tapestries for the Sistine Chapel,* London, 1972, p. 107.

Ascribed to Jean-Baptiste Corneille, *Frontispiece for Biography of Barocci*, engraving.
(Published in G.P. Bellori, *Le vite de' pittori, scultori, et architetti moderni*, Rome, 1672)

TRANSLATION OF

# Giovanni Pietro Bellori's

## *Life of*

## *BAROCCI*

*(Le vite de' pittori, scultori ed architetti moderni, scritte da Gio: Pietro Bellori, parte prima,*
Rome, 1672, pp. 169–196).

Ascribed to Pierre Simon, *Portrait of Federico Barocci*, engraving.
(Published in G.P. Bellori, *Le vite de' pittori, scultori, et architetti moderni*, Rome, 1672)

STVDIO·VIGILANTI

Ascribed to Jean-Baptiste Corneille, *Allegory of Study*, engraving.
(Published in G.P. Bellori, *Le vite de' pittori, scultori, et architetti moderni*, Rome, 1672)

Federico di Montefeltro, Duke of Urbino, who was renowned in his time for his studies of peace and arms, erected, among his other remarkable achievements, a most magnificent palace on the rugged terrain of Urbino which was considered the most beautiful that had ever been built. Not only did he embellish it with furnishings and ornaments, but he also decorated it with antique statues, both of marble and of bronze, and with outstanding paintings, and at great expense assembled a large number of very fine and rare books, which contained everything that dealt with the use of the body and of the spirit. For the purpose of the construction of the palace the Duke brought to Urbino various craftsmen and a great number of artists of different professions, among whom the Milanese sculptor, Ambrogio Barocci, who stayed for a long time and married a respected native of Urbino.

Ambrogio, founder of the Barocci family in Urbino, was the great-grandfather of the distinguished painter Federico, of whom we now propose to write, basing our account on the recollections of his life gathered by

Signor Pompilio Bruni, who most kindly presented them to me and who, being a maker of mathematical instruments, carries on both the school and the reputation of the Barocci in Urbino. Ambrogio lived in prosperity enjoying the esteem of Prince Federico, and left a son called Marcantonio, who pursued a legal career and with great pride dedicated himself to his country and state. To him were born Ambrogio, who took the name of his grandfather, and Giovanni Alberto, who, by good fortune, gave birth to an illustrious progeny of venerated artisans.

To Giovanni Alberto were born Giovanni Battista and Giovanni Maria Barocci who became clockmakers and practiced their profession proudly. Giovanni Battista reached the level of Cavaliere and Giovanni Maria became the most celebrated clockmaker that had hitherto practiced the trade. Among other aspects of his creative genius, Giovanni was the first to demonstrate how the planets move and how the sun and moon act and interact under the sign of the zodiac. With the same creative turn of mind

he made a clock for Pope Pius V which in its time was considered a great novelty and can still be seen in the Vatican palace.

Likewise from Ambrogio there descended two other accomplished men of talent. One was Simone Barocci, who is still considered the best modern maker of mathematical instruments. He learned his trade under the famous Federico Comandino from Urbino who restored the preeminence of the mathematical sciences. [Simone] made compasses, T-squares, astrolabes, and other instruments which earned him such a reputation that his name and his works became known everywhere, and his homeland was enriched by a fine workshop which still exists in Urbino. The other son of Ambrogio was our Federico Barocci, born in 1528 in Urbino.[1] His father, who worked in sculpture and in relief models, seals, and astrolabes, taught him the principles of draw-

1. Modern scholars have disputed Bellori's dating of the artist's birth and have suggested, on the basis of a notice in the Duke's Diary, that he was born ca. 1535. For a summary of opinions and evidence see Olsen, 1962, p. 20 n.2.

ing, an art to which he applied himself with so much enthusiasm and with such extraordinary ability that Francesco Mensocchi [or Menzocchi] from Forli, who was in Urbino to deliver his painting of the *Deposition of Christ* to the Confraternity of S. Croce, was so impressed with the youth that he encouraged him to become a painter.[2]

In fact, Federico's decision to do so earned the approval of his uncle, Bartolomeo Genga, architect of Duke Guidobaldo, who had him placed with Battista [Franco] Venetiano, who had been called by Guidobaldo to paint the vault of the choir of the Arcivescovato.[3] Being a scholar of antique statues, Franco continually made Federico practice the drawing of plaster casts and reliefs, a study to which [the young man] gave himself with affection and dedication; so much so, in fact, that at night he would forget to sleep and his mother would often find him awake in his room with a lantern burning until dawn, as often happens to those who take the greatest pleasure in learning. When Battista left Urbino, Federico moved to Pesaro to the house of Genga, who made it possible for him to study the paintings by Titian and other great masters in the Gallery of Duke Guidobaldo.[4] During that time Genga taught Federico geometry, architecture, and perspective, disciplines in which he became skilled.

At the age of twenty, stimulated by the desire for fame and by the name of his countryman, Raphael, Federico resolved to go to Rome where his father recommended him to a certain Pierleone, a painter from Acqualagna recently returned to Urbino, who

for some time kept him as his assistant in painting gilt stamped leather and in other humble tasks.[5] But meeting his uncle one day by accident in Rome, who was the Maestro di Casa of Cardinal Giulio della Rovere, he was received and brought to the attention of the Cardinal for whom he did a portrait and other paintings which were highly appreciated.[6]

He copied the works of Raphael alongside other youths who customarily competed there, but Federico was so modest and retiring because of a certain natural bashfulness that he kept to himself, without saying a word to anyone. It is worth mentioning the story that he himself tells about the time when he was drawing in the loggia of the Chigi [Sala di Psiche frescoes by Raphael and his school in the Villa Farnesina]. Giovanni da Udine happened by, who, recently returned to Rome,[7] and being very much interested in the students of his master Raphael, examined the drawings and encouraged the youths with helpful instructions. When he stopped to watch Federico and praised his style and proficiency, he inquired of his origins and background. As soon as he heard that Federico was from Urbino, and moved by the memory of his master, he embraced and kissed him, praising God to have found a young artist in whom the glory of Urbino would be revived. This scene was observed by everyone and thus Federico came to be regarded with respect by his comrades.

However, this same place was frequented by two young foreigners who came to draw, wearing clothes of rank and bringing with

them an attendant to sharpen pencils, so that everyone honored them and stepped aside to allow them space. Federico, new in Rome, and believing these two could sketch beautifully, did not dare to approach them to see their drawings. Nevertheless, drawn to them by his curiosity, he advanced little by little to where he could lay eyes on the paper and was shocked by their lack of ability. He reminded the two young artists that luxuries can be an impediment to one who desires to get ahead and that the pleasure of learning overcomes all discomfort and hardship.

Barocci used to tell the story about the time Michelangelo rode by on his small mule, as was his custom, while he and Taddeo Zuccaro were drawing from a façade by Polidoro.[8] Whereas the other young artists ran to meet Michelangelo and show him their drawings, out of timidity Federico stood still and did not step forward. As a result Taddeo grabbed his sheet out of his hand and took it to Michelangelo, who carefully inspected Barocci's drawings, among which was a copy of the master's *Moses*. Praising the copy, Michelangelo wanted to meet the artist and encourage him to continue the studies he had begun.

Barocci later returned to Urbino and spent several years there. His first work is believed to be the painting of *Saint Margaret* in the Confraternity of Corpus Domini in the same city. He depicted the saint in prison, holding a cross in her hand, stepping on the serpent, and looking up at the sky which opens between two angels.[9] His early works are still in the Cathedral: the *Martyrdom of Saint*

2. Menzocchi painted the *Deposition* for the high altar of the Oratorio of the Fraternità di S. Croce in Urbino in 1543–44 (see E. Calzini, "Francesco Menzocchi e le sue opere," *Rassegna bibliografica dell'arte italiana*, 1901, pp. 93–94).

3. For Battista Franco's work in the Marches see: W. Rearick, "Battista Franco and the Grimani Chapel," *Saggi e memorie di storia dell'arte*, II, 1959, pp. 105–139; A. Parronchi, "Una pala d'altare di Girolamo Genga," *Studi urbinati di storia, filosophia e letteratura*, Urbino, 1968, ser. B., no. 2, pp. 209ff; and L. Salomoni, "Battista Franco nelle Marche," *Arte Veneta*, XXVI, 1972, pp. 237–245.

4. For the specific paintings by Titian, Sebastiano del Piombo, Raphael, and the Bassani which Barocci saw, see J. Dennistoun, *Memoirs of the Dukes of Urbino*, III, London, 1851, pp. 440–450 and Gronau, 1936, pp. 61–81. Barocci's copy of the head and shoulders of St. Agatha in Sebastiano del Piombo's *Martyrdom of St. Agatha* now in the Pitti Gallery, located on the verso of Uffizi 11346F, may have been done during the artist's stay in Pesaro. Likewise, sketches on the verso of British Museum Pp. 3–201, which has figure sketches for the *Martyrdom of St. Sebastian* of 1557–60, derive from Sebastiano's painting; this fact suggests that the artist's stay in Pesaro may have taken place in the late 1550s.

5. This artist is likely to have been Pierleone di Giulio Genga who worked with Barocci at the Casino of Pius IV in 1561–63 (Friedländer, 1912, p. 131) and who later accompanied Federico Zuccaro to Spain (Bertolotti, *Artisti urbinati in Roma*, Urbino, 1881, p. 19).

6. Although neither the portrait nor any of the other works which Barocci executed for Giulio della Rovere (1533–78) has come to light, the Cardinal's coat-of-arms has been recently identified on a sketch in the Uffizi (907E verso) for a ceiling decoration (for which see G. Smith, 1977, p. 69).

7. Giovanni da Udine is recorded in Rome in March 1550, March 1552, and December 1555 (or earlier). He returned with Cosimo I de' Medici in 1560. Several copies made by Barocci from Raphael's Farnesina frescoes survive. They include Uffizi 11367F recto and verso (with Mercury and the head and shoulders of Galatea), Urbania, Biblioteca Communale no. I, 275 verso (with lower half of the putto with Neptune's trident and the foot of Mercury), Cambridge, Fitzwilliam Museum no. PD 70–1948 verso (with an angel in the *Galatea* fresco), and Uffizi 11374F (with a drapery study for Christ in the *Perdono* executed over a traced copy of the Mercury). In addition, Barocci sketched a few of the seated apostles and saints in the *Disputà* in Uffizi 11520F verso and made a colored

chalk drawing after the so-called head of Archimede in the *School of Athens* in the Ambrosiana Library in Milan (no. F.290, Inf. no. 6; see K. Oberhuber, *Raffaello: Il cartone per la Scuola di Atene*, Milan, 1972, p. 13 n. 17).

8. Taddeo Zuccaro left Rome in 1551 to complete the decoration of the choir of the Urbino Cathedral. He subsequently accompanied the Duke of Urbino to Verona, returning to Rome in the spring of 1553 to begin work at the Villa Giulia and on the Mattei Chapel. John Shearman, 1976, p. 52, has correctly identified the kneeling figures on Uffizi 11368F verso (repr. Bertelà, 1975, fig. 3), a drawing with architectural sketches for the Casino of Pius IV, as a copy from Polidoro's Palazzo Milesi frieze.

9. Untraced. This painting hung on an altar on the left side of the nave in the Church of the Corpus Domini. Elsewhere in the church were Joos van Gent's *Institution of the Eucharist* of 1473–74 and Titian's *gonfalone* of the *Resurrection* and *Last Supper* of 1542–44, all now in the Galleria Nazionale delle Marche. A final payment to the artist made on January 1, 1556, establishes a *terminus ante quem* for the execution (for which see E. Scatassa, "Chiesa del Corpus Domini in Urbino," *Reportorium für Kunstwissenschaft*, XXV, 1902, pp. 438–446).

*Sebastian,* and *Saint Cecilia* with other saints, inspired by Raphael.[10] During that period there arrived in Urbino a painter who was returning from Parma with some large sheets ["pezzi di cartoni"] and some exquisite heads drawn in colored chalks ["pastelli"] by Correggio, which Federico admired for the beautiful *maniera* which conformed perfectly to his own temperament; thereafter, he began to draw with colored chalks ["pastelli"] from life. These drawings by Correggio and others by Federico can be seen in Rome in the study of Signor Francesco Bene, a gentleman from Urbino.[11] Barocci profited from the excellent style of Correggio, and imitated it in the gentle expressions of his heads, and in the blending of his tones ["sfumazione"] and the gentleness ["soavita"] of the color.

Returning to Rome again in 1560, Barocci visited Federico Zuccaro, who was engaged in painting the friezes in the apartments [of Pius IV in the Vatican] commissioned on the occasion of Duke Cosimo de' Medici's visit. After they greeted one another, Zuccaro handed Barocci the paint brushes and put him to work. At first he declined modestly, but being pressed, Barocci painted two putti by blending the colors so well that they appeared to be done in oil rather than in fresco. Nonetheless, to Zuccaro Barocci's style seemed to have been too toned down ["troppo sfumato"]. Consequently, he took up the brush in Barocci's presence and proceeded to outline the contours and strengthen the colors, which apparently was all that was needed to perfect the work. Barocci watched this, and was not affected by it but instead gave thanks to his friend for having sincerely advised him in this way without malice.[12]

After 1561, the palazzetto of the woods of the Belvedere designed by Pirro Ligorio was being painted by order of Pope Pius IV, and Barocci was selected with Federico Zuccaro and others to take part in the project. In this building, in the four corners of one room, Barocci painted seated *Virtues,* each holding

a shield bearing the name of the Pontifex, and he also painted a frieze with small putti. In the middle of the vault he depicted the *Virgin with the Christ Child* in which the Child extends his hand playfully towards the young Saint John to present him with the reed cross. Also shown there are Saint Joseph and Saint Elizabeth.[13] In the vault of an adjacent room Federico represented the angel of the *Annunciation* descending to the Virgin, figures that are smaller yet skillfully executed. Subsequently Barocci began the story of *Moses speaking with God the Father* in a room in the [Vatican] Belvedere [now Museo Etrusco], but he was forced to abandon it before it was finished because of an unfortunate mishap that burdened him from that day forward and compelled him to drop the project.

It is believed that the misdeed occurred as the result of the perversity of a few painters, who, incited by jealousy, invited him to a light meal and poisoned his salad. Whatever actually happened, what is certain is the fact that at that moment he succumbed to such an incurable disease that not only could no remedies be found, but even the cures ordered by Cardinal della Rovere from the best doctors were all in vain.[14] After various medications proved ineffectual, the physicians finally advised the artist to return home to the mildness of his native climate. Even this hope proved in vain; before the acute pain subsided, four years transpired during which the artist suffered without ever being able to touch a brush. Lamenting above all the fact that he could not paint, one day he prayed to the heavenly Virgin with such conviction that he was heard.

Feeling an improvement in his health, he made a small painting with the Virgin and Christ Child who blesses the young Saint John [*Madonna di San Giovanni,* Galleria Nazionale, Urbino] and presented it as a votive offering to the Capuchin fathers of Crocicchia, two miles outside of Urbino, where he often would stay on a farm of his. Because of the departure of the friars, the

painting is now conserved in the convent [of the Capuchins] in the city.

Barocci was continuously bothered by his illness, which allowed him about two hours a day to practice his art. During this respite he painted a picture for the church of San Francesco of the Virgin holding the Christ Child. She is crowned by the angel and flanked on one side by Saint Thaddeus and on the other by Saint Simon; the patrons of the chapel are at her feet [*Madonna di San Simone,* Galleria Nazionale, Urbino]. Two gentlemen from Perugia happened to come to Urbino in the company of a painter who took so much pleasure in the finished picture, and praised it so much that the men resolved to bring Barocci back to their homeland. Not much time passed before they called him to Perugia, where he himself agreed to go and paint that work which renders him glorious among painters of great fame.

## *DEPOSITION FROM THE CROSS*[15]

Barocci painted for the Cathedral of San Lorenzo [in Perugia] the *Deposition of Christ* from the cross, which is an ordered composition full of figures, all of which are in movement and involved in action. Christ's body hangs suspended from one arm attached to the cross, with the other arm and the feet now loose; Saint John receives him by the feet; and behind on the ladder Joseph of Arimathea leans on the cross and lowers his hand behind Christ and supports his drooping shoulder in a sheet. In so doing, Joseph waits and watches with great concern Nicodemus on the other side, who is also behind the cross and above on a ladder. Nicodemus holds with one arm the wood of the cross and with the other hand grasps a hammer to unnail Christ's right hand. In front, on another ladder beside Christ, a young man holds up Christ's body in the sheet with one hand at his back and the other under the thigh. Seen with his head turned away, this figure reveals the strength

---

10. Both paintings are still in the Duomo. The contract for the *Martyrdom of St. Sebastian* signed on November 9, 1557, by Barocci's father with the heirs of Antonio de Bonaventura called for the artist to execute an altarpiece for the Chapel of St. Sebastian for the fair value established by a group of experts when the work was done, which was not to exceed 100 florins (for the text of the contract see A. Lazzari, *Memorie di alcuni celebri pittori d'Urbino,* Urbino, 1800, pp. 39–40, or Olsen, 1955, pp. 109–110).

11. Nothing is known of the drawings by Correggio and Barocci owned by Francesco Bene, nor are there any surviving examples of Correggio's use of pastels (A. E. Popham, *Correggio's Drawings,* London, 1957, p. 4).

12. Friedländer, *Burlington Magazine,* CVI, 1964, p.

187, has noted that this incident underlines the difference between the linear maniera style practiced by Federico Zuccaro and his followers and the more painterly, and advanced, approach of Barocci which sought a "baroque" union of the color scheme as well as uniplanar composition on the basis of crossing diagonals and three-dimensionality not only of the figures but also of space.

13. Barocci was responsible for the overall design of the decorations in the first room as well as the execution of six of the eight *Virtues* in the corners (all but *Justice* and *Immortality*), the *Holy Family,* the figures flanking the *Baptism,* the two putti over the Pope's arms at one end, and a portion of the frieze.

14. Bellori adopted the idea that Barocci was poisoned

from Borghini (1584, pp. 138–139) and Baglione (1642, p. 133) and described the symptoms of the illness in detail later in the biography. On the basis of Bellori's account, Jørgen Kringelbach has suggested that Barocci suffered from a chronic gastric or peptic ulcer (*ulcus ventriculi*), a condition described in M. Baillie, *The Morbid Anatomy of Some of the Most Important Parts of the Human Body,* London, 1793, p. 87. I owe this information to Professor Graham Smith (1973, p. 91 n. 16).

15. On 22 Nov. 1567 the Nobile Collegio della Mercanzia in Perugia sent Captain Raniero Consoli to Urbino to bring Barocci to the city to paint the altarpiece for the Chapel of St. Bernardino in the Cathedral. A contract was signed the following year and the finished work installed Dec. 24, 1569. Barocci received 325 scudi plus food and wine. The painting is *in situ.*

of all his members in supporting the greater weight of the dead body, arching his chest, tensing a knee, and exposing his legs to mid-thigh; his tunic and chlamys are swept into the air and his hair is lifted by the wind. Besides these convincing movements, this figure also casts a shadow over the chest of Christ, and in leaning backwards lets the rest of Christ's body come forward into the light. Opposite him a servant descends from the ladder of Joseph, and while descending looks below, with part of his shoulder and arm exposed. Resting his hand on the ladder, the servant bears the crown of thorns, and places the pliers on his arm, having just unnailed the right [sic: actually the left]hand of Christ.

All these figures are intent on their work and inspired in their actions, but the figure of Christ, which is the principal one and located in the middle, demonstrates in the limpness of every member the languor and weight of a body which has no life to sustain it. While the right arm hangs from the cross above, the other arm falls with the shoulder, and the head droops to rest on the shoulder. The chest is doubled over, the stomach is curved in shadow, and the legs and lifeless thighs are projected forward. The flesh, the veins, the nerves, and surrounding areas are still, without life. The whole face is dead, the dark hair falling behind the forehead, the eyes closed, and the lips slightly parted from having taken the last breath.

Among the emotions expressed by the other figures, John demonstrates his grief by weeping as he raises his face in profile toward Christ and holds onto the pierced feet. Behind him Saint Bernardino, deeply moved, throws open his arms as though desiring to provide support for the divine limbs. But beneath at the foot of the cross take place the lamentations and grief of the Maries, the figures in the foreground who bend to aid the stunned and fallen Virgin. Two move toward the Virgin with their arms open while another supports her from behind with her arm under the fallen head. This latter figure, in supporting the Virgin in this way from behind, kneels on the ground and bends forward with tearful eyes, wondering at the pale, cold face of the stricken Virgin. Such displays of emotion are accompanied by the exquisite appearances of the heads, and each figure is executed with well-defined contours which harmonize with the vigorous ensemble and soft coloring; Barocci merits every praise also for the excellent way in which he has handled the draperies and made the folds correspond to the movements of the figures, an aspect of painting which has come to be considered one of the most difficult parts.

Barocci remained in Perugia for three years under the benevolence and good care of those gentlemen, leaving there a finished work which has increased his reputation among foreigners. After returning to Urbino, he sent an autograph *Nativity* about four *piedi* high [ca. 140 cm.] to Signor Simonetto Anastagi as a gift in recognition of their friendship. [16] Barocci painted for the church of San Francesco in the same city the picture on the high altar which is also a work rendered in a perfect style. It represents Christ giving his consent to Saint Francis to pardon [''il perdono''] those who visit the Chiesa degli Angeli in Assisi.

## IL PERDONO DI SAN FRANCESCO D'ASSISI [17]

Barocci represented the interior of the church and in the middle Saint Francis in adoration. The saint kneels on a large marble stairs in the foreground and displays the internal fire of his celestial love. With opened arms he raises his face and spirit; and in looking at the Virgin above, he turns his head slightly in profile as he lifts up his face. The heavens glow above: in the middle is Christ, flanked by the Virgin and Saint Nicholas, and a glimmering light is diffused throughout the resplendent little clouds of cherubims. The Virgin kneels with her arms opened in the act of communicating the saint's request to Christ; her right hand is raised in prayer toward her Son, the left points downward toward the saint to denote her intercession on his behalf. The view of the Virgin is in profile; her blue mantle hangs down from her head and arms to her breast.

In the middle of the composition is the risen Christ in majesty, with luminous rays all around him. His entire figure, seen frontally, stands out against a large field and sphere of light, and he bends his right arm forward in the act of blessing and granting pardon [''perdono''] at the intercession of the Virgin and of the saint. On the other side his left hand is opened and his arm is covered with a red mantle, which, together with the tunic, is filled out by the wind, and which unfolds in a flourish from the left

shoulder behind the right hand. And the whole figure is supported by three cherubims, with one foot lightly placed on the middle cherubim and the other suspended in the air, so that the bottom of the feet can be seen from below, as if to show that Christ is supported by his own divinity. On the other side of Christ one sees Saint Nicholas in his episcopal dress kneeling on the clouds and looking at a book which he holds in one hand and upon which are the three golden balls, while in the other hand he holds his pastoral staff; below is the saint's mitre.

One must be careful not to disregard the ability of this painter without considering the smallest details of his creations which he continually changed for the sake of reproducing the exact imitation and rendering its natural quality. [18] The saint kneels on a marble stairway rising to the upper level with two additional small steps between two balustrades, over which material is draped here and there, while on one side there are two candles and a bell. He includes in the middle of the background a small chapel; and since the view is oblique, one can see through the open door only half of the altar, with half of a painted Crucifixion, the standing Virgin, and a lighted candle on the side. Barocci then took the opportunity to include a light passing through an open iron door in the dark wall, reverberating in a dazzling fashion on a column outside. In the middle is Saint Francis, lighted directly from above. His head is set off against the darkness of the wall, and his whole figure projects forward out of the dim light of the church. And although the light falls down upon the saint from above, Christ is not illuminated by his own glorious radiance but by natural daylight; with reasoned artistry Barocci took this license in order to give relief to the figures above, and thus be able to employ the shadows properly in the completely illuminated space.

Barocci finished this picture in the convent and worked on it for more than seven years, as much because of the attention he gave to it as because of the hindrance of his illness which slowed the work. [19] The artist himself showed his approval of the painting by issu-

16. This work is identifiable as the version of the *Rest on the Return from Egypt* (oil on canvas, 133 x 110 cm.) which Barocci sent to Perugia in 1573, with an accompanying letter of October 2nd, and which is now in the Pinacoteca Vaticana.

17. The painting, *in situ* on the high altar of S. Francesco in Urbino, was ordered from Nicolò Ventura, who died 5 Sept. 1574, and completed by June 2, 1576, when the artist reported to the rectors of the Misericordia in Arezzo that he was free to devote himself exclusively to the completion of the *Madonna del Popolo*.

18. In the case of the *Perdono*, the artist adjusted the

head of St. Francis many times before painting it on a separate piece of paper which he then pasted to the canvas.

19. If Barocci worked on the *Perdono* over a period of seven years, he would have received the commission in 1569 when still in Perugia finishing the *Deposition*. While there is no evidence to rule out this possibility, it would seem more likely that the commission dates from 1574, in all likelihood from a bequest of the donor who died in September of that year, and that Bellori thought the artist completed the work as late as 1581, the year in which the artist issued his own print of the composition.

ing the beautiful print on paper etched by his own hand and published in 1581. As a consequence of the rightful acclaim that the painting received, the friars who had only given him 100 scudi of gold, for which he was content because of their poverty, procured for him donations of another 100 scudi.

Thereafter Barocci executed the painting of the Misericordia for the Pieve in Arezzo [*Madonna del Popolo*, Uffizi] representing Christ seated on a cloud blessing through the prayers of the Virgin those who perform the seven acts of *Misericordia*. Many figures are depicted; among the poor who receive alms is a blind man who manages to look very realistic playing a viola with an iron bar.[20]

In order to see the works of the masters in Tuscany, and wishing to entertain himself, Barocci took this painting himself to Arezzo.[21] Having reached Florence, and being so inclined, he arranged to see the Palazzo [Vecchio] and the Gallery [Uffizi] of the Grand Duke. Ruling at that time was Grand Duke Prince Francesco [de' Medici], a most cultured person and lover of the fine arts, who, learning of the merit of Barocci and of the painting brought to Arezzo, conceived of doing something becoming his gentility, namely of disguising himself as an unknown person in order to talk and discuss freely with Barocci and to solicit his frank opinions about painting. On the assigned day Barocci went to the palace and after the Grand Duke introduced himself as an unknown, the artist was led, instead of to the Guardaroba, through the rooms, and was shown paintings and statues so that the Prince could learn which works the artist held in greatest esteem. The Prince behaved towards him in this way quite some time,

and it was only when, exiting from a room he was presented with a document ["memoriale"], that Barocci recognized the Grand Duke and wished to leave immediately. He was most kindly restrained by the Prince who took him by the hand and wished to continue talking with him on the same familiar basis as before. The Grand Duke embraced him and because he greatly appreciated his knowledge and modesty, he offered the artist favorable conditions to stay at his court. But Barocci expressed his unwillingness and spoke of the necessity of living in his native land. He then thanked the Prince and took leave for Urbino.

Barocci next put his hand to the painting of the *Deposition of Christ* for the monument of the Confraternity of S. Croce in Senigallia [*in situ*], depicting in it the Savior carried off to the sepulcher in a sheet.[22] The two figures holding him, one at the head, the other underneath, are joined by Saint John, who holds the sheet at the feet of Christ, and expresses the strain and the severity of the weight. As he moves and turns forward, he bends back his chest and arms and his hair is blown by the wind. Since the sacred body of Christ is carried in this manner, the upper part unfolds in a pitiful fatal languor, the cheek rests against the shoulder, the hair falls, and the divine eyes close almost as if in placid sleep. Behind St. John appears the Virgin who is held by one of the Maries while the other wipes her tears with a veil that she holds to her eyes with both of her hands. On the opposite side the kneeling Magdalene manifests her grief through her dishevelled hair and closed hands held up towards Christ. Behind her a figure bends over at the base of a cliff to clean the sepulcher, while in the distance one sees Calvary with some small figures who carry away the ladders of the cross. This work, be-

cause it came to be constantly copied for its beauty, was almost destroyed through the audacity of someone, who in polishing it, penetrated the color and contours and damaged the whole thing. It remained that way for several years until, at the request of the Duke of Urbino, Barocci took it back to his house; he took out of his study original sketches for the work and, in the last years of his life, repainted it.[23]

In the same city of Senigallia can also be seen the painting by Barocci of Saint Hyacinth who kneels to receive the scapular from the Virgin in glory with the Christ Child in her lap.[24] For the Olivetan church of San Vitale in Ravenna Barocci made the painting of the *Martyrdom of Saint Vitalis* [now Brera, Milan] in which the figure of the martyr who is being thrown into a well is seen foreshortened.[25] Behind the saint is the figure of the magistrate shown in the act of having given Vitalis the push, while up above the angel descends with the crown and a palm. There are other figures who, like the magistrate, are intent on the spectacle. Among them is the amusing scene of a young girl who feeds a magpie with a cherry held in her hand, and while her mother turns her away to look at the saint, the magpie opens its mouth, fluttering its wings. One cannot describe the grace with which Barocci adapted similar charming touches to his works from time to time; on this occasion, for example, the artist used the cherry to designate the Spring, since the martyrdom of Vitalis is celebrated on the 28th of April.

In the pontificate of Gregory XIII the church of Santa Maria in Vallicella of the Oratorians [the Chiesa Nuova, Rome] was built. Because of the fervor of their founder, Saint Filippo Neri, who desired that sacred

---

20. The artist agreed to paint the picture for 400 scudi in a contract signed in Arezzo on June 18, 1575 (reprinted below) and installed the finished work in the Fraternity of the Misericordia's Chapel in the Pieve in Arezzo in June, 1579. In 1786 Grand Duke Pietro Leopoldo purchased the principal panel for the Uffizi collection. The tondo of *God the Father* which decorated the space above the main painting remained in Arezzo and is now exhibited in the Pinacoteca Communale.

21. Barocci accompanied the *Madonna del Popolo* to Arezzo not only as a means of reaching Tuscany but also to fulfill his obligation under the contract to insure the painting's safe transport from Urbino (see below).

22. After initially requesting 600 scudi, the artist agreed on July 2, 1579, to furnish the painting within two years for 300 scudi. The artist finished the painting in late April or early May of 1582, after being granted a request for an extension of his deadline.

23. According to documents published by Vecchioni ("La Chiesa della Croce e Sagramento in Senigallia e la 'Deposizione' di Federico Barocci," *Rassegna marchigiana*,

V, 1926–27, pp. 497–503), the incident occurred in 1587. As a result, the brothers of the Confraternity instituted a ban on visitors climbing on the altar, and to protect the canvas from rodents, they covered the back with a metal shield. Damage apparently continued to deteriorate the condition of the painting, however, and the artist agreed to restore the painting in Urbino when the church was enlarged in the early seventeenth century. The painting was shipped to Urbino in 1606 and was returned in the spring of 1608. Barocci himself restored the painting, no doubt with the aid of the half-cartoon in The Hague and the oil *bozzetto* in the Galleria Nazionale, Urbino, as well as the artist's other compositional and individual figure studies in his studio, and received 150 scudi in payment.

24. Bellori refers here to the painting of the *Madonna del Rosario* which the artist contracted to paint for the high altar of the Confraternità dell'Assunta e del Rosario in Senigallia for 500 scudi in September 1588 and delivered after 1592, in all probability sometime between 1596 and 1599 when Antonio Viviani finished painting the frame. This painting, now in the Palazzo Vescovile in Senigallia,

shows the Virgin lowering the rosary to St. Dominic, who holds out a scapular, rather than St. Hyacinth. Bellori's confusion of the saints may reflect his knowledge of the composition through drawings rather than through the original. A compositional sketch in the Albertina in Vienna, which may be an early idea for the *Madonna del Rosario* rather than a study for an independent commission, represents the Virgin delivering her girdle to a kneeling saint who similarly holds a scapular and who may represent St. Thomas or St. Hyacinth (repr. Olsen, 1962, pl. 106a).

25. Barocci signed the contract on June 20, 1580, after having submitted a drawing of the proposed subject and finished the painting in the spring of 1583, the year he inscribed on the canvas. He received 640 gold ducats in payment. The painting remained in its original location on the high altar of the church of S. Vitale in Ravenna throughout the seventeenth century. In the eighteenth century it was moved into the sacristy and later was removed by Napoleon to France. It reached the Brera in 1811.

images be painted by excellent artists, Barocci received the commission for the painting of the altar of the *Visitation* [*in situ*].[26] He represented Saint Elizabeth at the top of the stairs outside her house embracing and shaking hands with the Virgin while Saint Zacharias comes out to meet her, and while Saint Joseph at the foot of the stairway, holding a small donkey by the reins, places his bags on the ground. Behind the Virgin is a young woman beginning to climb the stairs. She lifts her garment with one hand and holds a basket of chickens with the other. She is truly a very beautiful figure, carrying around her neck a straw hat to denote the summer month of July. It is said that Saint Filippo Neri was so pleased with this painting that he went to this chapel for his devout contemplations.[27] It is certain that Barocci had a special genius for painting sacred pictures. He indeed deserves to be commended, especially if one considers how rare it is to find paintings in churches which have the decorum and the sanctity necessary to incite devotion.

Meanwhile Barocci finished for the city of Pesaro a most worthy work: the painting of the *Calling of Saint Andrew* for the Confraternity of Sant'Andrea [Musée Royal des Beaux-Arts, Brussels].[28] He represented Christ on the beach beside the sea extending his hand to Saint Andrew, who, bending one knee to the ground and spreading his arms, demonstrates his desire to follow the divine voice. Meanwhile, behind them, a young man beaches the boat with an oar, while Saint Peter disembarks and puts one foot into the waves, eager likewise to go without delay to Christ. Barocci painted this picture on the order of the Duchess of Urbino who wrote to him about it in 1580, and

the payment was 200 gold scudi. Upon its completion, after 1584, the Duke liked it so much that he requested it from the brothers of the school and sent it as a gift to Philip II, King of Spain, since Saint Andrew was the protector of the Knights of the Order of the Golden Fleece. Today this painting is housed in the Escorial among the many other religious pictures by the early masters.[29] An *Annunciation* similar to the other in Loreto is also still preserved there, which, as we will note later, was given by the same Duke to King Philip.[30] Barocci painted a second version of the *Saint Andrew* for the abovementioned Confraternity in Pesaro,[31] and in the church of San Francesco there is also another painting by Barocci, the *Beata Michelina* [now Vatican Pinacoteca], tertiary of the Franciscan sisters, shown kneeling on Mount Calvary with her arms apart, rapt in contemplation of Christ's death.[32] Her pilgrim's staff and hat rest on the ground while her cape flutters in the wind on the hill beyond which can be seen the city of Jerusalem.

Duke Francesco Maria, a devotee of the Most Holy Annunciation, dedicated a chapel to it in the church of Loreto. The painting was executed by Barocci.

*THE ANNUNCIATION* [Vatican Pinacoteca][33]

The Virgin is momentarily transfixed, kneeling with her eyes lowered. She opens her right hand with modest wonder, placing her other hand with the book on the small table. In the foreground the Angel bends on one knee and places his left hand with the lily on the other knee. Extending his right

hand gently toward the Virgin, the Angel reverently announces the divine mystery. Barocci shows the most beautiful, sweet appearance of the Virgin and Angel, one facing out, the other in profile. One exudes complete modesty and virginal humility, with her eyes lowered and her hair simply gathered over the forehead. And without exceeding decorum, her sky blue mantle falls from her arm over the prie-dieu to the floor. The Angel in its beautiful profile is heavenly, its golden hair falling over its forehead and over the neck; not only in its contours and stance does it demonstrate itself to be agile and light, but also the color itself reveals its spiritual nature, tempered subtly in the yellow shirt and in the iridescent red tunic with the pale-blue wings, almost rainbow blue. The design of such a noble work can be seen engraved in an etching by Barocci, through which one can recall the beauty of the original painting. The Duke of Urbino was greatly satisfied with Barocci's work and rewarded him generously. Being a most virtuous and worthy prince, and in his time the honor of Italy, he attracted to his court the most famous men in every discipline. Among these he never failed to acknowledge Barocci as the principal figure in his region; the Prince showed great affection for him and often visited Barocci in his studio.[34]

In the Chiesa dei Cappuccini of Mondavia there is another *Annunciation* by Barocci, in which he added a Saint Francis reading a book,[35] and another one in Fossombrone in the church of the same fathers, the painting of the *Virgin on a Cloud with Saint John the Baptist and Saint Francis* kneeling below, partly colored in gouaches.[36] Afterwards Barocci carried out the painting of the *Cir-*

---

26. As early as 1582 the Oratorian Fathers of the Chiesa Nuova applied to Duke Francesco Maria II della Rovere for assistance in obtaining an altarpiece from Barocci; they also provided a "memoriale" showing what they wanted. On June 19, 1583, Barocci accepted the commission. The finished painting was sent to Rome in the late spring of 1586, where it was immediately admired by both artists and laymen.

27. Barocci's work had a strong appeal to the reformer and founder of the Oratorians, Filippo Neri (1515–95); consequently the Church Fathers elected him to execute several paintings in the church including the *Presentation, Incoronation,* and *Nativity of the Virgin* for the left and right nave and high altar respectively, only the first of which he completed (in 1603). Barocci's association with the Oratorians and their founder is further documented by two portrait studies of Neri, executed in colored chalks from death masks, which are preserved in Windsor Castle (no. 5228, Popham-Wilde no. 93) and in the Museo de Bellas Artes, Caracas (repr. Wm. Schab Gallery, New York, cat. no. 55, 1974, no. 13, in color). I wish to thank Professor Chandler Kirwin for assistance in identifying these drawings as portraits of Neri.

28. Signed and dated 1583. The painting was removed from Pesaro by the French in 1797 and deposited in Brussels in 1802.

29. From documents published by Gronau (1936, p. 160 and *passim*), we know that Bellori's account is in error in regard to the *Calling of St. Andrew.* The painting sent to the King of Spain, which is still in the Escorial, is a replica of the one delivered to Pesaro and was executed between 1584 and 1588.

30. This painting, which is now untraced, was a replica of the painting in the Vatican Pinacoteca. It was sent to the King in 1589.

31. See n. 29 above.

32. According to an eighteenth-century notice discovered by Krommes (1911, p. 128) in the Biblioteca Oliveriana in Pesaro, this painting was commissioned in 1606 from Alessandro Barignani to decorate the Chapel of Bd. Michelina Malatesta in S. Francesco in Pesaro. The artist received 150 scudi.

33. The Duke paid Barocci 150 scudi in three installments beginning in 1582 and ending in 1584. The picture was brought to Rome in the eighteenth century and replaced by a copy in mosaic.

34. This statement is supported from entries in the diary of the Duke which record various visits to the artist's studio: 17 Sept. 1597—"Andai a veder le pitture del Barocio in casa sua"; 11 Sept. 1598—"Andai a vedere le pitture del Barroccio"; 12 Sept. 1602—"Fui a vedere le

pitture del Barroccio in casa sua" (A. Alippi, "Documenti," *Rassegna bibliografica dell'arte italiana,* XII, 1909, pp. 70–73).

35. The original is untraced. The appearance of the composition is recorded in a small workshop copy formerly in the Esterhazy Collection and now in the Museum of Fine Arts in Budapest (no. 472, oil on canvas, 87 x 65 cm.).

36. Executed for the Capuchin church of Monte Abbato in Fossombrone in the mid-1560s, this painting came to Milan in 1806 where it was initially housed in the Brera and later lent to a church in Lentate sul Seveso. In 1913 di Pietro (fig. 90) published a sketch of it. This sketch and the developed compositional study in the British Museum (no. 1873–12–13–1937) provide the best evidence of the appearance of the work, whose present whereabouts are unknown.

37. Signed and dated 1590. From a *ricordo* recently discovered in a cupboard of the sacristy of the original church of the Nome di Gesù in Pesaro (published by Floriano de Santi in *Brescia Oggi,* 8 Nov. 1975), we know that the artist contracted to paint the picture for 550 scudi on Oct. 2, 1583. The painting was brought to France in 1797.

*cumcision* for the high altar of the Compagnia del Nome di Dio in Pesaro [Louvre].[37] Depicted there is a seated figure who holds the Christ Child at his chest while the figure who performs the circumcision, having cut the foreskin, holds the bandage on the wound and takes the powder to stop the blood. Behind them kneel the Virgin and Saint Joseph, while among the other figures there is one who replaces the knife in its case, a young boy who holds a candle and points at the foreskin in a small dish, a kneeling shepherd in front who offers a lamb, and above, two angels in adoration. On the hassock where the Virgin kneels one can read Barocci's name with the year in which the picture was done: FED. BAR. URB. PINX. MDLXXXX.

After 1596 Barocci completed the painting of the *Crucifixion* ordered by Signor Matteo Senarega, who was Doge of Genoa.[38] This painting has acquired great fame for its beauty as can be seen by the way it is admired in the Duomo of Genoa. Barocci painted in it mourning angels in the air, and at the foot of the cross, the prostrate Virgin supported by Saint John, plus the figure of Saint Sebastian to whom the chapel is dedicated. I will not describe the gestures of the figures other than to quote from the letter written to Barocci by the same Senarega, an illustrious man of learning.

*To Signor Federico Barocci from Matteo Senarega*
*This painting has but one defect: because it is almost divine, human praises cannot do it justice. Therefore it lives wrapped in silence and awe. The most holy Crucified One, although appearing to be already dead, nevertheless is breathing, alive in paradise; this demonstrates to us that in truth he willingly of his own consent suffered death, out of love for us, and for the well-being of all. The sweetness of the Virgin Mother is so great that at a single glance it wounds and heals, inspires compassion and consoles, and indeed it appears as if the divine spirit deep within the wounds of Christ enters her to know if it must pierce her again with the death of her beloved son or restore to her the salvation of the human race. Thus, driven by diverse feelings and stunned, she abandons herself in her reborn son who, moved tenderly by wonder and charity, also responds to her. In Saint Sebastian one sees the true colors and rhythms of art, to a degree that perhaps the ancients never attained, much less the moderns; and as a whole, the work is so rich in artifice and grace that it does not leave room for anything but a desire to imitate it. And these holy angels, how they too express vivid feelings of wonder and pity! I repeat and confess how, like something divine, the painting enraptures, divides, sweetly transforms. Whence my obligations to Your Excellency who has labored so greatly in this work press me and increase; and our Monsignore Ventura will have to provide further for it. I add that in Rome the Signori Giustiniani have the order to pay out the remainder of the cost to you, or to your agent. Not that this will extinguish my debts for which I intend to remain accountable, and which I will repay at the first opportunity that I can be of service to you. From Genoa, October 5, 1596.*

Barocci painted another similar *Crucifixion* for the Compagnia della Morte in Urbino [*in situ*], but the figures in the lower portion are by Alessandro Vitali, Barocci's pupil.[39] Barocci made another painting, the *Noli me tangere,* for the Buonvisi family, which was put in a church in Lucca.[40] The artist represented Christ as a gardener pulling back from the Magdalene who kneels and extends her hand to touch him. This work is regarded among the artist's best and most praiseworthy. As was said before, the painting of the *Visitation* in the church of the fathers of the Oratory [Chiesa Nuova, Rome] met with much satisfaction from San Filippo Neri. As a result, since the altars with the mysteries of the Virgin required decoration and Monsignor Angelo Cesi, Bishop of Todi (who had completed the façade of the church built by his brother Cardinal Pier Donato Cesi), was interested in decorating an altar on the right side of the transept, hence Barocci was selected to paint the *Presentation of the Virgin.* It was executed with care and great study.

## THE PRESENTATION OF THE VIRGIN[41]

The young Virgin, having climbed the stairs of the temple, kneels in front of the priest who places his hand on her head and proceeds to consecrate her to our Lord. She folds her hands over her chest and in turning her face in reverence, lowers her eyes and forehead, expressing in her face her celestial bearing and simplicity. In the vestibule of the temple young Levite boys in white ecclesiastical garments give assistance. Two of them on either side hold lighted candles. Two larger figures dressed in long white robes flank the old priest, and lift his golden mantle from his arms. The one at the left of the priest opens his hand and looks at the beauty and humility of the young girl elected by God; the other, turning to the side, extends his hand and signals for incense to be brought to consecrate the girl. Meanwhile one of those young boys keeps the censor suspended between his hands, and having closed it, watches it as he comes forward amidst the others who assist with the candles. Four steps below the Virgin and two from the ground kneels Saint Anne; she is shown in the act of bringing her parted hands together with a maternal, devout air. Beside her stands Saint Joachim with his head lowered, speaking to her and pointing out the priest. Saint Anne in her red mantle advances into the stronger light, displaying her profile, still beautiful at such an old age. Below on the first step sits a young country girl with her hands on a basket of doves to present at the Temple. Depicted in full-face and in a yellow shirt, she turns herself happily to an old woman who touches her shoulder and appears to ask her who the young girl is who is presented in the Temple. But only the old woman's head in profile and her hands can be seen at the edge of the painting. On the opposite side is a figure who pulls a ram by the horn to make an offering of it, and further behind, a young boy bends over placing one hand on the shoulder of a red calf, and with the other hand, feeds grape leaves to the animal, while above him is a blind man resting on a cane. Both latter figures are cut off by the edge of the painting. Over the door of the temple a cloud of cherubims and three flying angels create a celestial splendor. The little angel in the middle carries a wreath or diadem of gold to crown the Virgin with eternity, while another on the right throws roses and flowers, and the third on the left joins its hands in adoration. The upper figures are set within the dazzling field in front of the temple adorned with architecture, with the view of the interior through the door. In the middle the priest comes forward into the daylight, and in bending over to the right, casts a shadow over the arm of the Levite who raises his mantle, which, in turn, produces a shadow which falls on the two young boys carrying one candlestick and the

---

38. *In situ.* Signed and dated 1596. Although negotiations with the Duke of Urbino for Barocci to paint an altarpiece for the Chapel of St. Sebastian in the Genoa Duomo began as early as 1587, Barocci did not agree to accept the commission until 1590. In May he signed a contract to execute the work for 1000 scudi.

39. This painting is a pastiche of various works by the artist, in particular the Senigallia *Entombment,* the Genoa *Crucifixion,* and the *Crocifisso Spirante* in Madrid. It was painted between 1597 and 1604.

40. The composition of this work is best known through an engraving made by Luca Ciamberlano in 1609 (Olsen, 1962, fig. 122c). The painting itself, which belongs to Viscount Allendale, Bywell Hall, has suffered extensive damage and is in a state of near total ruin. A photograph of the work in its present state is published by Tschudi Madsen, 1959, opposite p. 274.

41. *In situ.* Signed and dated 1603. The signature and date were revealed in a recent cleaning (for which see Emiliani, 1975, p. 207). Angelo Cesi, Bishop of Todi, ordered the work in 1590–91, but the artist did not begin on the painting until after 1592.

censor while another boy in his white tunic comes forward in the light carrying the other candlestick. These figures serve as a background to Saints Anne and Joachim below. Although refined in all its individual parts, the work is weakened by the numerous reflections of light; for when the color attains its effect in such a subtle fashion, the subject becomes difficult to read.

The picture was done during the pontificate of Clement VIII, about 1594.[41] The Pope, on his way to Ferrara on the occasion of the recovery of the duchy, was received by the Duke of Urbino, who prepared him a most noble gift, a golden vase for holy water.[42] To increase its value, the Duke had Barocci paint, in gold leaf in the middle of the vase, the Infant Christ seated on clouds who holds in one hand the globe and with the other gives a blessing. The Pope was so pleased with the picture that he took it off the vase and kept it in a breviary to see it every day when he took his offices. Thus, when the Pope built the noble chapel in the Minerva, he went to the Duke to see if Barocci would paint the altarpiece of the institution of the holy sacrament.[43]

## THE INSTITUTION OF THE HOLY SACRAMENT[44]

Christ holds in one hand the paten and in the other the host of the divine bread. Standing in the middle of the supper-room, he appears to affirm his body in that food and to meditate upon the Passion. The apostles kneel at his feet. Saint John on his left lowers his head and opens his arms, with his hands toward the ground, humbled by profound adoration. His red mantle falls from his shoulder, his elbow is naked, and his feet are bare. Opposite him another apostle lifts his head and spirit to look at the celestial food, being already near to receiving it; his golden mantle reflects the brilliant light. Another apostle behind places his arms on his chest and lowers his eyes in veneration. Among all of these is Saint Peter, whose figure emerges and stands out over those who appear in front of Christ. He keeps his hands apart and watches the great mystery. Behind and to the right of Saint Peter can be seen other disciples at a table with a chalice and an amphora of wine. The one in the front is shown with one hand on the table and the other on his chest as he is about to get up to kneel down, while the others, moved by the words of Christ, beckon, stare, and gather together. One easily recognizes the wicked Judas with his head in shadows and his eyes lowered not out of humility but with the intent of plotting his betrayal. Being on the other side of Christ

behind Saint John, and bending over with one knee on the ground, Judas raises his other knee and holds his hand on his thigh with a thin purse. Resting his head in the cup of his hand, he remains motionless, absorbed in his thought of the betrayal of Christ. The dress of Judas is of a rancid color, and behind him in shadow are other apostles in adoration displaying the same gestures of humility and veneration as seen in the others. As one can see in the vivacious expressions of the figures, Barocci lacked neither diligence nor skill in showing the whole scene of the Supper in the hazy and nocturnal background light. Behind the Christ on the left there is represented another table bearing a candlestick and light which illuminates a servant who holds his hand there. And further away, in the last part of the scene, is another small light on the cupboard where the servants put back the vases. There are small details indicated in this background, where reflections play among the shadows on the walls, the jambs of the doors, pilasters, cornice, and on the carved ceiling. But since it is a night scene, one sees at the right [sic: actually left] edge of the painting part of a young man withdrawing into the shadow; he holds a torch and the flame stands out against the dark doorway. This torch provides light for the principal figures of Christ and the apostles at his feet. The floor of the supper-room is raised up three steps; and below in the foreground scene are two servants almost in shadow. One is bent over to clean tin dishes in a copper basin, while the other, bearing a basket with the leftovers of the dinner under his right arm, turns to his left with one foot on

the first step, and leans slightly to that side to pick up a copper pail on the floor, almost touching it with his hand. But in leaning over too much he shows his fear of dropping the basket he holds in his other hand. Although these two figures are in a dark area, they are somewhat illuminated by a candlestick on the floor in the center with a small amount of wick burning. Much harm is done by the fact that the painting does not have light in front. Not only is a great deal lost to view but one cannot appreciate its artistic quality. It is very unfortunate that one encounters this in Barocci's works in Rome and elsewhere, for his soft painting requires the strength of natural light.

Before Barocci painted this picture, the Pope wanted to see the drawing for it.[45] Since Barocci had represented the devil speaking in the ear of Judas, tempting him to betray his master, the Pope declared that he did not like the devil to be on such familiar terms with Jesus Christ and to be seen on the altar. As a result, he was removed, leaving Judas in that position in which he appears to be meditating his betrayal. This painting was sent as a gift from the Duke to the Pope, who, holding it in such high esteem, not only gave Barocci the highest praise, but also presented the artist with a golden necklace of great value.

Among the other paintings by Barocci which one can see on public view is the one in Cortona in the Chiesa di Zoccolanti showing *Saint Catherine* kneeling and looking at a shimmer of cherubims bearing the angel who brings her the crown of her martyrdom.[46] In Macerata on the high altar of the church of the Capuchins is another painting

---

42. Clement VIII was in Pesaro on May 3, 1598, and again on Dec. 7 in 1598. Barocci received payments in 1597 (May 5) for "un Christo nell' ornamento d'oro," and the following year (Sept. 7) he was paid to execute a replica—"il Christo nel 2 ornamento d'oro." No doubt one of the works served as the Pope's gift. Neither has survived, and the composition of the painting is known through a replica in the Glasgow Art Gallery (repr. Olsen, 1962, fig. 123b).

43. The Pope's choice of Barocci to execute the altarpiece in S. Maria sopra Minerva was probably due to several factors. One of them may have been the arrival in Rome of the *Presentation,* which was installed in the Chiesa Nuova in April 1593, four months prior to the Pope's selection of Barocci for the Minerva commission (for which see Shearman, 1976, p. 52).

44. The painting is *in situ* on the altar of the Aldobrandini Chapel in S. Maria sopra Minerva. Clement VIII's desire to obtain a painting by Barocci was communicated to the Duke of Urbino on Aug. 13, 1603. At the request of the Duke, who eventually paid for the work himself and sent the work to the Pope as a gift, Barocci accepted the commission and produced two sketches which were shown to the Pope in Rome in November of the same year. Barocci revised the design to accommodate the Pope's wishes—first to remove the devil beside Judas and later to create a dark interior—and completed the work in 1607–08. The painting was sent to Rome in 1609. The artist received more than 1600 scudi in payment.

45. Barocci made two drawings which Malatesta Malatesti showed the Pope in November 1603. Among these was probably the drawing in Chatsworth (Devonshire Collections, inv. 361) which shows Satan accompanying Judas who kneels before Christ (repr. Olsen, 1962, fig. 87a) and a drawing in an English private collection, which is closer to the final work but has a different lighting (repr. Emiliani, 1975, fig. 264). For the Pope's criticisms of these drawings see the letters published by Gronau, 1936, pp. 181–185.

46. This work is untraced. As noted in *Mostra,* Florence, 1912–13, p. 44 n. 43 a painting of the same subject—so completely repainted its attribution cannot be determined—is in the Palazzo Rosso in Genoa (Brogi neg. 11545).

of the *Immaculate Conception* with the Virgin in a glory of angels positioned above Saint John the Baptist who is pointing, Saint Francis, Saint Bonaventura, and Saint Anthony of Padua, all of whom are executed in an excellent manner.[47] Another work to be mentioned is the painting of the *Stigmatization of Saint Francis* in the church of the Capuchins in Urbino, which shows the saint pierced by the seraphic light, while he kneels by the cliffs of La Vernia with outstretched arms.[48] Further below his companion places his hand on his forehead to shield his eyes from the holy splendor. In the church of San Francesco on the altar of the Compagnia della Concezione is the image of the *Virgin Standing on the Moon* with open arms, while men and women of the Company gather below her in attitudes of devotion.[49] This painting was first executed in gouache, but since it did not come out well, Barocci repainted it in oil in the last years of his life. The last work that he completed was the painting of the sacramental *Supper* in the Chapel of the Archbishopric [Urbino, Duomo].[50] Christ is shown seated at dinner in the middle of his disciples. With one hand he holds the divine bread in front of the chalice, with the other he blesses, turning his eyes toward the light of the open sky where four angels adore him. Among the admiring apostles is a figure in the front who has been drinking, and upon hearing the divine words, he stops to dry his lips with his mantle and holds out his empty cup to a young boy. There is also a very natural figure opposite him who, after having eaten, replaces his knife in its sheath. And further in the foreground on either side are servants who clean and collect the vessels from the table.

It is certainly incredible to hear of the number of public works done by this master (not to mention his private ones which are greater in number), and to see how all of his works were done using great diligence and careful preliminary studies based on close observation of details and characteristics of nature. It is all the more incredible given the fact that the artist's incurable illness allowed him to work only one hour in the morning and one at night. He was unable to work beyond those two hours, even with his mind. Beyond those two hours he was unable to make the slightest mark, let alone pick up his brushes. And even if he had given his students all the time which was his custom to offer them, he separated himself during the only hour in which he was able to work. The rest of the day was spent with stomach pains and cramps, causing him to vomit constantly, which happened to him immediately after having eaten. Leaving the breakfast table and dinner table, little by little he lost all his food; and in the end he became so battered and stunned that he was unable to sleep. He never went to the dinner table with an appetite, but when he began to eat, unless the meats in front of him had been portioned, he was unable to satiate himself; and the more he ate, the more he would suffer pain and be wracked by vomiting. At night he slept very little and in the short time that he did, he was disturbed by terrible nightmares. At such times he cried and made mumbling noises, so much so that someone stayed by him to rouse him and free him from his anxiety. Such was his condition from the day that it is believed he was poisoned until his death, for a period of fifty-two years. It is indeed a stupendous fact that the artist, in spite of such a long, continuous, and atrocious illness, managed to keep up with the physical and mental strain of painting, without ever resting or amusing himself in leisure. It is likewise amazing that Barocci reached the ripe old age of eighty-four with a keeness of eyesight so strong that he never had to use glasses, and that he still retained every faculty of his mind.

Having lived a long life in this way, he was suddenly stricken by an apoplectic fit which within 24 hours took his speech and then on the last day of September 1612, his life.[51] He was buried in the church of San Francesco. With funereal pomp his body was displayed and his painting of the *Crucifixion "Spirante"* placed at his feet in the bier. The Barocci family has its sepulcher in the same church, on the right side, with the family arms of an eagle on a bar above a lion. Ambrogio, the nephew of the artist, placed the following inscription there: D. O. M./SIMEONI ET FEDERICO/DE BAROCIIS/ANIMI INGENVITATE PRAECLARIS/MANVVM OFFICIO PRAESTANTIBVS/QVORVM ILLE/NOVIS MATHESEOS INSTRVMENTIS/INVENIVNDIS FABREFACIVNDISQVE/ARTEM ILLVSTRAVIT/HIC VERO/VIVIS PICTVRAE COLORIBVS/OBSCVRAVIT NATVRAM/AMBROSIVS BAROCIVS/PATRI PATRVO AC EORVM PATRVELI/IOANNI MARIAE/HOROLOGIORVM ARCHITECTO/QVI ARCHIMEDEM AEMVLATVS/IN PARVA PYXIDE COELESTES MOTVS/PII V. P.M. AC SVCCESSOR. COMMODIS/ARTIFICIOSE CLAVSIT OMNES/P. C.[52]

Barocci was overtaken by death during the time that he was making the cartoon of an *Ecce Homo* and was about to finish the feet of Christ, who we can believe received Barocci in His great benevolence.[53] Barocci's death was accompanied by the tears of his fellow citizens who loved him tenderly and greatly and lamented so serious a loss, for they were to miss one who brought both glory and splendor to their country. A most worthy funeral was celebrated by the heirs. In the middle of the church was erected a catafalque with hieroglyphics, *imprese,* and verses which represented the virtues of his genius and of his painting, as the placement of his paintings and cartoons between the

---

47. Destroyed in 1799 when French soldiers set fire to the church, the painting was commissioned from Margherita Ricci who on her death in 1605 bequeathed to her heirs 200 fiorini for the purposes of paying Barocci for the altarpiece. The painting was installed Oct. 29, 1608. The composition is known through a painted copy formerly in the Trascinelli collection in Macerata (repr. Olsen, 1962, fig. 123c). Although the artist adopted figures from other works—principally the *Beata Michelina*, Urbino *Last Supper*, and *Madonna del Rosario*—in creating the upper part of the composition, he newly invented the poses for the four kneeling saints below; and numerous drawings for the individual figures below have survived.

48. Urbino, Galleria Nazionale delle Marche. Engraved by Villamena in 1597. Probably identifiable with the "quadro dei cappuccini d'Urbino" for which payments from the Ducal treasury were made in Feb. 1594 and Sept. 1595. Despite the contention of Emiliani (1975, p. 182), the execution of the work shows traces of studio intervention, as Olsen first noted.

49. Urbino, Galleria Nazionale delle Marche. Dateable on stylistic grounds to the mid-1570s (Olsen, 1962, p. 162), although presumably repainted by the artist later in his career, this painting appears to be totally autograph though somewhat damaged through abrasion. Lazzari, *Delle chiese di Urbino*, Urbino, 1801, pp. 107–108, identifies the figures depicted in the lower half as members of the Ambrosi family.

50. This painting, along with a Fall of Manna, was commissioned from Barocci by the Archbishop in 1590. Barocci's asking price was 2000 scudi, though the Duke persuaded him to settle for 1600. The *Last Supper* was finished and installed in the Cappella del SS. Sacramento in 1599. Because of the artist's poor health and other commitments, the church authorities decided in 1602 to commission the Fall of Manna to another artist. They considered Federico Zuccaro but finally awarded the contract to Alessandro Vitali in 1606.

51. The date of Barocci's death is confirmed by a note in the Diary of the Duke of Oct. 1, 1512: "Morì Federico Barocci da Urbino, pittore eccellente, di anni 77, nella quale età l'occhio e la mano il servivano come quando era giovane" (A. Alippi, "Documenti," *Rassegna bibliografica dell'arte italiana*, XII, 1909, p. 72).

52. "Ambrogio Barocci, to his father and his uncle, Simone and Federico, [who were] distinguished by nobility of spirit [and] outstanding in the work of their hands, of whom the former showed his skill by inventing and making new instruments of mathematics, while the latter outshone nature with the living colors of his painting, and their cousin, Giovanni Maria, the maker of clocks, who emulated Archimedes and enclosed all celestial movements in a small box for the advantage of Pius V, Pontifex Maximus, and his successors."

53. This cartoon is recorded in the description of the contents of the artist's studio made soon after his death as being on the back of the cartoon for the Gubbio *Annunciation* (Calzini, 1898, p. 106). Although untraced, the composition is known through a drawing in the Kupferstichkabinett in Berlin (Inv. 20447; Pacetti 4179: repr. Olsen, 1962, fig. 117a) and an oil painting in the Brera which has traditionally been ascribed to either Ventura Mazzi or Alessandro Vitali (repr. Olsen, 1962, fig. 117b).

black devices indeed demonstrated. In order to express the loss and the honors owed to the memory of such an illustrious citizen, an oration in his praise was recited by Signor Vittorio Venturelli from Urbino with the assistance of Monsignor Archbishop Benedetto Ala and with the intervention of the supreme magistrate of the Eight which had been elected by the Duke in his old age to govern each city of the state. Not only was the whole city drawn to the grandeur of the funeral, but also a large number of honorable persons from surrounding places came to Urbino, inspired by the name and by affection towards him who, with his brush, had brought glory to that region.

Barocci was of average height and bald-headed. He had a genial face and black eyes, and was rather lean.[54] He enjoyed the comforts of life and left a sizeable estate, since his works were bought at the requested price without any objections. He never thought of being avaricious; instead, he always worked to be proud of his reputation, continued to paint nobly, and never failed to undertake careful studies and give much time to his work, as we have said.

About his personal habits little is known; he was principally charitable to the poor, generous to everyone, affable and humble in conversation. And he even seemed to cultivate good manners: when he became violent with anger, he would suddenly temper his first impulse and transform himself, making out of his disordered appearance one of congeniality and mildness. He never had vain thoughts, nor did he ever draw or paint something that was indecent; on the contrary, with his good and pious mind he committed himself always to painting sacred images and holy subjects. And since he slept so little, during the winter he had a group of artists and *virtuosi* of the city come to his studio in the evenings and remain there up until the eighth hour in the night.[55] During those few hours that he did sleep, he was always tormented. And when he found time for rest, he had stories and poetical compositions read to him, which gave him pleasure and comfort.

Prince Duke Francesco Maria held Barocci in such high esteem that he awarded the artist an apartment for life. The artist lived there for some time, but after having found a house to his own taste, he retired there to live, and expressed his thanks to the Duke. The good prince never came to Urbino without personally paying a visit to Barocci, for he enjoyed seeing him paint, speaking with him, and lavishing favors upon him, something which he was not accustomed to doing with anyone else.[56] The Duchess shared this affection, and more than once she paid Barocci a visit. Barocci also requested a large room wherein his paintings and cartoons were displayed. Everyone who came to court desired to meet the artist, including the many foreigners who were attracted to Urbino by his fame and who wanted to meet him and to admire his beautiful method of painting.

Barocci did a portrait of the Duke,[57] one of the Marchesa del Vasto, one of the Marchese,[58] and one of Monsignor della Rovere.[59]

Among his dearest friends he painted Monsignor Felice Tiranni, first Archbishop of Urbino;[60] Count Cesare Mamiani;[61] Signor Antonio Galli;[62] and Galli's wife, Caterina, with twins who play with a jeweled necklace;[63] and many other similar portraits in *pastelli* which are very naturalistic.

Because of Barocci's fame the Emperor Rudolf II asked the Duke, through his ambassador in Rome, for a painting by this artist's hand. This was the *Burning of Troy* with Aeneas carrying around his neck his aged father Anchises, followed by the young Ascanius and by Creusa.[64] The work pleased the Emperor and he made repeated requests for Barocci to move to his court, which he would gladly have done if his sickness had not prevented it. Barocci did another version of this painting for Monsignor della Rovere, which today can be seen in Rome in the Borghese Gallery [*in situ*].[65] The King of Spain, Philip II, was so pleased with the painting he had of *Saint Andrew* and another of the *Annunciation,* that, after having extended Barocci invitations in letters, he ordered Cavaliere Leonardo Aretino to use every inducement to bring him to Spain to serve him. But on account of his bad health Barocci again refused the offer and stayed in Urbino.

At his death many of Barocci's works were left unfinished, notably the painting for the cathedral in Milan (preserved in the sacristy) wherein Christ is shown carried to the sepulcher [now Bologna, Biblioteca Comunale dell'Archiginnasio].[66] Barocci also had begun an *Annunciation* for the Confraternity

---

54. Bellori's description is borne out by the *Self-Portrait* preserved in the Uffizi and the colored chalk drawing in Würzburg which served as a preparatory study (for which see R. Linnenkamp, "Zwei unbekannte Selbstbildnisse von Federigo Barocci," *Pantheon,* XIX, 1961, pp. 46–50).

55. Bellori means by the "eighth hour of the night" one o'clock in the morning since, according to church practice, night began with vespers at five o'clock in the afternoon.

56. See n. 34 above.

57. Barocci actually executed two portraits of the Duke: the first, in the Uffizi, shows him as prince, dressed in full armor, after the Battle of Lepanto (1571); the second, in the Goethe Nationalmuseum in Weimar, ordered from the Grand Duke of Tuscany in 1583, shows him in a black velvet suit and cap, in his mid-forties (repr. Olsen, 1962, figs. 32 and 37a).

58. The Marchesa del Vasto was Lavinia, sister of Francesco Maria II della Rovere, who in 1583 married Alfonso Felice d'Avalos, Marchese del Vasto, and died in 1632. The portraits which Barocci did of her and her husband are untraced. Schmarsow (1909, p. 160) has argued that Bellori is referring in this notice not to Marchese del Vasto but to Ippolito della Rovere, the eldest son of Cardinal Giulio, who became Marchese of S. Lorenzo in 1584 when he married Isabella Vitelli dell'Amatrice. Evelina

Borea (1976, p. 61, fig. 3) has recently proposed identifying a painting in the Uffizi, for many years on loan to the Galleria Nazionale in Rome and considered by Olsen as a portrait of the mathematician Guidobaldo del Monte (Olsen, 1962, pp. 204–205, fig. 982), as Barocci's portrait of Ippolito della Rovere.

59. Monsignor della Rovere is identifiable as Giuliano della Rovere, son of Cardinal Giulio and Leonora di Ferrara and Prior of Corinaldo and Abbot of S. Lorenzo in Campo. He was born about 1559 and died in 1621. Barocci's portrait is in the Kunsthistorishes Museum in Vienna, having come to Florence in the seventeenth century with Vittoria della Rovere and having been exchanged with Vienna in 1792 (repr. Olsen, 1962, fig. 95).

60. Felice Tiranni was bishop of Urbino from 1551 and under him, in 1563, the seat of Urbino became an archbishopric. He died in 1578 and was succeeded by Cardinal Giulio della Rovere. The painting is untraced.

61. Untraced. Tentatively identified by Olsen, 1962, p. 151, as the *Portrait of a Young Man* in the Hermitage, Leningrad.

62. Antonio Galli was a poet and Prince Francesco Maria II della Rovere's teacher. Olsen, 1962, pp. 140–141, fig. 3a, has proposed identifying a painting traditionally ascribed to Titian in the Royal Museum of Fine Arts in Copenhagen as Barocci's portrait of Galli, a suggestion that has recently been rejected by Emiliani

(1975, pp. 56–57) and upheld by Shearman (1976, p. 51).

63. Untraced. Olsen, 1962, p. 142, identifies a painting in Copenhagen as an old copy of the head of Caterina Galli.

64. Barocci executed this work, his only mythological painting, for the Emperor who, through agents, applied to the Duke of Urbino for an example of Barocci's work in September 1586. Barocci finished the painting, of which no trace survives after it was sold in London in 1800, in January 1589 and received 400 scudi from the Duke in payment.

65. Signed and dated 1598, the painting is recorded in the Borghese collection as early as 1612 and was probably presented by Giuliano della Rovere directly to Scipione Borghese in the first decade of the seventeenth century.

66. Commissioned from Barocci as the altarpiece for the Chapel of S. Giovanni Buono in the Milan Cathedral in 1600, the artist left the painting unfinished at his death: "sono tredici figure, compreso un puttino et un diavolo sotto alli piedi di S. Michaele, cioè il Christo morto nudo finito, la Maddalena parte finita et parte abozata, il vescovo è finito ed il restante delle 10 figure sono abozate solamente" (Lonati's description of the painting Apr. 10, 1630, published in *Annali della fabbrica del Duomo di Milano,* V, Milan, 1883, p. 159). The painting was brought to its present state of finish by Ventura Mazzi in 1635.

of Gubbio, which, despite its unfinished state, nonetheless pleased the brothers [Gubbio, Santa Maria dei Laici].[67] As far as the other paintings which Barocci undertook to do and completed at other times, there are a few we should mention. For the father of Francesco Maria, Duke Guidobaldo, Barocci did a small easel painting of the Virgin resting from her *Flight into Egypt;* she sits and with a cup draws water from a spring while Joseph lowers a branch of apples [*sic:* actually cherries], offering it to the Christ Child who laughs and holds out his hand. This painting was sent as a gift to the Duchess of Ferrara [Lucrezia d'Este], and because it was so admired, a replica was painted [now Vatican Pinacoteca] and another one done in gouache with life-size figures, which Count Antonio Brancaleoni sent to his castle, the Pieve of Piobbico [Piobbico, Santo Stefano].[68] For Count Brancaleoni Barocci also painted another small piece, the Virgin seated in a room with the Christ Child at her breast. She draws the Child's attention to a cat which is about to jump up at a swallow held up with a string by the young St. John. Behind, Joseph leans with his hand on a small table and pushes himself forward to watch [*Madonna del Gatto,* London, National Gallery].[69] Barocci did other paintings for Duke Francesco Maria. Among these is a very beautiful *Visitation* of Saint Elizabeth with the Madonna, in which he seized the opportunity to depict the interior of the room: and he placed Joseph outside raising the curtain over the door for Elizabeth, who climbs up to the threshold to enter the room. Inside one can see the Virgin seated with a book in her hand and turned calmly toward her sister. The scene also depicts the Infant

Christ awakening as the Virgin stops swinging the cradle. Meanwhile the young Saint John ascends the stair beside Elizabeth and with the reed cross in his hand points out the inscription "Ecce Agnus Dei." Saint Zacharias behind sticks out his head and looks toward the room which is illuminated by a light which comes from the side, while, in sharp contrast, the figure of Joseph and the curtain remain outside in shadow. Included here at the foot of the Virgin is an amusing scene of a cat feeding her kittens. In fear of the presence of intruders, the cat rises up in defense, arching her back and appearing ferocious. Outside the stairs there are carpenter's tools, and through another door of the room opens the view of a small garden where Joseph's donkey feeds. Farther in the distance one catches a glimpse of the hill with the Ducal Palace of Urbino. The figures are no larger than three *palmi* [ca. 67 cm.], and the painting can be seen in Rome in the Novitiate of the Jesuit Fathers.[70]

For the same Duke Barocci painted the *Nativity* which shows the Virgin in adoration of the newly born Christ Child in the manger and Joseph opening the door of the stall to shepherds who turn toward the light with wonder [Madrid, Prado].[71] In addition, Barocci painted two other *Crucifixions:* one for Cardinal della Rovere with the Virgin and other figures standing, sent to Rocca Contrada [Arcévia];[72] the other for a chapel of Count Pietro Bonarelli in the church of the miraculous Crucifixion in Urbino. In the latter are two angels in the sky and the standing Virgin and Saint John.[73] For Count Francesco Maria Mamiani Barocci painted two half figures of *Saint Catherine* and *Saint Sebastian,* depicting the latter turned toward

the heavenly splendor with arrows in one hand while his other hand is pressed against his chest.[74] For Monsignor Giuliano della Rovere Barocci did the *Apparition of Christ to the Mourning Magdalene,* who is shown with her hand at her cheek [Munich, Staatliche Gemaldegalerie].[75] Many additional paintings by Barocci await the praises of whomever goes to admire them.

The methods used by Barocci in painting, notwithstanding his illness, required great effort and application. He always worked from life, not allowing himself to paint even a small part without having first observed it. This fact explains the great number of drawings which he left in his studio. Whenever he was in the piazza or in the street enjoying a respite from his sickness, he would observe the features and the images of people. When he noticed someone with an interesting feature, he arranged to take the person to his house, making a selection and taking advantage of the situation. When he saw a beautiful turn of the eyes, a good profile of a nose, or a fine mouth, he would use them as models to create a very beautiful head. He drew in chiaroscuro, using a stick of burnt wood, and he made even more use of *pastelli,* in which he became extremely proficient, shading the design in a few lines. When doing this, first he conceived of the scene to be represented, and before doing a sketch of it, he placed his youths according to the design, arranging them in accord with his idea and asking them whether they felt unnatural or if by turning more one way than the other they felt more at ease. In this process Barocci experimented with the most natural and unaffected movements and executed his drawings. In the same manner, if

67. From documents published by Umberto Gnoli (*Rassegna marchigiana,* III, 1924–25, pp. 42–44), we know that this painting was commissioned to the artist by the Fraternità dei Bianchi in 1609 for the price of 500 ducati and that having been left unfinished ("abozzato") at Barocci's death, it was completed in 1615 to 1619 by Ventura Mazzi, who received forty-five scudi.

68. Olsen, 1962, p. 154, has proposed that the first version of the painting, which is now untraced, was done for the wedding of Lucrezia d'Este and Francesco Maria II della Rovere on January 2, 1571. At Lucrezia's death in 1598, the painting passed to Cardinal Pietro Aldobrandini, in whose collection Raffaello Schiaminossi engraved the composition in 1612 (repr. Olsen, 1962, fig. 122b). The second version, done in gouache on the scale of a full-size altarpiece, is identifiable as the one in Piobbico, while the third one, now in the Vatican, appears to have been done for Simonetto Anastagi, a Perugian acquaintance, in 1573 (see n. 16 above).

69. Engraved by Cornelis Cort in 1577. A replica, probably executed by a studio assistant, is in the Musée Condé, Chantilly.

70. Bellori is describing a small replica—possibly the same as the picture once in the Orléans collection and the Metropolitan Museum of Art in New York and now in a private collection in Florence (repr. Emiliani, 1975, fig. 216)—of the painting which came to Florence in 1631 with the property of Vittoria della Rovere and is now in the storerooms of the Palazzo Pitti, in extremely damaged condition (see Borea, 1976, p. 60). Olsen has correctly identified this work with a painting of the "Madonna'" for which the Duke of Urbino paid Barocci 635 scudi between 1588 and Sept. 1592. Another copy of the painting is preserved in the Ringling Museum in Sarasota (1949 cat., no. 35; 133 x 99 cm.).

71. This work was done for the Duke of Urbino, in all likelihood in 1597 when the *Libro di Spese* records a payment to Barocci on August 19 of 272.44 scudi "per un quadro della Natività di N.S."; in 1605 it was sent by the Duke to Queen Margherita of Austria, wife of Philip III, who wanted a devotional painting to decorate her oratory. Copies of the painting were commissioned to Alessandro Vitali in 1598 and 1605, one of which was acquired by Federico Borromeo in the early seventeenth century and is now in the Pinacoteca Ambrosiana. An unfinished painting of the same subject in the Rasini Collection in Milan records a preliminary stage in the development of the composition (Olsen, 1962, fig. 89).

72. Untraced. Recorded by Borghini (1584, p. 569) as well as by Bellori. According to Olsen (1962, p. 149), this painting might have been similar to that represented by the artist on the altarpiece in the background of the *Perdono.*

73. Urbino, Galleria Nazionale delle Marche. On stylistic grounds Olsen dates this painting to the mid-1560s (1962, p. 147). A sketch for the composition in the Uffizi (11416F) is superimposed upon a developed study for the *Madonna di S. Giovanni,* providing a *terminus ante quem* of ca. 1562–66.

74. Untraced. The compositions may have been identical with that of a drawing of St. Sebastian by Barocci in the Kupferstichkabinett, Berlin (Inv. 15228; Pacetti 4195; Olsen, 1962, fig. 81) and a painting of St. Catherine by a follower of Barocci in the Borghese Gallery, Rome (Olsen, 1962, fig. 120b), as proposed by Olsen.

75. Signed and dated 1590. The reduced version of the composition in the Uffizi, considered an autograph replica by Olsen and Emiliani, may have served as a "bozzetto per i colori," later finished by the artist's nephew, Ambrogio, in order to market the work as a finished original (repr. Olsen, 1962, fig. 57; discussed in Pillsbury, M.D., 1976, p. 59).

he wished to add a group of figures to the painting, he would rearrange his young male models together to fit the action and from the sketches he then composed a finished drawing ["disegno compito"]. It is for this reason that one sees in his gestures a relaxed, natural, and gracious air. After making the finished drawing, he also did models for the figures in clay or wax that were so beautiful that they appeared to be the work of the best sculptor; not being content at times with only one, he sometimes made two or three wax models of the same figure. After dressing the models as he wished and, certain that they looked well, he would try the draperies on the live model to eliminate any trace of affectation. From all of these preparations Barocci would make a small cartoon in oil or gouache, in chiaroscuro, and afterwards he would make use of a full-scale cartoon in charcoal and chalk, or in *pastelli* on paper, laying it over the priming of the canvas and tracing the contours with the stylus so that the drawing never deviated from the original design.

As regards the coloring, after the large cartoon Barocci made another small one in which he distributed the hues in proportions and sought to find the right tones between one color and the next so that all the colors together would have a sense of harmony and balance among them, without one imposing on another. And he would say that just as the melody of voices delights the ear, so likewise the consonance of colors accompanied by the harmony of outlines brings pleasure to the eye. He therefore called painting "music," as, for instance, when questioned one time by Duke Guidobaldo, Barocci referred to what he was doing as making music, pointing out the picture he was painting. I know that some persons will ridicule these studies and efforts as useless and superfluous, but there are even others who will mock their ignorance, vainly persuading themselves that they can create a fine composition with a simple sketch or with a couple of strokes of the chalk on the canvas. This explains why in so many paintings one sees not only no well-ordered scenes, but not even a beautiful drapery fold, a good outline, a fine head, or a natural and real gesture. For the most part, such preliminary studies were carried out by all the great masters, who were never satisfied with only a caricature of the right color and contour; and whoever examines well the works of our Barocci will recognize how praiseworthy are his most exacting labors.

After he completed the preparatory work, Barocci was quick to color the form and he often shaded with the big finger of his hand instead of with the brush. He resembled, to some extent, Correggio both in theory and means of conception and in the pure and natural features, the sweet airs of the putti and women and in the folding of the draperies carried out in a relaxed and soft style. Although Barocci approached Correggio in the harmonization of colors, it is still true that he did not attain Correggio's mastery of shading. Whereas Barocci at times modified his tints with cinnabars and blues along the contours or blended his colors too much, Correggio's hues were more natural. Nonetheless, Barocci's works render him immortal; witness the fact that the greater share of those described are well endowed with strength and vitality. The beauty of his drawing can be seen in the intaglios etched by him of the *Annunciation,* the *Appearance of Christ to Saint Francis of Assisi* (in *foglio*), and another smaller etching of *Saint Francis* which shows him receiving the stigmata. His talent was more suited to delicate and devotional subject matters rather than to actions carried out with the boldness which best characterized Correggio's style.

Among Barocci's followers, Cavaliere Francesco Vanni of Siena succeeded in becoming a good painter. Many panels by his hand can be seen in a number of cities and localities in Tuscany, in Lucca, Pisa, and Siena. In the Vatican Basilica in Rome he painted a large panel of the *Fall of Simon Magus,* a work which is inferior, however, to his other works.

# Contract and Two Letters for the *Madonna del Popolo*

Federico Barocci, *Madonna del Popolo*, oil on panel, 1575-1579. Uffizi, Florence.

1. Contract dated June 18, 1575 between Federico Barocci of Urbino and the Eight Rectors of the Fraternità di Santa Maria della Misericordia in Arezzo (Arezzo, Archivio della Fraternità dei Laici, *Deliberazioni dal 1573 al 1577, BB 87,* filza 1486, cc. 107 recto–108 recto).

Die 18 Iunii 1575
Eisdem anno, indictione, pontificatu et magnoducatu, et die Sabati decima octava mensis Iunii. Actum Aretii, in edibus Fraternitatis Sancte Marie de Misericordia dicte civitatis, presentibus ibidem Hieronimo Ludovici de Caponsacchis et magistro Sebastiano Iohannis alias Giannone scultore aretino, testibus etc.

Univeris pateat qualiter Magnifici domini Rectores Fraternitatis Sancte Marie de Misericordia civitatis Aretii, videlicet Dominus Andreas Mattiae de Cencis, Dominus Nerozzus Joannis Antonii de Albergottis, Benedictus Bernardini de Spadaris, Carolus Domini Donati de Marsupinis, Ser Andreas Bartholomei de Subbianis, et Adrianus Domini Augustini de Recuperis collegialiter congregati in sufficiente numero et servatis servandis in eorum solito auditorio, absentibus tamen domino Cristoforo Hieronimi de Francuccis et Cammillo Leonardi de Rosellis eorum collegis, vigore cuius cumque eorum authoritatis pro dicta Fraternitate et omni meliori modo etc., volentes et intendentes pingi facere unam pulcram et speciosam tabulam pro capella Fraternitatis Sancte Marie Plebis de Aretio ultimo loco fabricata, omni meliori modo etc. locaverunt dictum opus et dictam tabulam sic pingendam et faciendam magnifico et celebri pictori Domino Federigo Baroccio de Urbino, presenti et conducenti et stipulanti, cum infrascriptis capitulis, qualitatibus, conditionibus et pactis solemnibus stipulationibus hinc inde firmatis et vallatis videlicet.

Quia convenerunt imprimis quod dicta tabula sit manu propria supradicti Domini Federigi picta ut vulgariter dicitur ad oleum et fabre facta cum omni studio et diligentia ac perfectione, prout ad celebrem et doctum pictorem pertinet et prout melius idem Dominus Federigus peritissimus pictor pingere et facere sciet et poterit. Item sit coloribus finibus et in tabulis ligneis antiquissimis, stabilibus et firmis et ex omni parte et respectu ydoneis, et cum ornamento ligneo inaurato solito poni in extremitate et circum circa tabulam ut bene adhereat et uniatur lapidibus vulgariter appellatis pietre concie supra dictae Capelle, a quibus ipsa tabula ambita et circundata erit. Historia ipsius tabulae sit gloriosissimae Mariae Deiparae semper Virginis intercedentis et orantis ad Dominum Yesum Christum filium eius be-nedictum pro populo ibi similiter picto et representato in dicta tabula cum decoro et venustate et gratia secundum conditionem et qualitatem figurarum ibi pingendarum, singula singulis congrue et respective referendo. Et omnes sumptus et expensae quae fient et fieri contingerint in coloribus et in tabulis et in materia qualibet et in omnibus instrumentis, fiant et fieri debeant de pecuniis dicti Domini Federigi pro ipsum Dominum Federigum, excepto ornamento deaurato ponendo in circuitu et ora ipsius tabule, quod ornamentum fieri debeat de pecuniis dicte Fraternitatis. Item dictus Dominus Federigus ultra tabulam principalem faciendam ut supra, facere teneatur et debeat quamdam tabulam parvam rotundam, secundum porportionem loci rotundi qui apparet incisus et sculptus in ipsa capella lapidea et in capite vel quasi ipsius [*canc.*: tabulae] capellae. In qua parva tabula pingere possit et debeat illam sive illas picturas et inmagines quas maluerit dictus Dominus Federigus, dummodo sit fabre facta, pulcra, ad oleum et manu propria ipsius Domini Federigi. Quam tabulam sive tabulas tam magnam quam parvam possit dictus Dominus Federigus laborare et facere extra civitatem Aretii, in civitate Urbini et sic in patria sua, seu alibi ubi sibi satius fuerit, dummodo ipse postea quam dictam tambulam [*sic*] pinxerit integre et perfecerit, deferat seu verius defferri faciat ad civitatem Aretii et illam ibi tradat finitam integraliter et affixam quoque capellae supradictae Fraternitatis, que sita est in dicta ecclesia Plebis et in suo lecto et loco, sive in suis lectis et locis ibi destinatis, omni periculo, risico, casu et fortuna supradicti Domini Federigi. Expensae tamen omnes que fient et facere oportebit in deferendo et deferri faciendo dictas tabulas de civitate Urbini vel de alia civitate et loco ubi fabricata fuisset [*sic*] ad ipsam civitatem Aretii in qua collocari et stari debet ut supra, videlicet victura iumentorum, mercedes et salaria hominum et instrumenta lignea, ferrea, linea et similia oportuna et necessaria in deferendo ipsas tabulas, fieri et solui debeant de pecuniis dicte Fraternitatis, absque eo quod in dictis et ad dictas expensas faciendas pro deferendo dictas tabulas concurrat dictus Dominus Federigus in aliquo. Et pro omnibus et singulis supradictis et pro dicta tabula pingenda et facienda ut supra, dictus Dominus Federigus habeat habereque debeat a dicta Fraternitate, ultra dictas expensas delationis ipsius tabulae, scuta quatringenta in bona moneta Florentina, videlicet scuta 400 de libris septem pro quolibet scuto, hoc modo videlicet: scuta ducenta similia quae ipse dominus Federigus extraxit actualiter de capsone ferrato Fraternitatis ad presentiam mei notarii et supradictorum testium, videlicet de pecuniis ibi depositatis partim sub die prima marti 1572 et sub die 24 octobris 1573, et partim in hac presenti die, de quibus scutis ducentis dictus Dominus Federigus presens fecit finem et quietationem. Item scuta centum habere et consequi debeat a dicta Fraternitate et a dominis rectoribus Fraternitatis infra octo menses ab hodie, et alia scuta centum pro residuo scutorum quatringentorum consequi et habere debeat finito integraliter toto opere et collocata et affixa dicta tabula sive tabulis in locis suis supradictis, et sic infra unum annum ab hodie. Infra quem annum dictus Dominus Federigus promisit dictam tambulam [*sic*] sive tabulas pingere, facere, defferre et collocare eam sive eas in locis suis supradictis et supradictae capellae Fraternitatis. Et si forte dictus Dominus Federigus desineret esse in humanis et moreretur (quod Deus advertat) antequam perficeret dictum opus, convenerunt in dicto casu quod heredes et successores suprascripti Domini Federigi teneantur restituere et solvere dictae Fraternitati totam quantitatem pecuniarum quam illucusque habuisset et recepisset pro dicto opere confficiendo dictus Dominus Federigus, et tabula incohata et semipicta et nondum finita remanere debeat supradictis heredibus dicti Domini Federigi, et ita convenerunt dicti contrahentes solemnibus stipulationibus hinc inde intervenientibus. Pro quo quidem Domino Federigo et eius praecibus et mandatis Michael filius quondam alberius Michaelis Petri de Tortorinis, lapicida Aretinus, presens et sciens ad supradicta non teneri, sed volons teneri et efficaciter obligari, ideo sponte, ex certa eius scientia, per se et suos heredes et successores solemniter et in forma iuris fideiussit et fideiussor extitit pro dicto Domino Federigo penes supradictos Dominos Rectores presentes et stipulantes pro dicta Fraternitate et pro omnibus et singulis quorum interest, intererit et interesse poterit quomodolibet in futurum, in omnibus et singulis supradictis promissionibus obligationibus et in omnibus et singulis promissis, actis, gestis et factis per dictum Dominum Federigum et in quolibet illorum menbro et capite, atque etiam ut principalis principaliter se obligavit dictus Michael ad omnia et singula supradicta. Quem indemnem etc. Quae omnia et singula supradicta promiserunt perpetuo attendere, adimplere et observare, sub pena dupli etc., quae pena etc., qua pena etc. Pro quibus omnibus etc. obligaverunt etc., videlicet dicti domini Rectores dictam Fraternitatem et ipsius Fraternitatis iura, res et bona presentia et futura et Rectores pro tempore existentes, dictis nominibus tantum, dictus vero Dominus Federigus et dictus Michael in solidum obligaverunt se ipsos et suos heredes et successores, iura, res et bona presentia et futura. Renuntiantes etc. Iurantes etc. Rogantes etc.

**2.** Letter dated October 26, 1578 from Federico Barocci in Urbino to the Rectors of the Fraternità di Santa Maria della Misericordia in Arezzo (Arezzo, Archivio della Fraternità dei Laici, *Registro di lettere, CCI,* filza 175, cc. 176 verso–177 recto).

Molto magnifici Signori Rettori padroni osservantissimi

Per dua cause son indugiato sin' hora à dimandare li cento scudi di cotesta moneta che io devo havere per il secondo pagamento. La prima causa é stata il non haverne hauto bisogno, et l'altra è stata che sin tanto non ho vista l'opera à un certo buon termine, non me son curato pigliare altri dinari, hora che Dio laudato la tavola è a bonissimo termine et ritrovandomi il bisogno di danari, prego le SS. VV. . Molti si voglino contentare quanto prima mandarli, essendovi persona fidata, che venisse di qua di corto sarebbe bene, caso che non li potranno dare al procaccio indrezzando la lettera à messer Rafaello Angelini d'Urbino, et il procaccio li potrà consignare à Fermignano Castello d'Urbino, à Marchione Horte, che lui subito li portarà à Urbino: et di grande quelle non manchino per loro cortesia farmi questo servitio, et favore qual mettarò fra gl'altri da loro riceuti. Circa la tavola penserò con l'aiuto del Signore che sarà finita à tempo nuovo et io non mancarò darli buon fine quanto à me serà possibile et sin tanto star io sane, et allegre, che nostro Signore Dio le contenti, e prosperi, e gli bacio le mani. D'Urbino allì 26 8bre 1578.

Di VV.SS. Molti
Servitore Affezionatissimo Federigo Barocci

Alli molto magnifici signori miei padroni osservantissimi li Signori Rettori della Fraternità

Post scritta mandando li scudi doro in oro farete che sieno di peso, perche qua il nostro Duca ha fatto un bando che se li perde assai; imperciò serà meglio avertirci acciò non vi venisse il danno mio
Servitore Federigo Barocci

**3.** Letter dated October 30, 1578 from the Rectors of the Fraternità di Santa Maria della Misericordia in Arezzo to Federico Barocci in Urbino (Arezzo, Archivio della Fraternità dei Laici, *Registro di lettere, CCI,* filza 175, cc. 176 recto–176 verso).

Molto magnifico messer Federigo
Haviamo riceuto la lettera di V.S. delli 26 dello stante, alla quale con brevità rispondendo diciamo, che li cento scudi che ella ci scrive che gli mandiamo per la seconda paga à conto del prezzo della tavola non segli mandano hora, si perche non ci troviamo à dua giorni al fine del nostro offitio, et si perche à noi pare, che l'opera della tavola, che conforme alla conventione fatta si doveva dar fornita, et condotta in Arezzo nel luogo, et nell'altare perciò fatto, come V.S. ha veduto, fra termine di un'anno, et così per tutto il dì 18 del mese di Giugno 1576: non solo non sia fornita condotta, et messa nel detto suo luogo, et altare, ma si pensi di darla fornita à tempo nuovo, cosa invero tutta contraria alla sudetta conventione: et nondimeno poi che la tavola si trova ancora imperfetta, et noi desideriamo haverla compita, non mancaremo lasciare la cura, et ordine al nuovo Magistro delli signori Rettori, che entraranno il primo di Novembre prossimo, che mandino detti denari à V.S., quali non doverano mancare di fare quanto sarà conveniente, et honesto: et non essendo questa per altro di core ce li raccomandiamo.
D'Arezzo allì 30 ottobre 1578.
Di V.S. molto magnifica
Affezionatissimi
Li Rettori della fraternità d'Arezzo

Al molto magnifico messer federigo Barocci, nostro osservantissimo

1

# Catalogue of Drawings

**1** *The Vision of Saint Cecilia, with Saints Mary Magdalene, John the Evangelist, Paul, and Catherine of Alexandria*

Pen and brown ink, and brown wash, heightened with white, with traces of a preliminary drawing in black chalk and (on right) red chalk, on beige paper, 316 x 229 mm. Annotated in black chalk at lower right: *Nr. 1437*; in pen and brown ink at lower left: *10/z*. Annotated on reverse in pencil: *von einem Schüler Santis.* Laid down; red chalk stains on right; white (on Magdalene and John's eagle) partially oxidized; surface abrasion, especially on left; traces of central horizontal and vertical folds; small repaired holes and tears in upper right, lower left, and lower right corners; tear along right contour of Cecilia; shoulder of John reworked in black chalk; small red paint spots in left corner.

Stuttgart, Staatsgalerie Stuttgart, Graphische Sammlung, Inv. 1338

Published: Olsen, 1969, pp. 49–54, fig. 2; Pillsbury, *M.D.*, 1976, p. 57; C. Thiem, *Die italienischen Zeichnungen in der Graphischen Sammlung des Staatsgalerie Stuttgart*, Stuttgart, 1977, no. 369.

The recent discovery of Barocci's *modello* for his earliest surviving composition, the *St. Cecilia* altarpiece of ca. 1556 in the Urbino Cathedral, has made an important contribution to our knowledge of the artist's formation and development as a draughtsman. Identified among the anonymous Italian drawings in the Staatsgalerie in 1966 by Christel Thiem and subsequently published by Harald Olsen *(loc. cit.),* the delicately executed pen and wash study betrays a strong debt to the calligraphic drawing style of Barocci's first teacher, Battista Franco (see Cat. 2). According to Bellori, Franco put the young student to work copying from plaster casts and reliefs. Through Franco, who was prolific as an engraver, Barocci also probably became aware of the prints of Marcantonio Raimondi,[1] in particular the engraving after a lost drawing by Raphael for the *St. Cecilia and Four Saints.*[2] As Schmarsow, Krommes and di Pietro were the first to observe, Barocci relies upon this model, as much as that of Raphael's painting of 1516 in the Bologna Pinacoteca, for developing his composition. The Stuttgart drawing supports this conclusion by establishing new links with the engraving. As in the Marcantonio engraving, the last saint on the left looks downwards and to the right, with one arm extended from its body at a right angle; the saint closing the group on the right gazes upwards at the appearance of music-making

angels; the figure of St. John stares out at the viewer; and the sky is filled with two large angels. In the final work Barocci altered these and other details producing a work whose linear rhythms, dry coloring, and elongated forms have more in common with the Central Italian mannerist style of Franco and Bolognese artists like Prospero Fontana than it does with the more three-dimensional, strongly modelled art of Raphael.

There are no other drawings by Barocci that can be connected with the *St. Cecilia.* One may deduce that at this stage in his career the artist's working method did not include the use of detailed studies from nature, which the artist began to employ on a regular basis only in the next decade, with the Casino of Pius IV decorations in Rome. Given the nature of the commission, and the artist's treatment of the subject, the absence of life studies should come as no surprise.

1. W. Rearick suggests that Franco recieved his training as an engraver from Marcantonio ("Battista Franco and the Grimani Chapel," *Saggi e memorie di storia dell'arte,* II, 1959, p. 112, n. 36).
2. Reproduced in F. di Pietro, "La 'Santa Cecilia' di F. Barocci nel Duomo di Urbino," *Studi e notizie,* 1913, pp. 101–111, fig. 34.

2

## BATTISTA FRANCO (Venice ca. 1510–1561)

**2** *The Virgin and Child with St. Catherine of Alexandria and an Elderly Female Saint (possibly Anne)*

Pen and brown ink, brown wash, heightened with white, over a preliminary drawing in red chalk, on white paper, 260 x 262 mm. (280 mm. in diameter at widest point). Reduced to a circular format, bordered with pale blue watercolor, and mounted against a gold background; some oxidation of whites; horizontal crease; scattered stains and repairs; according to a note on the reverse of the mount: "In July 1862 the lights were restored by an artist under the advice of Mr. Colnaghi when the small figure near the child appeared—this Cheney thinks was not part of the design and purposely rubbed over—'I Pentimenti' in the Child's head then appeared also."

Cleveland, The Cleveland Museum of Art, Delia E. Holden Fund, no. 65.16

Provenance: Jonathan Richardson, Sr., London (Lugt 2183); Earl Spencer, Althorp (Lugt 1531); William Roscoe, Liverpool (Lugt 2645); Studley Martin; O'Byrne.
Published: L. Richards, "Drawings by Battista Franco," *The Bulletin of the Cleveland Museum of Art,* LII, no. 8, Oct. 1965, pp. 107, 110, 112, illus. p. 106.

Battista Franco's relevance to this exhibition is as Barocci's teacher. In his biography of the artist, Bellori relates that Barocci's natural ability and enthusiasm for drawing, which he had acquired from his father, a sculptor and maker of mathematical instruments, were so great that he was encouraged to become a painter and, with the approval of his uncle, the architect Bartolomeo Genga (1516–1558), he went to study with Battista Franco. Venetian by birth, Franco had come at an early age, probably in the early 1530s, to Rome, where he fell under the spell of Michelangelo and classical antiquity and came into contact with Martin Heemskerck (1498–1574) and other younger artists visiting the eternal city.

In 1545 Duke Guidobaldo invited him to Urbino to decorate the vault of the cathedral (completely destroyed by fire in the eighteenth century), and except for brief trips to Rome he remained in Urbino for at least the next seven years, receiving the commission to paint the vault of the Chapel of the Sacraments in the Duomo (which later would house Barocci's *Last Supper*), executing designs for the ducal majolica factory in Castel Durante, and executing other pictures for the Duke (e.g. those in the Cathedral sacristy today). Franco returned to Venice before 1554.[1]

In all likelihood Barocci became apprenticed to the older artist around 1550 and remained with him for no more than a few years. While Franco's influence is critical in the *St. Cecilia*, as is evident both in the drawing in Stuttgart and in the finished work, it is considerably less (although not entirely erased) in the *Martyrdom of St. Sebastian* which was commissioned in 1557 and shows the impact of Venetian art (seen in the Ducal collections in Pesaro after Franco's departure) and the artist's first visit to Rome.

Although the *Virgin and Child and Two Saints* cannot be identified with a known work (as is the case with the majority of Franco's figural drawings), its style is characteristic of Franco with its reliance upon large Michelangelesque forms and thin contours tightly hatched and crosshatched with low diagonal penstrokes and further modelled with brown wash and white highlights. It has been suggested that it was done in the 1540s, and the connection of the sleeping child under Christ's left hand (in the upper right corner of the design) with Michelangelo's so-called *Madonna of Silence* (London, Duke of Portland) would seem to support this view.[2]

The stylistic connections of this work with that of Barocci's modello for the *St. Cecilia* in Stuttgart (Cat. 1) are numerous. The engraver-like neatness of outline, the emphatic shading by means of wash and body-color, the rich patterning of the drapery folds as well as the oversized, Michelangelesque character of the forms themselves, all are qualities shared by the two works. It should be noted, however, that Barocci's drawing style, even at this early point in his career, is distinct from that of Franco. While Franco's lines are insistent, Barocci's tend to have a certain degree of lightness and delicacy. Moreover, whereas the modelling in Franco's drawing reinforces and strengthens the definition of the forms, in Barocci's it flickers evenly across the surface, creating an abstract pattern of light and shade. In Barocci's drawing, in short, the forms have less tactility; they exist as a function of the form-defining power of light. They are conceived pictorially rather than sculpturally, and the overall effect is less one of a harsh brittleness than of a tender arabesque.

1. This information is based upon W. Rearick's study of the artist in *Saggi e memorie di storia dell'arte*, II, 1959, pp. 105–139, and L. Salomoni, "Battista Franco nelle Marche," *Arte Veneta*, XXVI, 1972, pp. 237–245.
2. As noted by L. Richards, *loc. cit.* The technique of the drawing is closely related to a drawing of the *Madonna and Child and a Female Figure* in the British Museum (no. 1895–9–15–855). In style the Cleveland drawing should be compared with the artist's painting of the *Pietà* in Lucca.

## 3 *Virgin and Child Seated on Clouds*

Black chalk, on blue paper, 220 x 169 mm. Annotated (? by E. G. Harzen) in pen and brown ink at lower right: *federici Barocci/Ita est. Ce'sander Ad . . .* (edge of sheet). Laid down; small repaired hole at middle of right edge; light stain (from verso) across lower center; scattered light brown oil spots at lower right.

Hamburg, Hamburger Kunsthalle, no. 21054

Provenance: E. Harzen, Hamburg.
Published: Olsen, 1955, p. 111; Olsen, 1962, p. 140.

In this black chalk sketch the Virgin is shown seated on a bank of clouds bending over slightly to the left with her arm round the standing Christ Child; a *pentimento* reveals that the artist first wanted the Virgin to support the raised foot of the Child with her left hand. Traditionally ascribed to the artist, this drawing is identifiable as a preliminary idea for the Madonna and Child group in the upper half of the *Martyrdom of Saint Sebastian* in the Cathedral at Urbino. In the painting the Virgin sits in the same position as in the drawing, now with the Christ Child moved to her left hip and shown embracing his mother from a seated rather than standing position.

3

Barocci was commissioned to carry out the altarpiece from the heirs of Antonio Bonaventura on November 9, 1557. The date of the painting's completion is unknown, but it must be placed before his departure for Rome in 1560. The fact that the commission for the painting was made with Barocci's father rather than with Barocci himself has been considered a reason to think that Barocci was in Rome in late 1557. It is equally possible, however, that, if Barocci was born in the mid-1530s, as most scholars now contend he was, his age in 1557 would have been only twenty-two; as the age of majority in most Italian cities was twenty-five, his father's signature on the contract would have been required by law.

It is likely that Barocci went to Rome as well as Pesaro sometime during the interval between the completion of the *St. Cecilia* and his work on the *Martyrdom of Saint Sebastian*. The influence of Correggio is still not evident in the *Sebastian* altarpiece, but the combined effect of Venetian art and Taddeo Zuccaro's recent frescoes in S. Maria della Consolazione, Rome, is manifest. Sebastiano del Piombo's *Martyrdom of Saint Agatha* in the Pitti, which Barocci saw and sketched in Pesaro, provided the general inspiration for the dramatic gathering of figures in the lower part of the picture.[1] Titian's *Madonna* in Ancona served the same purpose for the upper half of the composition. Other paintings by Titian, like the Compagnia di Corpus Domini *gonfalone* of the *Last Supper* in Urbino, account for the richly colored vestments, expressive heads, and naturalistic details like the dog in the foreground. Barocci incorporated many of these features into his works done in Rome in the following decade, particularly in the *Holy Family with Saints John, Elizabeth, and Zacharias* in the Casino of Pius IV. On the other hand, the exaggerated contortions of the St. Sebastian and archer figures, their strongly foreshortened limbs, and the donor portrait at the front edge of the picture reveal a knowledge of Taddeo Zuccaro's Mattei Chapel frescoes completed in 1556.[2] Taddeo was in Urbino from 1551 to 1553 and, according to Bellori, took Barocci to visit various monuments when the latter came to Rome for the first time.

The *Sebastian* altarpiece is, nonetheless, not completely free of elements reminiscent of Franco. In the upper part, the half-circle of putti that surround the Virgin form a decorative frieze that recalls Franco's engravings after antique cameos;[3] likewise the coloring and design of the Virgin's garments have a metallic coldness reminiscent of Franco's paintings, and the basic division of the scene into separate zones connected abstractly—not dramatically—by means of a central armature (the tree) is a device inherited from Franco and Central Italian art.

The Hamburg drawing reveals a similar multiplicity of sources. The use of black chalk (not the usual pen) as the sketching medium and the choice of a colored paper, a natural blue like that commonly used in Venice and other parts of North Italy, show Barocci's receptivity to new ideas and the beginning of his conversion to a more pictorial style, while the actual forms depicted are at least in part inherited from Barocci's first teacher. The Christ Child, as represented in the drawing, comes directly from an etching by Franco: the lovely circular composition of the *Madonna and Child with the Infant Baptist.*[4]

As in the case of the *St. Cecilia*, it would appear that Barocci developed the composition and executed the picture without making numerous life studies of the individual parts. The only other drawings for the picture which have come to light are Uffizi 11600 recto and verso for the right leg of Christ and the right arm of the angel on the far left and, possibly, Albertina, Inv. 17,653 (R.384), a pastel study of a bearded man similar in pose and features to the man with white beard located in the background between the martyred saint and the magistrate.

1. British Museum no. Pp. 3–201, which contains a well-known study for the later *Madonna del Popolo* on its recto (repr. Olsen, 1962, fig. 43b), shows on its reverse two chalk sketches of a martyrdom scene which is derived from Sebastiano's painting. These sketches are dateable to the period in which Barocci was working on the *St. Sebastian* altarpiece because of the brief outlines of

a figure, similar to that of the archer in the right foreground of the painting, seen on the left side of the recto when the sheet is rotated ninety degrees to the right.
2. In particular, the *Flagellation* (for the torso of St. Sebastian and the pose of the figure nearest to the saint on the right), the *Ecce Homo* (for the pose of the magistrate and Sebastian) and the *Crucifixion* (for the donor portrait), repr. by J. Gere, *Taddeo Zuccaro: His Development Studied in his Drawings,* London, 1969, figs. 73, 72, and 75 respectively.
3. E.g. Bartsch XVI.148.82.2, a copy of which belongs to the British Museum, no. 1874–8–8–413.
4. Repr. Pittaluga, 1930, fig. 231.

**4** *Study for a Wall Decoration with Female Figures on either side of a Rectangular Panel who hold a Canopy; Small Angel Turned to Right, Full-face; Small Figure (Angel?) Seen from Behind*

Black chalk, stumped, pen and brown ink, and dark brown wash, heightened with white, with traces of incised stylus lines under the figures, on greenish-blue paper, 240 x 217 mm. Inscribed in pen and brown ink at lower center: *B.* Annotated in pen and brown ink at lower right: *Federigo Zucceri* [?] (the latter name erased); in pencil on reverse of mount: *Zucchero Federigo 1542–1609 No. 147;* in another hand: *F. Zuccero o. Eleve 1542–1609;* in red chalk: *115.* Partially laid down; whites partially oxidized; trace of central vertical crease; gray spot at lower center edge.

Detroit, The Detroit Institute of Arts, William H. Murphy Fund, no. 34.138

Provenance: Unidentified collector's stamp, an arrow in blue, on reverse (cf. Lugt 2200a); H. Voss, Berlin; acquired in 1934.
Exhibited: Ann Arbor, The University of Michigan Museum of Art, April–May 1973, no catalogue.
Published: Smith, 1973, pp. 83–88, fig. 2; Smith, 1977, pp. 69–70, fig. 55.

Barocci's first major commission was for the interior decoration of the small villa of Pius IV in the Vatican gardens. Payments to the artist for work at the Casino extend from November 1561 to October 1562 (a final payment is dated June 10, 1563); other artists involved in the undertaking were Federico Zuccaro, Santi di Tito, Orazio Sammacchini, and a group of young assistants. Early sources give to Barocci individual stories and figures in the first two rooms on the ground floor. On the evidence of drawings, Friedländer and other scholars have concluded that Barocci was responsible for the overall design of the decorative plan of the two lower rooms as well. And as we shall try to show (Cat. 6–7), Barocci may also have participated in the decorations of two further rooms on the upper floor: the Galleria (over the portico) and the so-called Santi di Tito

room bearing an oval representation of the *Agony in the Garden* in the center of the vault.

The Detroit drawing was only discovered, and connected with the Casino, by Graham Smith in 1973 (*loc. cit.*). Smith correctly identified the sheet as a preparatory study for the central section of one of the long coves of the large room, or Stanza Grande, on the ground floor of the Casino, noting that the figure on the right side of the sheet compares closely, both in pose and in the arrangement of the draperies, with the woman to the right of the *Baptism;* and it is of interest that of the two figures in the drawing only the righthand one is developed to a finished state in wash and white highlights. In the completed fresco the artist altered both the pose of the lefthand figure and many of the elements in the overall decorative setting. In the final work the figure sits with a rod in her hand and with her legs crossed, holding a garland of fruit, flowers, and vegetables, rather than a tasseled canopy; while the central panel is transformed into a horizontal, not vertical, format embellished with volutes, and an escutcheon, and crowned by a segmental pediment framing a trophy (not a burning chalice). As Professor Smith has noted, the reason for altering the composition of the two figures may have been to avoid the repetition of gestures in the drawing. The unused motifs were adapted for other parts of the room, in particular for the tops of the coves in the four corners where a similar tasseled and knotted baldachin appears—supported by a pair of small angels, however, rather than by two adult females.

In style and technique this drawing owes a debt to the work of Barocci's elder countryman, Taddeo Zuccaro. We have already noted the influence of Taddeo's Mattei Chapel frescoes on the lower half of the *Martyrdom of St. Sebastian,* the altarpiece Barocci completed just before coming to Rome. The figures in the Detroit drawing can also be related to the same project, especially the sibyls represented on the arch leading to the chapel.[1] Moreover, the use of pen and wash with white bodycolor over black chalk on blue paper in the Detroit drawing is one that Zuccaro used in the drawings to prepare his S. Maria della Consolazione frescoes and other contemporary works.[2] In view of the close stylistic affinity with Taddeo, it is not surprising that the Detroit drawing bears an old attribution to Taddeo's young brother, Federico, who served as Taddeo's assistant in the late 1550s and early 1560s and whose early drawings often employ a similar technique.

1. J. Gere, *Taddeo Zuccaro: His Development Studied in his Drawings,* London, 1969, fig. 65.
2. *Ibid.,* pp. 66–67, figs. 63–64, 66.

4

5

6

## AFTER FEDERICO BAROCCI

**5** *Virgin and Child*

Black, red, and white chalks colored with yellow, rose, and salmon-pink pastels, on light gray-blue paper, 250 x 195. Laid down; light stains at lower edge and along right edge.

New York, The Pierpont Morgan Library, no. IV, 154

Provenance: C. Fairfax Murray; J. Pierpont Morgan.
Exhibited: Northampton (Massachusetts), Smith College Museum of Art, *Italian Drawings 1330–1780*, 1941–1942, no. 11.
Published: *J. Pierpont Morgan Collection of Drawings by the Old Masters Formed by C. Fairfax Murray*, IV, London, 1912, no. 154.

The large rectangular panel in the center of the ceiling in the first room on the ground floor of the Casino of Pius IV represents the *Holy Family with Saints John, Elizabeth, and Zachariah*. In it Barocci created a work that immediately established him, in Vasari's words, as ''giovane di grande aspettazione.'' Incorporating elements from the artist's new environment, in particular the works of Raphael and Giulio (e.g. the Farnesina frescoes and Giulio's *Madonna della Gatta*), the fresco introduces a system of modelling in color that was new in Rome.

The Morgan Library drawing has been traditionally considered a study for the central Virgin and Child, and, in fact, the design and coloring have a close affinity with the painting. The decorative handling of the colored chalks (or pastels), however, is foreign to Barocci, as is the characterization of the individual parts of the body, especially the faces and hands. It would seem more likely that the drawing was made as a copy after the fresco rather than as a working drawing and possibly, as a note on the mount has suggested, the work of the Sienese artist Francesco Vanni. Vanni, although never a direct disciple of Barocci, emulated Barocci's style of painting, especially that of his early works, with great success and had a strong influence on a generation of artists in Siena.[1]

It is worth noting in regard to this drawing that Barocci's technique of using colored chalks, or pastels, was quite distinct. While in this work the pastel shades are arbitrarily applied to create a decorative effect, in Barocci's the use of artificially produced chalks, or pastels, was restricted to specific modelling functions such as suggesting skin tone (usually a buff or light pink pastel) or giving hair texture and local color (a deep ochre pastel). The rest of the color values Barocci created by stumping, blending or wetting the three traditional chalks—black, red, and white; and it is in these three basic colors that most of Barocci's drawings are done, often with a natural blue or brown-tinted paper serving as a middle tone.

1. The style of the Morgan drawing should be compared with that of Vanni's early chalk studies, for example Uffizi 9337S, 1696E, and 4783S (repr. P. Riedl, *Disegni dei barocceschi senesi*, Florence, Gabinetto Disegni e Stampe degli Uffizi, 1976, figs. 5, 8–9).

**6** *Individual Studies for Four Putti Seated on a Cornice: Two Angels with a Cartouche and Two Putti with a Cord*

Pen and brown ink, point of the brush and brush and brown wash, on white paper, 180 x 255 mm. (including 10 mm. extension at lower edge). Inscribed in pen and brown ink within a cartouche: *quanto se puo dir/ antiamodo bella fanno quanto se/mai possibille/di talle vallor/bella mani(e)ra;*[1] at lower left: *...uallo marovillia/...scho quanto in mani...* (indecipherable; crossed out); at lower right: *quest ...* (end of sheet). Annotated in pen and brown ink on mount at lower right: *Correggio.* Laid down. Watermark: similar to Briquet no. 749.

Chatsworth, The Trustees of the Chatsworth Settlement, no. 769

Provenance: N. Lanière, London (Lugt 2886); William, 2nd Duke of Devonshire (Lugt 718).
Exhibited: London, Royal Academy, *Drawings by Old Masters*, 1953, cat. by J. Byam Shaw, p. 35, no. 116; Bologna, 1975, no. 12, p. 60.
Published: Olsen, 1955, p. 113; Olsen, 1962, p. 144; Pillsbury, *M.D.*, 1976, p. 60.

This sheet of putto studies bears an old attribution to Correggio, an idea suggested by the technique—pen, point of the brush, and wash—and fluidity of execution.[2] Its authorship as the work of Barocci, however, is in little doubt. The figures themselves bear a close relationship with the small angels represented in the corners of the first room on the ground floor in the Casino of Pius IV and the technique is comparable to that used by Barocci to make large-scale compositional and figure sketches.[3] Taddeo's influence on the younger artist's drawing style is still evident at this point.

The precise identification of the drawing with a known work by Barocci is more problematic. On the basis of the resemblance of the figures with the small frescoed angels in the large downstairs room of the Casino and with those sketched on a drawing in the Uffizi (no. 907F), believed to contain a first idea for the first or second downstairs rooms, modern writers (loc. cit.) have associated the drawing with the commission to decorate the ground-floor rooms and have assumed the drawing was done at an early stage in the planning. The recent identification of the arms of Cardinal Giulio della Rovere, Barocci's Roman patron and protector, on the Uffizi sheet, however, places this theory in doubt.[4] A more convincing case exists for identifying the drawing as a study for the stucco figures in the corners of the so-called Santi di Tito room on the second floor of the casino. This room contains representations from the Life of Christ in the vault and standing female personifications of the Cardinal and Theological Virtues in the corners. Tucked between each pair of Virtues sit two stuccoed putti, their legs projecting over the cornice, engaged alternately in holding the papal escutcheon or binding a cord through the papal keys. Although there is no exact correspondence between a figure in the drawing and its counterpart in stucco, the overall similarity of function and postures, especially if certain poses are reversed, is sufficient to imagine that the drawing served as a model for the stucco workers. None of the early sources (Vasari, Borghini, or Bellori) mentions Barocci's activity at the Casino beyond the two rooms on the ground floor, but this, in itself, does not rule out the possibility of his involvement since the sources give an incomplete account of the work there.

Graham Smith has recently concluded a study of the Casino in which he has revised many of Friedländer's attributions of the paintings. Among his changes has been to attribute the room under discussion to Federico Zuccaro, based on Vasari's testimony and a re-reading of the payments.[5] While it is possible that Federico Zuccaro,

rather than Santi di Tito or some other assistant in the project, was responsible for the overall plan of the room's decorations and the designs for certain individual parts (like the Transfiguration, Last Supper, and First Temptation of Christ), there is nothing to preclude Barocci's intervention in the execution or planning of the individual parts. The monthly payments preserved in the Archivio di Stato in Rome establish that Barocci began work in 1561 in the "prima stanza . . . del primo piano," then he went to the "terza stanza" (identified elsewhere as the "terza stanza di sopra"), from there to unspecified rooms, and ended up in the "stanza grande."[6] If we identify the "terza stanza" as the large room on the upper floor—an hypothesis which is plausible from other points of view as well—then it is possible to associate Barocci with the group of assistants who worked with Federico Zuccaro to decorate the upstairs room.[7]

1. This transcription is based upon that of Bertelà and Emiliani in the 1975 Bologna exhibition catalogue, no. 12, p. 60.
2. Cf. A. E. Popham, Correggio's Drawings, London, 1957, pls. XXXIb, XLVIb, and XCa.
3. E.g. Edinburgh, National Gallery of Scotland, Inv. D.725 and Louvre, Inv. 2861 (repr. Bologna, 1975, figs. 40 and 23).
4. Smith, 1973, pp. 88, 91 n. 15.
5. Smith, 1977.
6. The documents are catalogued and annotated by Friedländer, 1912, pp. 123–132.
7. One of the most perplexing problems has been the interpretation of the room numbers mentioned in the payments to the individual artists in regard to work at the Casino. The only certain identification is that of the Galleria, which is mentioned as the fourth room. The others are open to question. Both Friedländer and Smith have attempted to give numbers to the individual rooms, but neither account is entirely satisfactory. I would propose the ground-floor room where Barocci and Santi di Tito worked (with the Annunciation in the vault) be identified as number two, the large adjacent room painted mostly by Barocci number one, the room on the upper floor with the Life of Christ and Virtues three, either the chapel or portico on the ground floor five, and the stairway vault (by Santi di Tito) six.


## 7 Temperance

Pen and brown ink, brown wash, heightened with white, on blue paper, 226 x 101 mm. Annotated in pen and brown ink at lower left: Barocj. Laid down; whites oxidized on right arm and vases; brownish spots at lower left. An old copy is at Windsor (4788; Popham-Wilde, Cat. no. 754, as "attributed to Giuseppe Porta; repr. Arte Veneta, XVII, 1963, p. 164)

Ottawa, National Gallery of Canada, no. 6896

Provenance: unidentified mark (not in Lugt); acquired from P. & D. Colnaghi & Co., Ltd., London, on the recommendation of Paul Oppé (no. 338), in 1957.
Published: A. E. Popham and K. M. Fenwick,

European Drawings in the Collection of the National Gallery of Canada, Toronto, 1965, no. 40, p. 31, repr.; J. Gere, Taddeo Zuccaro: His Development Studied in his Drawings, London, 1969, no. 153, p. 182; Smith, 1970, pp. 108–110, fig. 55; Smith, 1977, pp. 65–66.

Traditionally ascribed to Barocci, this drawing has more recently been given to Taddeo Zuccaro by Popham, Gere, and Graham Smith.[1] The latter related the work to the frescoed figure of Temperance in one of the corners of the coves in a room on the second floor of the Casino, painted with scenes from the Life of Christ and the Cardinal and Theological Virtues. Smith concluded that Taddeo provided the drawing to his younger brother as a guide in carrying out the fresco. While in the Zuccaro workshop there may be a precedent for this kind of collaboration and the drawing's relationship to the fresco is indisputable, a question arises about the drawing's attribution to Taddeo. In rejecting the traditional attribution of the drawing to Barocci in 1965, Popham noted that "the handling of the drawing does indeed come near to that of Barocci at a stage when his style of drawing closely resembled that of his contemporary and fellow townsman, Taddeo Zuccaro . . ." (loc. cit.). Popham's observations were made without the knowledge of the drawing's purpose and date and without the knowledge of some of the works by Barocci closely related in style and technique, like the Detroit Study for a Wall Decoration (Cat. 4). This drawing and others by Barocci of the same period, like the Adoration of the Magi in the Van Altena Collection (Cat. 9), executed with pen, wash, and bodycolor on blue paper, rely on long, controlled penstrokes that are repeated, and then strengthened with low parallel hatching, and finally covered by broad applications of wash and white highlights. Whereas similar drawings by Taddeo, like those for the Mattei Chapel sibyls, are built up systematically in different media to enhance the plastic effect,[2] Barocci's drawings are conceived in terms of light and dark; the wash and the whites play a role in refining the design as well as putting the forms into relief. Also characteristic of Barocci is the way in which the artist conceived of the figure: first as a sketch of a naked torso—one, in fact, reminiscent of Michelangelo's Risen Christ in the Minerva—executed to establish the pose and subsequently as a study of the drapery covering the figure to fix its final form.

Yet once we accept the traditional attribution of the Ottawa drawing to Barocci, we must confront the question of the authorship of the related fresco. As has already been noted, the paintings in the room have been given to Santi di Tito and, more re-

34

cently, to Federico Zuccaro. In regard to this room, Vasari mentions not only the latter but also Orazio Sammacchini and Lorenzo Costa.[3] An examination of the actual room would suggest that not only these but other artists as well may have collaborated in the execution. Among the eight Virtues, *Fortitude, Justice,* and *Peace* (holding a dove) seem to be by one hand; *Wisdom* and *Hope* another; and *Faith, Charity,* and *Temperance* by three further artists. And certain of these show the characteristics of identifiable hands. The *Charity* has an elegance of stance and lightness of coloring that suggests the works of Santi di Tito; the *Faith* would appear to be by a Bolognese, possibly Sammacchini; the *Justice, Love,* and *Fortitude* are more apt to be by a close follower of Zuccaro's (Lorenzo Costa?); while the *Wisdom* and *Hope* may be by the same artist who executed the parts of the first room downstairs which Barocci did not carry out himself (who has been identified as Pierleone Genga). The figure of *Temperance* has possibly the most pronounced stylistic features of any of the eight Virtues. Its draperies are softly and delicately executed without the calligraphic, or purely abstract, flourishes of the other figures. The pose is simple and logical with the large torso of the figure poised naturally on one leg, while the head inclines slightly downwards to follow the flow of water from one vessel to another. And the colors are light and airy: the transparent veil is beige, the blouse pink and ochre, and the skirt a bright, almost turquoise, green. Moreover, all of the colors are suffused with a brilliant white light which shimmers across the surface. In all these respects one is reminded of Barocci's allegorical figures in the large room below, which have similar softly textured but richly colored draperies. The pose of the figure even brings to mind that of one of the figures in Barocci's nearly contemporary *Martyrdom of Saint Sebastian;* compare, for example, the position of the hands and legs in the *Temperance* with the limbs of the bearded man carrying the sheath of arrows on St. Sebastian's left.

If Barocci were responsible for both the drawing and the painting of one of the eight Virtues, and for the design of the stuccoed angels in the corners as well, his role in the entire Casino project must have been considerably greater than has been previously believed. Barocci might have quickly demonstrated his remarkable gifts when he arrived at the Casino and consequently received a greater part in the formulation and execution of all the decorations than the other assistants of Federico Zuccaro.[4] If the room is identifiable from documents as the "terza stanza di sopra," as would seem likely, Barocci worked in the upper-floor

7

room from November 1561 to January 1562 and received 45 scudi for his efforts.

1. According to a note written on the drawing's mat, John Gere now acknowledges that the traditional attribution of the drawing to Barocci may be correct. I am grateful to Mimi Cazort Taylor, Curator of Drawings at the National Gallery of Canada, for conveying this information to me.

2. J. Gere, *Taddeo Zuccaro: His Development Studied in his Drawings,* London, 1969, pls. 62–64.

3. Vasari-Milanesi, VII, p. 92.

4. It is tempting to consider the possibility that Barocci's lively pen sketch for an *Agony in the Garden* in the Uffizi (No. 11482F; repr. Olsen, 1962, fig. 14b), which has a preliminary drawing for an escutcheon on its verso and hence has been associated with the Casino decorations, was executed with the central panel of the upper-floor room, which bears an oval representation of the same subject, in mind. Barocci's treatment of the scene in the drawing is analogous to his handling of the *Annunciation* fresco on the ground floor.

**8** *Study for the Drapery of Saint Catherine of*
*Alexandria Kneeling in Profile to the left*

Black and white chalks, stumped, squared in
black chalk, on light brown paper, 350 x 257 mm.
Annotated in pen and black ink at upper left: *N.⁰*
*13;* in pencil at lower left: *N⁰. 412 p. 20;* in pen and
brown ink at lower center: *Barocci;* in pen and
brown ink at lower right: *N.7.* Laid down; large
gray and brown stains along upper and lower
edges and scattered throughout; two small holes
along bottom hem of cape.

London, Trustees of the British Museum, no.
1946–7–13–20

Provenance: Sir Thomas Phillipps; T. Fitzroy
Fenwick, Cheltenham; acquired in 1946.
Published: A. E. Popham, *Catalogue of Drawings in
the Collection formed by Sir Thomas Phillipps, now in
the possession of his grandson, T. Fitzroy Phillips Fenwick of Thirlestaine House, Cheltenham,* London,
1935, pl. XXI; Olsen, 1955, p. 225.

Although Olsen excluded this drawing from
Barocci's oeuvre, there is no reason to doubt
its authenticity. In technique, in handling,
and in style, it bears a close affinity with his
works of the 1550s and early 1560s. The pose
of the upper half of the figure recalls the
standing St. Catherine in the *St. Cecilia* altarpiece, while the use of white and black
chalks to model the drapery of the kneeling
saint may be compared with similar studies
of drapery for figures in the Casino decorations, like Uffizi 11405F verso and 11613F. In
the latter works and in other Barocci chalk
drawings for the Casino—for example, Uffizi 11330F and 11281F and Urbino, Galleria
Nazionale, no. 1673—the shadows are conceived in broad areas of low diagonally-
hatched lines and then carefully smoothed
with the stump to produce a continuous surface, and the highlights occupy large areas
bordered by thin, delicately-rendered contours. And like so many of the artist's early
works, especially those in the Casino, the
pose is borrowed from a school of Raphael
work, Giulio Romano's *Deësis above Saints
Paul and Catherine.*[1] Moreover, Barocci conceived of a related pose for the kneeling
figure of St. Lucy for the altarpiece commissioned in the late 1580s for the Danzetta
Chapel in S. Agostino, Perugia, and now in
the Louvre.[2] And a drawing at Windsor (no.
5425) represents a female head similar to
that in the ex-Fenwick study.[3]
   While the available evidence supports the
attribution, the problem of the drawing's
function remains unsolved. The saint kneels
in profile to the left with her martyr's palm
held next to her chest in her left arm and her
wheel on the ground to the side under her
extended right arm. Her head was first
drawn in a vertical position, possibly turned
slightly to the viewer, and was then set in
profile and inclined upwards. Such a figure

8

might have occupied a composition with a
Madonna and saints, as Popham suggested
*(loc. cit.),* or one with the appearance of
Christ, as in the Giulio drawing, or possibly
also a Marriage of St. Catherine. Although
there are no documented works by the artist
in which a St. Catherine appears, a pen
sketch in the Uffizi, among the drawings
traditionally ascribed to the artist, shows
three alternate ideas for a composition
with the Virgin holding the Christ Child on
her lap beside Saint Catherine who kneels
slightly below and faces to the right, in two
sketches, and to the left, in one.[4] The small
sketch in the right corner showing the figure
kneeling in profile to the right bears a close
relationship to the figure in the British

Museum drawing. Olsen and Bertelà have
proposed that this sketch was done for the
*Madonna of St. Lucy,* and a developed compositional model by a follower of Barocci
shows the St. Lucy composition transformed into the Marriage of St. Catherine.[4a]
Another possibility is that the drawing
served as a study for the ceiling of the Galleria in the Casino of Pius IV, formerly ascribed to Federico Zuccaro and more recently given to Barocci himself.[5] This fresco
shows the Virgin and Child seated in a
wooded landscape flanked by the Infant
Baptist, who sits with a dog at his side, and
by St. Joseph standing with his legs crossed
and leaning on a staff. The Virgin holds out
the ring-bearing right arm of Christ to St.

Catherine, who kneels on one leg with her left arm at her side holding the attributes of the wheel and palm and with her right extended upwards to receive the ring. As has been noted, this small frescoed panel is executed in the same rich rose-pinks, lime-greens, and ochres as the frescoes in the lower-floor rooms of the Casino, and the frieze-like composition is comparable to other works of the period by the artist.[6] One might therefore consider the London drawing as a possible study for St. Catherine at an early stage in the composition's development. Although this identification must be regarded as hypothetical because of the discrepancies from the frescoed figure, it has the advantage of placing the drawing in the early part of the artist's career, which would accord with its technique and style.

1. Louvre no. 3867, repr. F. Hartt, *Giulio Romano*, I, New Haven, 1958, p. 286, no. 6; II, fig. 1.
2. Repr. Olsen, 1962, fig. 118b.
3. Popham-Wilde, no. 106, as a possible study for the righthand saint in *Saint Cecilia*. Although heavily damaged and restored, this drawing seems to be acceptable as by Barocci; it is not mentioned by Olsen.
4. Uffizi 11483F, repr. Bertelà, 1975, no. 126, fig. 142, as a study for the *St. Lucy Madonna*, following Olsen, 1962, p. 226.
4a. Uffizi 11431F.
5. Pillsbury, *M.D.*, 1976, p. 60. Reproduced by Friedländer, 1912, pl. XXXX and Smith, 1977, fig. 74.
6. Cf. Louvre 2848 recto (Olsen, 1962, fig. 2a).

## 9 *Adoration of the Magi*

Pen and brown ink, brush and brown wash, white and pink gouache, over black chalk, on blue paper, 290 x 209 mm. Annotated on reverse of mount: *Barroccio*. Laid down.

Amsterdam, Professor J. Q. van Regteren Altena

Provenance: Th. Dimsdale, London (Lugt 2426); Sir Thomas Lawrence, London (Lugt 2445); W. Esdaile, London (Lugt 2617); Th. Thane, London (Lugt 2433).
Exhibited: Amsterdam, Rijksmuseum, *Italiaansche kunst in Nederlandsch bezit*, 1934, no. 475; Amsterdam, *Italiaanse Tekeningen*, 1970, no. 44, repr.
Published: Olsen, 1955, p. 116; Olsen, 1962, p. 147.

9

This beautiful modello for an Adoration of the Magi probably derives from the same period as the *Holy Family with Saints John, Elizabeth, and Zachariah* in the Casino of Pius IV and the *Moses and the Serpent* fresco in the Belvedere apartments in the Vatican, that is to say 1561–63. There are reminiscences of the *Martyrdom of Saint Sebastian* in the dense clustering of the figures around a central void, and in the close-up view of the scene through a repoussoir figure (at the right) and a cut-off figure moving into the composition (the boy with the horse at the left). Yet the diagonal emphasis, the Correggesque figure

at the right, and the more monumental, and classical, proportions of the Virgin, all suggest the work was done in Rome. Conceivably, if Barocci executed a picture from the drawing, the commission came from Cardinal Giulio della Rovere, Barocci's protector and patron in Rome for whom the artist did several paintings which have not been traced. The *Adoration of the Magi* also bears similarities with the drawings done for the Wilton House *Madonna and Child*, a work whose design prefigures the *Madonna di San Giovanni* but which, like the *Adoration*, was probably planned in Rome.[1]

A preliminary sketch for the composition is preserved in the Louvre.[2] In this version there are no animals in the foreground and the architectural setting has greater prominence.

1. This commission is discussed in detail by Anna Forlani Tempesti (in "Una scheda per il Barocci," *Prospettiva*, 1975, no. 3, pp. 48–50), although wrongly dated to ca. 1575. Further drawings for this commission are: Uffizi 11457F, 11464F and 11572F, all preliminary pen sketches done to establish the pose of the Virgin and Child and Berlin (Dahlem), Kupferstichkabinett 20347 and 20351 and Uffizi 11646F, chalk drawings for the drapery of the seated Virgin.
2. No. 2845 (repr. Olsen, 1962, fig. 13a).

**10** *Mountain Landscape with a Road leading to a Town*

Pen and brown ink, brown wash, heightened with white gouache, on blue paper, 272 x 401 mm. Annotated in pen and brown ink at lower center: *48;* at lower right: *Frederico Barrotio d'urbino;* in same place but in another hand: *175£–15–0* [?]; in red chalk on reverse of mount: *13.* Laid down; whites partially oxidized; repaired tears at lower center and along bottom and right edges; trace of vertical fold in center.

Hamburg, Hamburger Kunsthalle, no. 21056

Provenance: E. G. Harzen, Hamburg. Published: Olsen, 1955, p. 115; Olsen, 1962, p. 146; Olsen, 1965, p. 27, fig. XII, repr.

This beautiful drawing records the artist's impressions of the undulating hills and richly varied play of curves and planes in the landscape of his native Marches region. The artist began the sketch by setting down, in very controlled penstrokes, the profiles of the two hilltowns in the distance; he then added, in a more informal, summary, fashion, the wooded hillside with the meandering path and travellers. The contrast in handling between the two parts of the drawing makes it clear that the primary interest of the artist lay with the distant view of the town silhouetted against the mountains, which Olsen has suggested may be Ascoli Piceno. Broad panoramic views of this kind are not common in Barocci's work, and it would seem that this drawing was done early in the artist's career, conceivably on his way to or back from Rome in the mid-fifties or early-sixties. The general arrangement of the scene with trees flanking a view into a distant landscape recalls the work of Domenico Campagnola and possibly, as Olsen has suggested, Paolo Veronese. [1] And the penmanship, with its thin lines and restrained strokes, is closely related to that of the artist's earliest drawings, like the *Agony in the Garden* and *St. George and the Dragon* in the Uffizi and Louvre *Holy Family*. [2] Olsen has suggested that the drawing served for the landscape in the background of the *Madonna di S. Giovanni,* but the relationship is at best generic and the drawing has all the qualities of an independent work. The closest relationship that this drawing bears to a painting by the artist is with the *St. Jerome in the Wilderness* in the Museo del Duomo in Urbino—a little known picture that has a good claim to be regarded as an autograph work from the first part of the artist's career. [4]

1. Olsen, 1965, p. 27.
2. Repr. Olsen, 1962, figs. 2, 14.
3. Olsen, 1955, p. 115 and 1962, p. 146.
4. Repr. Olsen, 1965, fig. XIX, as a work whose attribution to the artist is "problematic."

ATTRIBUTED TO FEDERICO BAROCCI

**11** *Seated Angel Preparing to shoot a Bow and Arrow*

Black and white chalks, colored in ochre and pale pink pastels, with traces of lavender pastel (on wings of angel) and brown pastel (on hair), stumped, over incised outlines, squared in black chalk, on grayish blue paper, 421 x 266 mm. Annotated in pen and brown ink at lower left: *R. Liguori* [?; partially erased]. Paper lightly faded and restored; creased at upper right corner; scattered foxing.

The Cleveland Museum of Art, Dudley P. Allen Fund and Delia E. Holden Fund, no. 69.70

Provenance: unidentified collector's mark (shield with cardinal's hat; not in Lugt); A. Mouriau (Lugt 1853); Giuseppe Vallardi (Lugt 1223).
Exhibited: The St. Louis Art Museum, *Italian Drawings from Mid-Western Collections,* St. Louis, 1972, cat. by N. Neilson, no. 8, repr.

Although the pose of this figure is closely related to that of Barocci's Christ Child in the *Martyrdom of Saint Sebastian* and *Madonna di San Giovanni* and bears a resemblance to several putti frescoed in the Casino of Pius IV, neither the style, technique, nor subject matter accords with any known work of the late 1550s or early 1560s. One possibility is that the drawing was done independently of a painted commission as an experimental piece to explore the technique of mixing artificial and natural chalks on one surface. Bellori, Barocci's biographer, states that the artist started making drawings in pastels or colored chalks as a result of a visit to Urbino of an artist from Parma who had in his possession several cartoon fragments and head studies by Correggio.[1] Purportedly this experience affected not only the way Barocci saw nature and prepared his works but also his method and technique of drawing. Bellori dates this visit to the period in which Barocci was painting the *St. Cecilia* and *Martyrdom of Saint Sebastian,* but it may have occurred later, after Barocci returned to Urbino in 1563. In any case, while there are few large-scale studies done in colored chalks for the Casino frescoes, they become a part of his regular working process with the *Madonna di San Giovanni,* which is the first work Barocci is supposed to have executed in paint after leaving Rome. And the tentative handling of contours, the prevalence of ochre pastel, and the extensive, rather academic, modelling in black chalk around the figure in the Cleveland drawing bear comparison with Barocci's earliest documented pastels, e.g. those for the *Madonna di San Giovanni.*[2] It would therefore not be implausible to date the drawing in the early sixties, not long after Barocci left Rome and during a time in his career when, for reasons of health, he was incapable of producing much in paint. It is worth mentioning that there are more drawings for unexecuted pictures from this period than from any other time in the artist's life.[3]

While the drawing possesses many of the qualities of Barocci's autograph work, one cannot easily explain certain aspects as a product of the artist's youth or technical inexperience. For instance, the pastel flesh tints extend over an unusually large portion of the figure and receive extensive modelling in black chalk rather than serving as a means

11

of adding local color to finish the drawing. Moreover, it is uncharacteristic of the artist to develop a large-scale figure in colored chalks without using red chalk to describe certain critical features like the nose, eyes, or mouth. It is also difficult to find other examples of the artist using a yellowish ochre pastel tone for the flesh tints; the artist normally used ochre only for hair and drapery and applied the flesh tones in a pale pink or light beige pastel. In view of these qualities it is conceivable that the Cleveland drawing was

12

**12** *Virgin and Child Appearing to Saints Francis and John the Baptist*

Pen and brown ink, light and dark brown washes, over a preliminary drawing in black chalk, heightened with white, squared in black chalk and incised for transfer, on beige paper, 380 x 244 mm. Water-stained and faded; red stain at lower center; five-inch vertical tear at upper center; one-inch hole at upper left and scattered losses on edges.

London, The Trustees of the British Museum, no. 1873–12–13–1937

Published: Schmarsow, IIIA, pp. 18–19, pl. V; Krommes, 1912, pp. 78, 105; Olsen, 1955, p. 119; Olsen, 1962, p. 151; Emiliani, 1975, p. 253, no. 323; Bertelà, 1975, p. 33; Pillsbury, *YUAG Bulletin*, 1976, pp. 21–22, fig. 4.

As Bellori relates, after Barocci experimented with the poses by making life sketches in his studio, he prepared a finished drawing of the composition, or *disegno compito;* this drawing served as the model for further study and refinement of the coloring and lighting of the overall composition, and for the elaboration of the many parts of the individual figures like the limbs, head, draperies, and accessories. The drawing in the British Museum exhibited here, which is prepared in pen and wash and white highlights and squared in black chalk, served such a role for the painting which originally hung in the Capuchin church of Monte Abbato in the small town of Fossombrone outside Urbino, a work which is now lost.[1] The drawing agrees with the final painting in everything but small details like the left hand of John the Baptist, which was restudied in the drawing in Philadelphia shown here (Cat. 14) and modified in the final work. Although modern writers have dated the commission as late as the 1580s, most scholars now agree that the work was done in the 1560s.[2] Such an opinion is supported not only from the stylistic affinities with other compositions of the period like the *Madonna di San Giovanni* and *Crucifixion* in the Galleria Nazionale in Urbino, but also from the fact that two of the drawings for the painting bear studies related to the Casino of Pius IV decorations of 1561–63, while a third records a copy after a Raphael fresco in Rome.[3] In view of this, one should not rule out the possibility that Barocci undertook the project in Rome, possibly through the sponsorship of Cardinal Giulio della Rovere, and, for reasons of health, executed the painting only after a considerable delay. The project was one of the artist's most important commissions and in it he abandoned the abstract division of heavenly and earthly realms employed in the *Martyrdom of St. Sebastian* of 1557–60 by bringing the figures together into

made by a studio assistant or close follower rather than by Barocci himself. One of his assistants, Ventura Mazzi, is known to have made large-scale drawings in colored chalks based upon putti represented in Barocci's work of the 1560s.[4]

1. The kinds of drawings by Correggio which Barocci would have seen were probably not pastels as such but works done in colored chalks like the red chalk study in the Loùvre for Eve in the Parma Cathedral (A. Popham, *Correggio's Drawings,* London, 1957, no. 53, pl. LXb). Among the cartoon fragments Barocci might have seen, and one which shows a head—which, according to Bel-

lori, the artist emulated—is the drawing in black and white chalks for the Parma Cathedral in the École des Beaux-Arts, Paris (*ibid.,* no. 71, pl. LXXXIV). Both of these drawings are characterized by their subtle light effects achieved through rubbing of the chalks, which creates a smooth, continuous surface.
2. Berlin (Dahlem), Kupferstichkabinett, no. 20392 recto and Stockholm, Nationalmuseum, no. 405/1863, both for the head of John the Evangelist and the study in the Metropolitan for the Virgin's head (here Cat. 16).
3. These are drawings for an *Adoration of the Magi* (Cat. 9), *Adoration of the Shepherds, Agony in the Garden, Holy Family, Madonna and Child with Sts. Roch and Sebastian,* for which no paintings are known to have been executed (see Olsen, 1962, Cat. nos. 10, 12, 13, and 18, and *passim*).
4. Baldinucci-Barocchi, VI, p. 78.

13                                           14

a tightly-knit pyramidal structure reminiscent of Raphael's *Madonna di Foligno* in the Vatican and its counterpart by Titian, the *Madonna in Glory* in Ancona—both of which Barocci could have studied in the original—and by allowing the light, which falls from the upper left, to strike all three figures from the same angle, thereby creating a formal as well as psychological union of the figures. These experiments reach their fruition in the *Perdono* and *Madonna del Popolo* altarpieces, the artist's crowning achievements from the following decade.

1. The best record of the appearance of the painting is the sketch made after the painting at the beginning of this century published by di Pietro, 1913, fig. 90.
2. The painting was dated ca. 1590 by Krommes and ca. 1585 by di Pietro; Olsen, Emiliani, and Bertelà place it in the 1560s *(loc. cit.)*.
3. For a discussion of the development of the composition, see Pillsbury, *YUAG Bulletin*, 1976, pp. 20–25.

**13**   *A Standing Monk in Right Profile Holding a Cross and Looking Upwards.* VERSO: *Half length Infant Turned to Viewer with Right-Arm Extended; Drapery Fragment*

Pen and brown ink, with traces of black chalk (near Saint's feet), on greenish-blue paper, 178 x 116 mm. Annotated in pen and brown ink at lower left: *Federigo Baroc/ci fece.* Paper lightly stained in brown. Verso: black chalk. Annotated in pen and brown ink at upper left: *cercata del S. Francesco/dipinto nella Deposizione/dal Duomo di Perugia* (within cartouche)/*Ales. Maggiori comprò in Urbino l'anno 1817.*

New Haven, Yale University Art Gallery, Everett V. Meeks, B.A. 1901, Fund, no. 1975.31

Provenance: Alessandro Maggiori; unidentified collector with initials CA'(Lugt 486b); unidentified collector with initials PGB (Lugt 2079b); Caselli Collection (according to information supplied by

A. Matthews to Dr. Malcolm Bick); Alastair Matthews, Bournemouth; Dr. Malcolm Bick, Longmeadow, Massachusetts; Leonard Baskin, Northampton, Massachusetts; acquired from Lucien Goldschmidt, New York, in 1975.
Published: Pillsbury, *YUAG Bulletin*, 1976, pp. 20–25, figs. 1–2; *idem, M.D.*, 1976, p. 61.

While the early nineteenth-century annotation on the drawing's verso suggests that this sheet was done for the figure of St. Bernardino (not St. Francis) in the *Deposition* in the Perugia Cathedral—an idea which is supported by the similarity of pose and drapery—a closer link exists with the St. Francis in the artist's lost *Fossombrone Madonna* of a few years earlier (see Cat. 12); and the drawing's verso bears an outline sketch for the Christ Child in the latter painting. The drawing, which is related in style to genre drawings as well as other drapery studies by the artist,[1] would appear to have been done at an early stage in the development of the saint's pose and drapery. It shows the saint standing rather than kneeling. The source for this idea is a little-known drawing in the Fitzwilliam Museum, Cambridge, in which St. Francis appears to be standing at the foot of the Christ Child.[2] In the final work Barocci abandoned the intimate, Correggesque grouping of figures of the drawing in favor of a more classical solution employing monumental figures set in isolation. Having made this decision, he moved the Francis to the right side of the foreground and showed him in a kneeling rather than standing position. A faint recollection of the earlier version of the composition is present in the British Museum modello (Cat. 12) in the form of a pentimento showing St. Francis' small cross next to the Baptist's right hand. Further individual studies for the St. Francis are in Urbino and Florence.[3]

1. For example: The Pierpont Morgan Library, New York, no. IV, 155A (here Cat. 39); Biblioteca Ambrosiana, Milan, no. F.271, Inf. no. 81; and Uffizi nos. 11481F, 11498F, and 11512F.
2. Inv. PD 70–1948; repr. Pillsbury, YUAG Bulletin, 1976, fig. 6.
3. Ibid., pp. 22ff.

**14** *St. John the Baptist Kneeling in a Landscape and Pointing Upwards with His Right Hand*

Pen and brown ink, brown wash, heightened with white, over black chalk, squared in black chalk, on brownish ochre-tinted paper, 238 x 113 mm. Annotated in pen and brown ink on the reverse of the mount: *Parmigiano/Original drawing/by Parmigiano/From the collection of Wm. Carey Esq. purchased of him by John Neagle Feb'y 13th 1838. Philad.*[a]. Laid down; whites partially oxidized; loss in upper right corner repaired; tears along horizontal crease in center and elsewhere.

Philadelphia, Philadelphia Museum of Art, Pennsylvania Academy of the Fine Arts Collection, no. 121

Provenance: William Paulet Carey (1759–1839); John Neagle (1796–1865), Philadelphia; John S. Phillips.
Published: Popham, 1966, pp. 149–150, pl. 17.

The traditional attribution of this developed study for the figure of Saint John the Baptist in the *Fossombrone Madonna* is to Parmigianino, whose John the Baptist in the *Vision of St. Jerome*, now in the National Gallery in London, inspired the pose. Correctly identified and published for the first time by Popham in 1966 *(loc. cit.)*, this drawing gives the appearance of being a fragment from a larger compositional model. The design cor-

responds more closely with that of the figure in the painting than does the British Museum modello (Cat. 12). For example, in the left hand of the Saint in this drawing is a ribbon, as in the final work, while in the British Museum modello the limb rests simply against the pastoral staff. One also notices that the draperies are more fully and definitively articulated in this work, and all the pentimenti in the area around the left hand in the London drawing have disappeared. The modelling on the face has also become more precise, leaving a clear division between the few areas of the body which receive the heavenly radiance and the large part which remain in shadows.

Although the figure of St. John underwent less radical change than the St. Francis in the course of developing the composition, at one stage the figure assumed a profile position similar to that of Titian's St. Alvise in the Ancona altarpiece, while in another the saint stepped emphatically toward the viewer with his left leg, in almost direct imitation of Parmigianino's counterpart in the *Vision of St. Jerome*.[1]

1. Urbino, Galleria Nazionale, no. 1662 and Florence, Uffizi, no. 11286F. For a discussion of these see Pillsbury, YUAG Bulletin, 1976, pp. 23–24, n. 8.

**15** *Virgin and Child in a Landscape with Kneeling Saint John the Evangelist ("Madonna di S. Giovanni")*

Black, red, and white chalks, with traces of ochre pastel coloring (on John's mantle, Christ's hair, and on the basket at the lower left), over squaring in red and black chalks, incised for transfer, on grayish-brown paper, 481 x 403 mm. Annotated in pencil on reverse: *Francesco Vanni; Barocci* (cancelled). Laid down; varnished; severely rubbed; paper discolored (from original blue); repaired losses in upper right corner, lower left corner, and in lower center; trace of central horizontal crease.

New York, Mr. Janos Scholz

Provenance: Mary Brandegee (Lugt 1860c).

This unpublished modello executed in colored chalks records the composition of the votive picture of the Virgin and Child with Saint John the Evangelist which the artist executed for the Capuchin Church at Crocicchia. According to Borghini and Bellori, this small painting was the first work that the artist was able to complete after recovering from the illness which forced him to leave Rome. If, as Bellori maintains, the mysterious malady prevented him from painting for as long as four years, the work may not have been executed until 1567. In this work Barocci has abandoned the classical formula of the Casino *Holy Family* and *Fossombrone Madonna* in favor of a more intimate group-

ing of the figures along a simple diagonal, reminiscent of the works of Correggio.[1] Since this is the first work for which pastel studies survive, it is possible that the exposure to Correggio's drawings, which purportedly caused him to change his drawing style and begin making drawings in colored chalks, occurred between 1563 and 1567.

The Scholz drawing is unusual in the artist's oeuvre because it is a highly finished modello executed in colored chalks. The purpose of it may have been to study the relationships of color. Bellori relates that the artist often did a small cartoon to investigate the color juxtapositions after making the full-scale model and this helped him when he came to executing the final work. Less finished drawings of this kind exist for the *Annunciation* in the Vatican and the Allendale *Christ Appearing to the Magdalene*.[2] Although the Scholz drawing appears to follow the design of the final work in all details, there is at least one pentimento—in the foot of the Evangelist—and slight changes in the draperies and landscape. These qualities would appear to exclude the possibility of the drawing's being a copy, and a glance at the expressive handling of the chalk in the area of the curtain and landscape—despite the overall rubbed and varnished state of the drawing—supports this identification of the drawing.

1. Compare, for example, the *Holy Family with St. Francis* in the Uffizi or the *Giorno* in Parma (repr. C. Gould, *The Paintings of Correggio*, Ithaca, 1976, pls. 89, 157).
2. Uffizi 11391F and 11425F (repr. Bertelà, 1975, figs. 61, 68).

**16** *Head of a Young Woman Turned Three-Quarters to the Right*

Black and red chalks, colored in ochre pastel (for hair), stumped, on light beige paper, 240 x 188 mm. Annotated in pen and brown ink at lower right: *Correggio* [?]; in pen and brown ink in an old hand on reverse: *Barocci*. Paper soiled and abraded; repaired damages on left eye and in upper left corner; lower left corner made up.

New York, The Metropolitan Museum of Art, Gustavus A. Pfeiffer Fund, no. 64.136.3

Provenance: Pratt Institute of Art, New York.
Published: *Pratt Alumnus*, LXVIII, no. 2, 1966, p. 12, repr.; Pillsbury, M.D., 1976, p. 60.

The *Madonna di San Giovanni* is among the first works for which Barocci executed colored chalks or pastels for the heads of the individual figures. Two drawings of this type were known for the head of Saint John[1] and to this group can now be added this drawing acquired by the Metropolitan Museum in 1964. The drawing is executed in a characteristic manner: the outlines are first

15

16

put down with black chalk, then red chalk is used to define and accent the nose, eyes, lips, chin, and ear—and finally colored chalks, in this case ochre, are applied to add local color to the hair. What the New York drawing lacks is the usual white and pastel tints on the flesh parts, although these additions are the first to wear off over the course of time. By this method Barocci's drawings approximate the coloring in the painting. And Barocci seems to have made these drawings specifically as a type of auxiliary cartoon, after preparing the principal cartoon and before painting the figure. Such drawings served to refine the lighting and modelling and make last minute adjustments in the pose. In the case of the New York drawing for the Virgin's head, there exists at least one preliminary drawing which may represent the artist's life study from the model;[2] this drawing is characteristically done in simple red and black chalks and exhibits a sense of particularity and

realism that the New York drawing foregoes in favor of color and light effects. By proceeding in this way from life studies to more abstract color studies done in the studio, the artist transformed the life model into an ideal type suitable for the context of the religious subject of the painting.

1. Berlin (Dahlem), Kupferstichkabinett, Inv. 20392 recto (not in Olsen) and Stockholm, Nationalmuseum, no. 405 1863 (as a copy by Olsen). See Pillsbury, *M.D.*, 1976, p. 60.
2. Louvre 2864. An even earlier drawing for this figure, again done from life, may be Louvre 2865, a portrait-like representation in black and red chalk of a young girl seen with her head turned three-quarters to the right; Olsen, 1962, p. 234, fails to connect this drawing with a known work but says that it is "perhaps by Barocci from ca. 1555."

**17** *Virgin and Child Enthroned Under a Baldachin with Saints Roch and Sebastian*

Pen and brown ink, light and dark brown washes, over a preliminary drawing and squaring in black chalk, heightened with white, with traces of indented contours, on white paper, 327 x 272 mm. Annotated in pen and brown ink at lower right: *i 155;* on mount: *Federico Barocci.* Laid down; badly foxed; repaired tears at lower left edge and along right edge; horizontal crease across center.

Chatsworth, The Trustees of the Chatsworth Settlement, no. 358

Provenance: Lord John Somers (Lugt 2981); William, 2nd Duke of Devonshire (Lugt 718). Exhibited: Bologna, 1975, p. 75, no. 37, illus. Published: Schmarsow, IIIB, p. 38; Olsen, 1955, pp. 45, 115, 118; Olsen, 1962, pp. 57, 146, 151.

It is not known whether Barocci ever made a painting of this subject; given the absence of detail studies for the individual parts of the composition, it would seem implausible.[1] In the seventeenth century Cornelis Bloemaert (1603–1688) engraved the drawing in Rome and added the inscription: *Federicus Barotijus Vrbinas inventor. Cornelius Bloemart Vltrajectinus sculpsit . . .''*[2] In technique and style, the drawing may be compared with that of Barocci's *disegno compito* of the same period for the *Fossombrone Madonna* in the British Museum (Cat. 12). An approximate date *post quem* for this drawing is established by the underdrawing which Olsen correctly identified as a sketch for the *Madonna di S. Giovanni;* on the octagonal base next to Sebastian's leg is visible the indented lines of the Evangelist's chalice. The available evidence would suggest a date for the drawing sometime after the artist received the commission for the *Madonna di S. Giovanni,* which may have been in Rome, and before 1567, by which time he was supposed to have finished the votive picture. The reliance of the compositional arrangement and poses of individual figures upon Giulio

17

Romano's *Holy Family and Saints* in S. Maria dell'Anima in Rome, which the artist probably saw, would support a dating closer to 1563 than to 1567.[3] Other aspects of the composition such as the framing doric columns, the Christ Child's pose, and the Virgin's draperies seem to have drawn inspiration from Correggio's *St. Francis Madonna* in Dresden,[4] which the artist may have come to know, through drawings, in the early 1560s, soon after leaving Rome.

1. Olsen's tentative association of Uffizi 1391, *Study of a Male Head,* with the head of St. Roch is unconvincing (Olsen, 1962, p. 151).
2. Repr. Schmarsow, I, p. 24, pl. I.
3. Repr. F. Hartt, *Giulio Romano,* II, New Haven, 1958, fig. 94.
4. Repr. C. Gould, *The Paintings of Correggio,* Ithaca, 1976, pl. 11.

**18** *Nude Study of Standing Youth with Hands Clasped, Inclined Backwards, Looking Upwards to the Right; Nude Study of Boy Seated to Left and Reclining on Right Arm.* VERSO: *Half-length of Saint Mary Magdalene Holding her Salve-Box, Partially Draped*

Black and white chalks, stumped, contours (of large study) incised, on light blue paper, 394 x 270 mm. Watermark: crossed arrows (cf. Briquet, II, 6280–6281). Small repair at left center. Verso: black and white chalks, stumped. Annotated in black chalk at upper left: *Barocci.* Paper lightly abraded across top; small repair at lower right; light brown stain across central crease.

U.S.A., Private Collection

Provenance: Stefan von Licht, Vienna (Lugt 789b; sold Helbing, Frankfurt-am-Main, 7 December 1927, no. 90); Prof. Otto Benesch, Vienna; Private Collection, Stockholm.
Published: Olsen, 1955, p. 117; Olsen, 1962, pp. 148–149, fig. 196.

According to Bellori, Barocci executed the *Crucifixion with the Mourning Virgin and Saint John* in the Galleria Nazionale in Urbino for the Church of the Miraculous Crucifixion in Urbino on the order of Pietro Bonarelli della Rovere, a courtier of Duke Guidobaldo II and a member of the Accademia degli Assorditi. The large compositional sketch for the painting in the Uffizi (no. 11416F) is executed in pen, wash, and white over a developed study for the Virgin in the *Madonna di S. Giovanni,* establishing a relative date *post quem* of ca. 1565 for the composition. The starting point for the design was Titian's altarpiece of the same subject delivered to the church of San Domenico, Ancona, in 1558.[1] Barocci's first ideas for the figures of Mary and John, in fact, call for standing figures reminiscent of those in Titian's painting.[2] In the final work, after making a long

18 recto

series of drawings for each figure, however, Barocci transformed the two isolated saints into an integrated, unified pair that through their gestures draw the eye spirally upwards to the Crucified Christ and, at the same time, express the pain and suffering of Christ. Here Barocci not only elongates the proportions of his figures for expressive effect but exaggerates the foreshortening and movement of the figures to eliminate the barrier between the space depicted and that of the viewer.

The double-sided chalk drawing exhibited here contains a large-scale study from life for the pose of the Virgin. Executed in black and white chalks on natural blue paper and

modelled by softening the contours and shaded areas with the stump, this drawing represents a critical step in the artist's creative process. As described by Bellori, the artist asked his young male models to pose in his studio according to the design and then asked them whether they felt unnatural or, if by turning more one way than the other, they found a better pose. "In this process," Bellori goes on to say, "Barocci experimented with the most natural and unaffected movements and executed his drawings." The pentimenti in the head, arms, and legs reveal the artist's experimentation during the process of making the study. There followed from this drawing a further

18 verso

modello in the British Museum.[7] Barocci's figure has more slender proportions, and the position of the head, right arm, and right leg are somewhat altered, but the general conception and handling of the body is similar and each has the foreshortened trunk contrasted to the elongated left leg. If the Correggio composition was among the drawings and cartoons which Barocci saw in Urbino when a Parmese artist stopped in the city in the 1550s or 1560s, it is conceivable Barocci adapted the figure and then, in the present work, developed it by making a life study based upon the pose and figure type; and Barocci's later studies for the angel next to Christ in the *Madonna del Popolo* recall this figure.

The half-length Magdalene drawn on the reverse also raises questions of identification. No independent painting of the subject by the artist nor composition in which such a figure might have served, save the early *St. Cecilia,* exists. The right arm of the figure bears a certain relationship to the Virgin's in the Wilton House *Holy Family* of the early sixties, but the latter is shown draped rather than naked.[8] The artist's main concern seems to have been in showing the arm, shoulder, and chest; the rest of the figure appears to be sketched as if the artist were making a composition based upon the study of a single piece of anatomy. Like the study of the boy on the recto, one might look for a possible Correggio source, but no such close relationship exists, unless one wishes to see in the figure a reflection of the Parma Cathedral *Eve,* for which Correggio made numerous chalk studies.[9]

1. Repr. H. Wethey, *The Paintings of Titian: I. The Religious Paintings,* London, 1969, cat. no. 31, fig. 114.
2. Cf. Uffizi 11554F and Louvre 2861 plus the already mentioned Uffizi 11416F (repr. Emiliani, 1975, nos. 23 and 24 and Bertelà, 1975, no. 8, fig. 12, respectively).
3. Uffizi 11375F verso, repr. Bertelà, 1975, no. 7, fig. 10.
4. Berlin (DDR), Staatliche Museen, Inv. 2–1974, repr. Emiliani, 1975, no. 25.
5. Urbania, Biblioteca Communale, I, 305 and Berlin (Dahlem), Kupferstichkabinett, Inv. 20502 and 20266.
6. Berlin (DDR), Staatliche Museen, Inv. 1–1974 recto and verso and Uffizi 11375F recto (repr. Emiliani, 1975, no. 26 and Bertelà, 1975, no. 7, fig. 11.
7. Repr. A. E. Popham, *Correggio's Drawings,* London, 1957, pls. CV and CVI.
8. This painting is discussed and reproduced, although wrongly dated, by A. Forlani-Tempesti, 1975, p. 50, fig. 7.
9. Popham, *op. cit.,* pls. LXa, LXb, and LXI.

study—based on lines incised from the present sheet[3] which elaborated the figure's drapery; then the pose of the upper half of the body underwent revision in a drawing now in East Berlin.[4] This further refinement required the production of a new set of drapery studies before the artist was ready to paint the figure.[5] There are fewer surviving drawings for the St. John, but this figure also was restudied in a variety of positions before the final design was reached.[6]

The study of the young boy reclining at the side of the standing male nude has yet to be successfully connected with a figure in one of Barocci's compositions. It would appear to have no part of the development of the *Crucifixion,* even though a kneeling boy is present as a donor figure behind St. John in Uffizi 11416F; nor is Olsen's suggestion of a possible connection with the figure of St. Joseph in a sketch of an *Adoration of the Shepherds* in Berlin convincing *(loc. cit.)*. The rather androgynous features of the boy might suggest that the drawing is a copy made from an existing design, yet the realistic characterization of the head and arms seem to reflect the experience of a living model. One possible explanation for the drawing lies in the resemblance of the pose to the boy on the far right in Correggio's *Allegory of Vice,* as it appears in the painting itself now in the Louvre and in the red chalk

**19** *Christ Lowered from the Cross by Three Figures; a Figure on a Ladder, Behind a Bar, Reaching Downwards to the Right.* VERSO (visible through mount): *Swooning Virgin between Two Maries and Saint Bernardino*

Pen and brown ink, brown wash, on white paper, 280 x 209 mm. Annotated in pen and brown ink at upper left: *6.2* [?]; at lower right: *Barocci;* on mount: *Federigo Baroccio/di Urbino Pittore.* Laid down; strip added along upper left edge; repaired hole at upper right; upper part stained in light brown. Verso: pen and brown ink, over black chalk. Annotated in pen and brown ink at upper left: *Baroccio in Perugia . . ./n. 223;* in lower right: *Federigo B.*

Edinburgh, National Gallery of Scotland, no. D725

Provenance: Sir Joshua Reynolds, London (Lugt 2364); (W. Young Ottley); Sir Thomas Lawrence, London (Lugt 2445); David Laing (Lugt 1656d); Royal Scottish Academy (Lugt 2188); ceded in 1910 to the National Gallery of Scotland (Lugt 1969f).
Exhibited: Bologna, 1975, p. 75, no. 40.
Published: Andrews, I, 1968, p. 12; II, fig. 110; Emiliani, 1975, p. 75, no. 40.

The altarpiece of the *Deposition* in the Chapel of Saint Bernardino in the Perugia Cathedral represents the climax of the artist's development in the first decade of his activity as a painter. Barocci received the commission soon after finishing the *Madonna di S. Simone;* according to Bellori, two gentlemen and a painter from Perugia took so much pleasure in the latter and praised it so much that they decided to invite Barocci to Umbria. From documents we know that an emissary was sent in November of 1567 to bring the artist to Perugia, where, according to Bellori, he resided for three years; the contract was signed the following year; and the painting installed on Christmas Eve, 1569. The work derives various elements from Daniele da Volterra's altarpiece in the Orsini Chapel of S. Trinità dei Monti and Jacopino del Conte's painting in the Oratorio di S. Giovanni Decollato, both in Rome,[1] but transcends the two Roman prototypes by its emotional treatment of draperies, faces, and colors and by its dramatic unity of action and expressions. For example, the sudden release of Christ's body from the cross is reflected in the windblown draperies of the figure standing on the ladder at the left while St. Bernardino's meditation upon the event is underlined by the placement of the ladder as a link between his face and that of Christ. Moreover, the head of Christ can be read as the center of a series of concentric rings of figures who embody different levels of grief and comprehension, while the cross and ladders serve as the connecting spokes

19

of the wheel. The abstract armature is also buttressed by the rigorous patterning of drapery, the exaggerated excitement in the poses and gestures, by the idealizations of the facial expressions, and by the interaction of local color and reflected light. Bellori particularly admired the *Deposition:* for the

order achieved in the composition, for the fictive logic of the actions (and movements) of the figures, for the exquisiteness of the heads, and for the expressive quality of the draperies.

All these effects Barocci worked out through the systematic study of the various

20

of Nicodemus. In the lower left corner of the drawing is a sketch for the figure of Joseph as he appears in the final work.

One further observation about this drawing is that the verso, visible through the mount when the drawing is held to the light, contains a black chalk study for the swooning Virgin in the foreground. In the drawing she reclines to the right supported by a seated figure and attended by a kneeling figure; a standing figure with arms folded can be seen behind the ground. Other drawings for this group are preserved in Florence and Berlin, but neither the well-known pen sketch in the Louvre, which is usually identified as the artist's first idea for this group, nor the chalk drawing in Urbino appear to be autograph. [2]

1. Repr. S. Freedberg, *Painting in Italy 1500 to 1600,* Penguin Books, Middlesex, 1970, figs. 188, 205. In addition, Barocci was probably aware of Taddeo Zuccaro's fresco of the *Swooning Virgin at the Foot of the Cross,* preserved in a drawing in Budapest (repr. J. Gere, *Taddeo Zuccaro: His Development Studied in his Drawings,* London, 1969, figs. 74–75) and Marcantonio's engraving of the *Descent from the Cross* after a lost drawing by Raphael (Bartsch XIV. 37.32).
2. Louvre 2851 recto (repr. Emiliani, 1975, no. 38) and Urbino, Galleria Nazionale, no. 1652.

**20** *Figure on Ladder Supporting Christ.*
VERSO: *Drapery Study*

EXHIBITED IN NEW HAVEN ONLY

Black and white chalks, stumped, contours (of principal figure) incised for transfer, on light blue paper, 365 x 215 mm. Annotated in pen and brown ink at lower edge: *p.° Schizzo della deposizione di croce f. . . . da federico Baro . . ./per Senigall . . .* [?]; at lower right, in a different hand: *cento settant'ott . . .* Verso: black and white chalks. Annotated in pen and brown ink at lower left: *di federico Bar . . . zzi.*

England, Mr. and Mrs. H. M. Calmann

Provenance: P.O. Dubaut, Paris (Lugt 2103b).

The function of this hitherto unknown figure study for the Perugia *Deposition* was to establish the pose of the muscular young man who supports the weight of Christ's torso from the ladder on the left. The numerous pentimenti and re-workings of the contours attest to the process of refinement. The artist began the drawing by sketching the figure according to the pose established in a recently published sheet in the Biblioteca Hertziana in Rome, which shows the figure looking toward Christ with his left arm upraised and his left leg in a kneeling position. [1] From this model the artist evolved a nude figure whose pose closely resembles that of the final work except for minor adjustments in the placement of the legs and

parts of the composition. Because of the complexity of the composition, the number of figures, and the importance and variety of expressions, Barocci produced more drawings for this composition than for any of his previous works. These can be divided between the first sketches made to study the overall composition, the sketches for individual figures, the nude studies, drapery studies, studies of hands, arms, legs, and other parts of the anatomy, head studies, the cartoon, the chiaroscuro *cartoncino,* and finally pastel studies of heads. It is the first opportunity we have to view the full extent of Barocci's meticulous method of preparing his compositions.

The Edinburgh drawing is one of the earliest in the series. It represents a rapidly executed, imaginary sketch of the principal figures. In the center is Christ being lowered from the cross by a figure kneeling on a ladder at the left and by two standing figures below; a fourth figure who ascends a ladder at the right (presumably to release Christ's left hand that is still attached to the cross) looks on with fear from the side. This conception of the principal event incorporates one of the prominent features of Daniele's altarpiece: a figure on a ladder carrying the Dead Christ. In the final work the artist gave greater emphasis to the roles of Joseph of Arimathea and Nicodemus at the top of the ladder; the former holds the shoulder of Christ, while the latter hammers out the final nail that holds Christ to the cross. In this way the weight of Christ is suspended equally between four points and all the figures (except the boy at the right descending the ladder with the pliers and crown of thorns) direct their attention to the activity

rotation of the shoulders. With the incised contours of this figure as guide the artist continued to develop the pose in three further drawings, all in Berlin, which contain nude studies of the whole figure and of the legs.[2] All of these drawings are characteristically executed in black and white chalks on blue paper, with extensive use of the stump. The latter serves as a means of not only softening the contours and blending the areas of shade and light to create a continuous surface but also erasing—or at least diminishing—the disfiguring effect of the pentimenti. In the lower portion of the drawing can be seen a small sketch of the whole figure with the position of the arms and head already transformed to accord with the final work. Around the principal study are sketches of the surrounding figures. In addition to Christ and the standing figure below who holds the ladder and cross, these include a pair of figures on the left who do not appear in the final work.

1. Inv. 3, repr. Emiliani, 1975, no. 46.
2. Berlin KK 20462 (3747), 20465 (4270), and 20466 (4286).

21

**21** *Study of Dead Christ; Separate Study of Each Leg.* VERSO (visible through recto): *Two Figures (possibly Swooning Virgin and Attendant Mary)*

Red chalk, on white paper, 270 x 170 mm. Verso: black chalk.

New York, The Metropolitan Museum of Art, Robert Lehman Collection, 1975

Provenance: F. A. Drey, London.
Published: Olsen, 1955, p. 120; Olsen, 1962, p. 153.

The technique of this study for Christ in the Perugia *Deposition* is unusual for Barocci. It is executed exclusively in red chalk, and the contours are softened with a delicate web of hatched and cross-hatched lines. It would appear to be a sketch made to study the reflection of light from the surface of the torso. The design follows that of the finished work, and there is little concern for anatomical detail. Evidently the drawing was not done from life. The separate leg studies on the sides may represent an attempt to rearrange the folds of the loin cloth which falls between Christ's thighs.

Barocci made a long series of studies for the figure of Christ, several of which are preserved in Berlin. These reveal him working out effects of lighting, musculature, and pose, especially the problem of the foreshortening of the calves. All are done from life with the exception of a drawing in Berlin which has an outline sketch of the whole

22

figure, transferred from a study in the Biblioteca Hertziana, Rome, and a pair of sculpture fragments of a right leg similar to that of Christ's leg in the painting.[1]

1. Berlin KK 20468 (4406).

**22** *Head of the Swooning Virgin.* VERSO: *Partial Squaring; Fragment of a Composition with a Column in the Left Foreground*

Black and white chalk, charcoal, stumped, incised for transfer, on two pieces of coarse beige paper, 295 x 239 mm. Generally rubbed; upper left corner repaired with a piece of cartoon from another part of the composition; horizontal tear through figure's left eye; residue of buff-colored accretions at upper right; scattered light stains; traces of foxing; two brown spots at lower left; paper damaged along incised contours of face. Verso: charcoal. Stained and repaired.

Chicago, The Art Institute of Chicago, Leonora Hall Gurley Memorial Collection, no. 22.5406

Provenance: E. Chesney (according to note on former mount, bought at Sotheby's, London, in 1885); Leonora Hall Gurley, Chicago (not in Lugt).
Exhibited: Newark (N.J.), Newark Museum, *Old Master Drawings*, 1960, no. 29.
Published: Middeldorf, 1939, pp. 11–12, fig. 1; H. Tietze, *European Master Drawings in the United States*, New York, 1947, cat. no. 47, repr.; Olsen, 1955, p. 120; Olsen, 1962, p. 153.

Although in the preparation of a multi-figured composition like the *Deposition* the full-scale cartoon represented the synthesis of the artist's sketches and life studies, Barocci continued to experiment with the design and lighting at this stage. The cartoon fragment in Chicago is for the head of the swooning Virgin. In it, the artist has drawn and redrawn the essential contours of the facial features and drapery, and with the addition of white chalk and rubbing has softened and smoothed the modelling. The coarse fibre of the beige paper assists in achieving the desired effects of tone. It is important to point out that the artist deliberately restricted his medium to black and white chalk on beige paper in his cartoons. To study the relationship of the colors, the artist went on to make large-scale studies in pastels on blue paper which are themselves based on outlines transferred from the cartoon. A head study of this type (in Besançon), and the cartoon fragment from which it was made (in Vienna), survive in the case of one aspect of the *Deposition:* the head of the Mary holding the Virgin.[1] A further cartoon fragment of a head in the *Deposition* is preserved in the Biblioteca Communale in Urbania.[2] This drawing is of special interest since it served a double function. Not only did the artist use it for the head of St. John the Evangelist at the foot of the cross in the *Deposition* but he reused it—and altered the

*49*

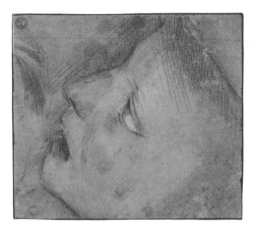

23

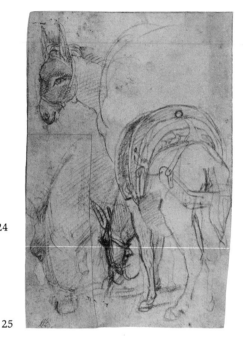

24

25

design accordingly—for the head of the Magdalene in the *Christ Appearing to Mary Magdalene* of more than two decades later in Munich. This circumstance suggests that the artist himself, rather than a subsequent owner of the cartoon, may have been responsible for dividing the large sheet into smaller fragments similar to those related to the *Deposition* now in Chicago, Urbania, and Vienna.[3] It is possible that the artist, after completing the cartoon, incised the contours to transfer the design to the surface to be painted and then removed individual sections of the cartoon for further, more detailed study, either in colored chalks or in some other media. The way the sheet has been cut down and pasted together with fragments from other parts of the same cartoon lends support to this hypothesis.

1. Besançon, Musée des Beaux-Arts, Inv. D.1516 (repr. Emiliani, 1975, no. 42) and Vienna, Albertina, cat. R.376 (Inv. 287) (repr. di Pietro, 1909, pp. 297–301).
2. Biblioteca Communale, no. II, 206 (repr. Bianchi, 1959, no. 10, pl. 22).
3. Ulrich Middeldorf (*loc. cit.*) came to the same conclusion, arguing that this would have made the cartoon easier to copy. He failed to notice, however, that the contours of the drawing are, in fact, incised for transfer, which is the means by which Bellori says the artist transposed his design to the paint surface.

## 23 *Head in Profile Looking Upwards*

Black, red, and white chalks, colored with a pinkish pastel (on flesh parts), lightly stumped, on light greenish-blue paper, 130 x 156 mm. Laid down; lightly stained in brown at upper center; other light stains at lower right and lower left.

New York, Mr. Janos Scholz

Provenance: Count(?) Gelozzi or Gelosi (Lugt 545).
Exhibited: Hagerstown, Washington County Museum, *Four Centuries of Italian Drawings from the Scholz Collection*, 1960, cat. by J. Scholz, no. 30; Oakland, Mills College Art Gallery, *et al, Drawings from Tuscany and Umbria 1350–1700*, 1961, cat. by J.

Scholz, no. 5; Hamburg, Kunsthalle *et al, Italienische Handzeichnungen der Sammlung Janos Scholz*, 1963, cat. by W. Stubbe, no. 9; Washington, D.C., National Gallery of Art and New York, The Pierpont Morgan Library, *Sixteenth Century Italian Drawings from the Collection of Janos Scholz*, 1973–74, cat. by K. Oberhuber and D. Walker, no. 16.

This delicate pastel study seems to have been done for a figure in one of Barocci's early compositions. Similar upturned heads in profile appear in the Urbino *Crucifixion*, the Perugia *Deposition*, and the *Immaculate Conception*, all of the late 1560s and 1570s. The closest correspondence exists with the St. John the Evangelist in the *Deposition*, who stands at the foot of the cross gazing upwards at the body of Christ.[1] While the head is further back in the painting than in the drawing—which may only be the result of the fragmentary nature of the drawing— the raking light, the gaping mouth, and the long, pointed nose are closely related. The diagonal line cutting across the upper right corner of the drawing could possibly represent the ladder, which appears in a similar place behind the figure in the painting; and the piece of drapery at the end of the figure's nose in the drawing may depict a portion of the saint's upheld right sleeve. A comparison of the drawing with the cartoon for the same figure in the Biblioteca Communale in Urbania, which shows similar pentimenti on the ridge of the nose, would also appear to support this identification; moreover, it is plausible the drawing was made after the Urbania drawing, and based upon it.[2]

1. This conclusion was also reached by Oberhuber and Walker in 1973 (*loc. cit.*).
2. II, no. 206, repr. Bianchi, 1959, no. 10, pl. 22.

## 24 *Holy Family Seated in a Landscape*

Pen and brown ink, light gray wash, heightened with white, over a preliminary drawing in red chalk, on buff paper, with some indented contours, 228 x 240 mm. Laid down; worm hole at lower center.

Chatsworth, The Trustees of the Chatsworth Settlement, no. 363.

Provenance: Sir Peter Lely (Lugt 2092).
Exhibited: London, Royal Academy, 1953, no. 104.
Published: Schmarsow, III B, p. 38; Krommes, 1912, pp. 62, 106; Olsen, 1955, pp. 176, 221; Olsen, 1962, p. 225.

The place of this pen sketch of the Holy Family in the artist's oeuvre is difficult to establish with certainty, and one must regard its attribution to the artist with caution. While Schmarsow, who accepted the drawing as an original, noted the apparent relationship of the composition to that of both the *Rest on the Return from Egypt* and the *Madonna del Gatto* of the 1570s, Olsen rejected the drawing as the work of Barocci and suggested it was done by either Francesco Vanni or the artist who painted the *Adoration of the Shepherds* in the Galleria Nazionale in Perugia, a work which bears an eighteenth-century attribution to Baldelli, Barocci's nephew. Olsen further drew attention to the drawing's stylistic affinity with a pen and wash sheet of figure studies in the Uffizi (no. 93698F). In view of this, it would seem that the drawing is likely to be either an early study for the *Rest on the Return from Egypt* of which the artist did three versions before 1573 (the best known of which, but the latest, is the one in the Pinacoteca Vaticana) or a later pastiche based on its composition and that of the *Madonna del Gatto* of ca. 1575. Both of the latter works were well known through Cort's engravings published in 1575 and 1577 respectively and had an influence on younger artists throughout Italy, as well as in the North. In support of the attribution to Barocci one may compare the application of gouache highlights, the pyramidal structure of the design, the summary treatment of the landscape, and the individual facial expressions to aspects of other pen, wash, and gouache compositional sketches done on blue paper.[1]

1. Cf. Uffizi nos. 11414F, 11416F, and 11556F (repr. Bertelà, 1975, figs. 4, 12, and 13) and Uffizi no. 11516F (repr. Emiliani, 1975, no. 14).

**25** *Donkey Grazing; Two Separate Studies of the Head.* VERSO: *Landscape Fragment with a Hill and Bushes*

Black chalk, on two pieces of white paper, 177 x 121 mm. Repaired hole at lower left; light brown stains on left and right edges; some dark spots at upper left. *Verso:* black chalk.

Amsterdam, Professor J. Q. van Regteren Altena

Provenance: Sir Thomas Lawrence, London (Lugt 2445); William Esdaile, London (Lugt 2617). Exhibited: Paris, Institut Néerlandais, *et al, Le Dessin Italien dans les Collections Hollandaises*, 1962, no. 133, pl. IC; Amsterdam, 1970, no. 45. Published: Olsen, 1955, p. 122; Olsen, 1962, p. 156, pl. 292; M. Jaffé, Review of Exhibition, *Burlington Magazine*, CIV, 1962, p. 232.

One of the first ducal commissions which Barocci received was for a small easel painting of the Virgin resting on the return from the flight into Egypt. Commissioned from Duke Guidobaldo II della Rovere and sent to Lucrezia d'Este, Duchess of Ferrara, possibly in 1571 on the occasion of her wedding to Prince Franceso Maria, this painting was so admired—a fact to which Bellori attests—Barocci himself executed two replicas and allowed Cornelis Cort to engrave the composition in 1575. The work illustrates the account of the sojourn of the Holy Family in Egypt given in the Gospel of Pseudo-Matthew: according to this source, Mary, on the way from Egypt, saw a palm with fruit on it and told Joseph she would like some of it, and the Christ Child responded by telling the palm to give Mary some of its fruit—which it did—and also water—whereupon a spring came forth.[1] While Barocci adapts the motif of the Virgin reaching for water from Correggio's well-known altarpiece of the *Madonna della Scodella* in Parma, in other re-

spects he re-interprets the event to create a pyramidal grouping in space which gives greater emphasis to the action of the Christ Child and accords a more significant role to the landscape and to the accessories of the figures—the donkey, the canteen, sack of bread, and straw hat.

This study in the van Altena Collection belongs to a series of preparatory drawings for the donkey in the background. In the lower right the artist has sketched from life the animal, seen with a pack on its back and eating from the ground. To the left is a study of the head on a larger scale while in the upper portion of the sheet is the outline of the animal's torso with a detailed study of the head, now turned back in profile to the left as in the final painting. Four further studies preserved in the Uffizi served to refine and develop the individual parts of the animal according to the pose as established in the van Altena drawing.[2] As a group these drawings are among the most naturalistic in the artist's oeuvre, as he rarely did purely genre drawings, and they demonstrate that his powers of direct observation were the equal of Andrea del Sarto, an artist who specialized in such kinds of chalk drawings from life.

1. M. R. James, *The Apochryphal New Testament*, 1926 edition, p. 75.
2. Nos. 924–926 orn, 928 orn (repr. di Pietro, 1913, figs. 36–39).

**26** *Seated Man in Armor with a Helmet*

Black and white chalks on blue paper, 287 x 180 mm. Annotated in pen and black ink on the mount: *Fed. Barocci.* Laid down; trace of small tear at left center edge; small gray spot at lower left.

U.S.A., Private Collection

Provenance: Nathaniel Hone (Lugt 2793); Charles Rogers (Lugt 625); Private Collection (sold London, Sotheby's, 4 July 1977, lot 175, illus. p. 25).

This delicate chalk study of a seated man in armor appears to have been done from life, possibly as a costume study. The emphasis in the drawing is upon the representation of the shoulder and arm coverings; the remaining parts of the figure are only schematically drawn. This aspect of the drawing raises the possibility it might have served as an early study for the artist's well-known *Portrait of Francesco Maria II delle Rovere* in the Uffizi, painted soon after the young prince returned from the Battle of Lepanto (in 1571). This picture is Barocci's only portrait of a man in armor, and, as in the drawing, the figure turns to the right and looks at the viewer over his right shoulder, with his helmet in the foreground. Although the resemblances would seem to end here, there

26

are other instances of Barocci basing a preliminary study for a three-quarter-length portrait on a full-length sketch or making a major change in the pose or setting between the costume study and final work.[1]

To accept this identification of the drawing, though, we must be willing to believe that the artist first conceived of the principal figure reaching back passively into space rather than gripping his helmet—an idea that might have been in keeping with Duke's passive temperament but one that, to official tastes, may have seemed to represent too radical a departure from the tradition of military portraiture established by Titian's portrait of the future Duke's grandfather and Bronzino's of his father in the Uffizi, both of which were before the artist (in Pesaro) when he began work on the commission.

1. Cf. Uffizi 11363F verso and a drawing formerly in the Morelli Collection in Bergamo which served for the *Portrait of Francesco Maria II* in Weimar; Uffizi 11340F for the presumed *Portrait of a Man* in the Italian Embassy, London; and Berlin KK 20446 (4373) and Uffizi 11649F for the *Portrait of Giuliano della Rovere* in Vienna.

**27** *Apparition of the Virgin and Child to Two Saints (St. Paul and a Monk with a Book) and a Donor in a Landscape*

Pen and brown ink, brown wash, heightened and corrected in white, over black chalk, on beige paper, 380 x 261 mm. Annotated in black chalk in lower center: *Barocci*; in pencil in lower right: *Baroche.* Laid down; bordered in pen and brown

27

*Simone* or Perugia *Deposition*. This dating would account for the conservative structure of the composition, which recalls Titian's *Pala Ancona* and Raphael's *Foligno Madonna,* combined with the advanced handling of the draperies (especially the saint on the right and the Virgin) and subtle lighting effects achieved through the use of different tones of wash and additions of white. Nonetheless, one should not rule out the possibility of a dating in the middle or later seventies, contemporaneous with the *Perdono,* Urbino *Immaculate Conception,* and the Fossombrone *Stigmatization of St. Francis,* when the artist retreated from the position taken in the Perugia *Deposition* and *Return from Flight* and sought the naturalism and simplicity of his classical forerunners like Andrea del Sarto; the *Madonna del Popolo* and *Madonna del Gatto* are products of this change in emphasis in the artist's work.

In regard to Olsen's attribution of the drawing to Viviani, it should be pointed out there is no stylistic evidence to support this suggestion and Viviani's association with Barocci began much later than the 1560s and 1570s.

1. Repr. Emiliani, 1975, nos. 32, 37, 82, and 323 and Bertelà, 1975, figs. 4, 12, 35, and 36.

**28** *Head of Young Woman, Turned Three-Quarters to Right and Inclined Slightly Downwards*

Black, red, and white chalks, colored in pink, ochre, and brown pastels, stumped, on grayish paper, 330 x 246 mm. Reinforced with blue paper and laid down on thin board; discoloration of original blue paper; large restoration of loss above head; scattered smaller repairs of worm holes and tears; light foxing.

Northampton (Massachusetts), Smith College Museum of Art, no. 1960.99

Provenance: C. A. Mincieux, Geneva;[1] N. Rauch, Geneva (sold 13–15 June 1960, sale no. 26, cat. no. 9, repr. p. 4, bt. H. Calmann); acquired in 1960. Published: *Smith College Museum of Art Bulletin,* 1961, no. 41, repr. p. 24; *Art Quarterly,* Winter 1960, p. 400 (recent acquisitions); Olsen, 1962, pp. 158–159; Bertelà, 1975, pp. 40–41.

Although the original blue paper has discolored to a grayish tone and there are several restored losses around the head, this drawing is among the finest and best preserved pastel studies by the artist. The head is conceived from a light outline sketch in black chalk, with red chalk markings to indicate the mouth, eyes, and nose, ochre and brown pastels the hair, and pink and white the flesh parts. The hair was then re-worked and strengthened in a soft black chalk (or charcoal), the curls on the forehead added in

ink; scattered small tears and insect holes; whites partially oxidized.

New York, Professor and Mrs. Richard Krautheimer

Provenance: Thomas Bewick (Lugt 416a); Lord Overstone; M. C. Loyd, Wantage; Arthur Thomas Loyd (sold, after his death, Sotheby's, London, 28 Nov. 1943, lot 1).
Exhibited: London, Burlington Fine Arts Club, *Drawings by Barocci,* Nov. 1923–Jan. 1924, no. 8; New York, Institute of Fine Arts, NYU, 1961; Duke University, The Gallery, *Italian Master Drawings,* Mar.–April, 1966, no. 8.
Published: Olsen, 1962, p. 289.

Although ascribed by Olsen to Viviani, this fine modello for an unknown altarpiece of the Virgin and Child appearing to two saints in a landscape has all the characteristics of an authentic drawing by Barocci of the 1560s or early 1570s. In technique and style the drawing has a close relationship with the artist's compositional studies for the Casino *Holy Family,* the *Madonna di S. Simone,* the Fossom-

brone *Madonna,* the Urbino *Crucifixion,* and the *Immaculate Conception.*[1] The Virgin and Child are modelled upon the *Fossombrone Madonna, the Madonna di S. Giovanni,* and *Madonna and Child with Saints Roch and Sebastian;* the saint at the right compares with the St. Francis in the *Fossombrone Madonna,* the St. Bernardino in the Perugia *Deposition* and the St. Simon in the *Madonna di S. Simone;* the donor figure recalls the foreground couple in the *Madonna di S. Simone* and the boy in the *Martyrdom of St. Sebastian;* and the landscape with the town in the distance is similar to that in the *Fossombrone Madonna.* The drawing is skillfully composed over a preliminary drawing in black chalk, which shows numerous pentimenti (e.g. the feet of St. Peter), and is modelled in different shades of transparent brown wash and heightened and corrected in white. The most probable date for the drawing would be in the late sixties, after the *Madonna di S. Giovanni* and *Fossombrone Madonna* but before the Urbino *Crucifixion,* the *Madonna di S.*

52

28

29

red chalk, and the background shaded in low parallel strokes of black chalk (or charcoal). The various colored chalks, although rubbed by the artist himself, maintain a strength and density that allows one to appreciate the disciplined buildup of forms employed by Barocci to study, on paper, the actual color relationships of the final painting. The only color missing from the Smith drawing is the blue of the original paper, now faded to gray, which would have provided a ground, or middle tone, to unify and blend the bright local hues.

While Harald Olsen expressed reservations about the drawing's authenticity—evidently on account of a misleading description of the drawing in the 1960 Rauch sale catalogue—[2]there can be no question about the drawing's authorship, and its critical role as a preliminary study for the artist's *Madonna del Gatto* in the National Gallery in London. Recently Giovanni Bertelà has suggested that the Smith drawing was the final, or penultimate, step in the preparation

of the Virgin's head and was preceded by several pastel drawings, including a newly identified one in Dijon.[3] Her conclusion may be correct, but it does not account for the discrepancy in the treatment of the hair between the drawing and the painting.

Barocci's use of colored chalks to study the heads of the figures in his paintings may be inspired from Venetian, or at least North Italian, practice, in particular that of Jacopo Bassano.[4] As a type of drawing, the head studies in pastel are analogous to Raphael's auxiliary cartoons, and like the latter they were probably done in the final stages of preparation, possibly even after the artist had begun to execute the painting. These drawings were the most prized collector's items in the seventeenth and eighteenth century—the lion's share now residing in Paris and Stockholm—and were highly valued by the artist himself. This drawing and others like it remained in the artist's studio as a source of reference in executing subsequent works. The Smith drawing appears

to have served as the model for the head of the nursing woman in the foreground of the *Martyrdom of St. Vitalis* of 1580–83.

1. According to information supplied to the museum by Janos Scholz (letter dated 23 Aug. 1960).
2. The sale catalogue (*loc. cit.*) describes the technique of the drawing as: "Dessin à la pierre noire et au pastel, légères reprises du pastel probablement au XVIIIe siècle." Olsen, who evidently never saw the drawing in the original, translated this statement as follows: "It has been retouched, probably in the XVIII century." The principal drawing has not been retouched, but the large losses and rough edges were restored with pastels when the drawing was removed from its traditional backing, possibly in the eighteenth century, and laid down on a piece of natural blue paper similar in hue to that of the original sheet.
3. Windsor 5230, Louvre 2866, Uffizi 9319S and 11475F and Dijon 1750, plus the Smith drawing. A further drawing that can be added to the series is Windsor no. 5229, which is incorrectly associated in the literature with the *St. Lucy Madonna.*
4. See A. Ballarin, "Introduzione a un catalogo dei disegni di Jacopo Bassano-II," *Studi di storia dell'arte in onore di Antonio Morassi,* Venice, 1971, pp. 145ff.

**29** *Standing Virgin with Arms Outstretched*

Pen and brown ink, brown wash, over a preliminary drawing in black chalk, on light beige paper, 260 x 178 mm. (sight). Lightly foxed; light brown stains on edges; two brown spots at lower right; scattered small, repaired holes.

Los Angeles, Mr. Vincent Price

Provenance: Sir Thomas Lawrence, London (Lugt 2445); Lord Northbrook, Earl Drax; JFVM (in monogram; not in Lugt).
Exhibited: Los Angeles, University of California at Los Angeles, 1956; Oakland, Oakland Art Gallery, 1957; New Haven, Yale University Art Gallery, *Paintings, Drawings and Sculpture Collected by Yale Alumni*, May–June 1960, no. 165.

After having completed the *Madonna di S. Simone* for S. Francesco in Urbino in 1566–67 and having begun work on the *Perdono* for the high altar of the same place in the early 1570s, Barocci received a commission to execute a third altarpiece for the Franciscan church in Urbino: this one for the private altar of the Compagnia della Concezione.[1] Evidently Barocci's first idea for the altarpiece was to depict the Madonna della Misericordia, in which the Virgin stood in the center in clouds, embracing under her outstretched mantle the members of the company arranged in a circle below, and receiving a crown from an angel above. The artist rejected this subject for his *Madonna del Popolo* because of its lack of dramatic potential,[3] and for similar reasons may have decided here to transform it into an Immaculata. By doing this, he was able to represent the Virgin standing on a crescent moon, surrounded by cherubims, delicately balanced above the circle of witnesses with her arms outstretched and her mantle blowing freely in the wind.

The drawing in the collection of Mr. Vincent Price is one of the artist's final studies for the critical element in the revised composition: the wind-filled cape. Executed in pen and wash over a preliminary drawing in black chalk, it corresponds closely with the final work and evidently served to refine and simplify the lighting effects as conceived in the finished drawing in the Uffizi, upon which the drawing was based and from which it may have been traced.[4] Between the Price drawing and the final work—which, according to Bellori, the artist repainted at the end of his life—the artist adjusted the angle of the head and gave more emphasis to the triangularity of the billowing mantle.

1. The altarpiece can be dated to the mid 1570s on the basis of a drawing in the Uffizi, no. 11668F, which bears studies related to both the *Immaculate Conception* and the *Madonna del Gatto* (see Emiliani, 1975, p. 106) and one in Berlin (KK 20412, Pacetti 4329) which has a study for the

30

first donor on the left and an early sketch for the beggar in the *Madonna del Popolo* of 1575–79.
2. Cf. Uffizi 11446F recto (repr. Bertelà, 1975, no. 33, fig. 35).
3. In one of the first letters exchanged with the rectors of the Fraternità dei Laici of Arezzo in regard to the proposed altarpiece of the *Madonna del Popolo*, Barocci stated that the mystery of the Misericordia was not a suitable subject with which to make a beautiful altarpiece—" . . . il voler fare il misterio della Misericordia non pare a me che sia sugietto troppo a proposito per fare una bella tavola" (letter of 5 Nov. 1574, published by M. Qualandi, *Nuova raccolta di lettere*, I, Bologna, 1844, p. 137).
4. Uffizi 11410F (repr. Bertelà, 1975, no. 34, fig. 36). The drawing's measurements are proportionately the same as the Price drawing and it is executed in pen and wash, with white highlights, over squared lines. Moreover, its contours appear to have been indented for the purposes of transferring the design to another surface.

**30** *Stigmatization of St. Francis*

Pen and brown ink, light and dark brown washes, heightened in white, over a preliminary drawing in black chalk, on light blue paper, 390 x 270 mm. Partial oxidation of whites in upper left and lower right; some abrasion.

London, The Trustees of the British Museum, no. Pp. 3–203

Provenance: P. J. Mariette (Lugt 2097; three times); Marquis de Lagoy (Lugt 1710); bequeathed by Richard Payne Knight in 1824.
Exhibited: Bologna, 1975, no. 80.
Published: Mariette, 1741, p. 24, no. 247; Schmarsow IIIA, p. 21; Krommes, 1912, pp. 105–106; Olsen, 1955, p. 182; Olsen, 1962, p. 161; Olsen, 1965, p. 34, n. 25; Jaffé, 1977, p. 52, n. 78, pl. 79.

See entry for Cat. 31 below.

# ATTRIBUTED TO FEDERICO BAROCCI

**31** *Stigmatization of St. Francis*

EXHIBITED IN NEW HAVEN ONLY

Pen and brown ink, brown wash, over a preliminary drawing in black chalk, heightened with white, on light blue paper, 365 x 277 mm. Laid down; partial oxidation of whites.

New York, The Pierpont Morgan Library, no. 1973.31

Provenance: Unidentified collector with initials "T.B." (Lugt 416a); A.T. Loyd; Lord Wantage (sale, London, Sotheby's, 28 Nov. 1945, lot 10); Janos Scholz, New York.
Exhibited: New York, The Pierpont Morgan Library, *Landscape Drawings and Watercolors. Bruegel to Cézanne*, 1953, cat. by F. Stampfle, no. 11; Bloomington, Indiana, University Art Museum, *et al. Drawings of the Italian Renaissance from the Janos Scholz Collection*, 1958, cat. by C. Gilbert, no. 47; Oakland, Mills College Art Gallery, *et al, Drawings from Tuscany and Umbria 1350–1700*, 1961, cat. by J. Scholz, no. 6; Hamburg, Kunsthalle, *et al, Italienische Handzeichnungen der Sammlung Janos Scholz*, 1963, cat. by W. Stubbe, no. 8; New Haven, Yale University Art Gallery, *Italian Drawings from the Janos Scholz Collection*, 1964, checklist by E. Haverkamp-Begemann and E. Sharp, no. 23; Durham, Duke University, Art Department, *Italian Landscape Drawings from the Collection of Janos Scholz*, 1965, cat. by J. Scholz, no. 4; London, Arts Council Gallery, *et al, Italian Drawings from the Collection of Janos Scholz*, 1968, cat. by C. White, no. 3; Middletown, Wesleyan University, Davison Art Center, *Master Drawings from the Collection of Janos Scholz*, 1969, no. 13; Washington, D.C., National Gallery of Art and New York, The Pierpont Morgan Library, *Sixteenth Century Italian Drawings from the Collection of Janos Scholz*, 1973–74, cat. by K. Oberhuber and D. Walker, no. 17; Santa Barbara, University of California, The Art Galleries, *et al, Drawings by Seventeenth Century Italian Masters from the Collection of Janos Scholz*, 1974, no. 4; Los Angeles County Museum of Art, *Old Master Drawings from American Collections*, 1976, cat. by E. Feinblatt, no. 111.
Published: Olsen, 1955, p. 182; Olsen, 1962, p. 161; Olsen, 1965, p. 34, n. 25, pl. XVIII, as a "second version or copy" of the British Museum drawing.

There are several versions of this composition, all of them executed in pen, wash, and white on blue paper and all of them of sufficient quality to have been considered the work of the master at one time. The best of the known examples is the sheet from Mariette's collection in the British Museum which Olsen has tentatively identified as a study for the unfinished painting of the mid-1570s belonging to the Museo Civico in Fossombrone and now on deposit in the Galleria Nazionale in Urbino.[1] The Morgan Library version, which comes from the Janos Scholz collection, is executed in a more summary fashion with fewer pentimenti and

31

greater contrasts of light and shade and appears to have been based on the London drawing, although it is by no means a straightforward copy. The principal saint has been moved forward and his proportions enlarged and the landscape passages further dramatized by the addition of varying tones of brown wash. A third version from the Santarelli Collection in the Uffizi, although considerably weaker in execution than the aforementioned, nevertheless seems to have been produced in the artist's studio; it introduces a different architectural setting in the landscape background on the left.[2] The existence of these three drawings raises a fundamental question: did Barocci ever copy his own drawings? We know that he preserved his drawings to refer to them and transferred his designs from one sheet

to another for further elaboration or, in cases of excessive changes, clarification, but there are no known, or even documented, instances of his actually reproducing, or directly imitating, one of his own drawings, especially a large compositional study like the *Stigmata*. If the Scholz drawing is by Barocci, it must have been done as a presentation piece rather than a working drawing, probably on the commission of a friend or collector; in which case the *Stigmatization* represents a stituation analogous to the *Return from Flight* of which the artist himself executed three, closely related, though not identical, painted versions during the same period. An hypothesis of this kind gains support from the fact that Olsen's identification of the function of the British Museum sheet as a study for the undocumented, and unfinished, Fossombrone painting is far from certain and there also exists an etching (Cat. 72) of a related composition from the same time which has the appearance of being the reproduction of a pen sketch.[3]

The *Stigmatization of St. Francis* drawing is a critical document in the development of Barocci's landscape drawing style. As we have already noted in relation to the Hamburg sheet (Cat. 10), Barocci's landscapes are North Italian in inspiration and are particularly indebted to the prints done after Titian by Campagnola.[4] The British Museum drawing reveals an explicit use of one of Titian's own prints, the large woodcut of *St. Jerome in the Wilderness* of ca. 1525–30.[5] The landscape masses defined by a tall tree at the left and a steep bank lined with bushes at the top on the right closely follow those of Titian's composition. Barocci's treatment of the individual parts of the landscape, however, is very different from Titian. Whereas the latter builds up the composition through an accumulation of carefully observed and graphically rendered landscape details, Barocci conceives of the scene in terms of atmosphere and light and the individual elements are treated in a generalized, impressionistic fashion. Michael Jaffé (*loc. cit.*) has noted that the London *Stigmatization* drawing served as the source for Rubens' transformation from a Venetian style of rendering details of landscape to his mature landscape drawing style.

1. Olsen, 1962, p. 161, fig. 41b. Krommes, 1912, p. 106, took exception to the general assessment of the London drawing as Barocci's primary version and concluded it was a school-piece.
2. Uffizi 1342S (Santarelli, 1870, p. 638, no. 32, as a study for the print).
3. Repr. Olsen, 1962, pl. 40b.
4. Barocci's interest in North Italian landscape prints may have inspired Duke Francesco Maria II to write the letter dated 23 Jan. 1581 to Giovanni Agatone in which he stated: "Noi desideramo havare tutte le sorti de paesi di Gio: Battista Pittoni Vicentino, di Titiano, del Campagnola, et altri Auttori, ma vorressimo esser sicuri che fossero in buone carte, delle prime stampe, et ben intagliati; . . ." (G. Gronau, "Die Kunstbestrebungen der Herzöge von Urbino," *Jahrbuch der Königlich Preuszischen Kunstsammlungen*, XXV, Beiheft, 1904, p. 32). This letter may provide an approximate date for Barocci's print of the *Stigmata* as well.
5. Repr. M. Muraro and D. Rosand, *Titian and the Venetian Woodcut*, Washington, National Gallery of Art, *et al*, 1976–77, no. 22. The relationship of the Barocci composition to the Titian print was noted by Ebria Feinblatt (*loc. cit.*).

## 32 *Two Trees*

Black chalk, point of the brush and brown ink, light and dark brown washes, heightened with white and gray gouaches, on cream-colored paper, 405 x 262 mm. Annotated in pencil on old mount in hand of Skippe: *Poussin*. Laid down; lightly foxed; gray stains from verso on edges;

32

specks of black paint at lower right; creased at lower left; scattered light brown stains.

Paris, Fondation Custodia (Coll. F. Lugt), Institut Néerlandais, no. 7216

Provenance: John Skippe; J. Martin; A. C. Rayner Wood; E. Holland-Martin (sold Christie's, London, 20 September 1958, no. 15, bt. Matthiesen); acquired by F. Lugt (Lugt 1028) in 1958.
Exhibited: London, Royal Academy, *Exhibition of XVIIth Century Art in Europe*, 1938, no. 352; London, Royal Academy, *Drawings by Old Masters*, 1953, no. 117, pl. 16, repr.; Paris, Institut Néerlandais, *et al*, *Le Dessin Italien dans les Collections Hollandaises*, 1962, no. 134, pl. XCVIII; Rome, Villa Medici, "Il paesaggio nel disegno del cinquecento europeo," 1972–73, cat. by F. Viatte, R. Bacou, and G. Delle Piane Perugini, no. 144; Bologna, 1975, no. 317.
Published: A. E. Popham, Review of Exhibition, *Burlington Magazine*, LXXII, 1938, p. 15; Olsen, 1955, p. 182; M. Jaffé, Review of Exhibition, *Burlington Magazine*, CIV, 1962, p. 232; Olsen, 1962,

pp. 117 n. 242, 234; R. Bacou, Review of Exhibition, *L'Oeil*, LXXXV, Jan. 1962, p. 61, repr.; *Critica d'arte*, no. 55, Jan.–Feb. 1963, repr. no. 2; Olsen, 1965, p. 31, pl. XVI; J. B. Shaw, "Two Drawings by Barocci," *Miscellanea J. Q. van Regteren Altena*, Amsterdam, 1969, p. 88 n. 7; W. Wegner, "Bemerkungen zu Zeichnungen Niederländischer Künstler um 1600," *Miscellanea J. Q. van Regteren Altena*, Amsterdam, 1969, p. 92; F. Viatte, *Il paesaggio nel disegno del cinquecento europeo*, exhibition catalogue, Villa Medici, Rome, 1973, p. 205 n. 144; M. Chiarini, *Disegni italiani di paesaggio*, exhibition catalogue, Uffizi, Florence, 1973, p. 15, under no. 3; Jaffé, 1977, p. 52, no. 73, pl. 151.

This beautiful study of two trees, and the following one in the Cleveland Museum (Cat. 32), seem to belong to the 170 landscape studies which the artist made from the countryside round Urbino and left in his studio at his death, only a fraction of which have survived.[1] In the inventory taken soon after the artist died, they are described as: *Paesi coloriti a quazzo di colori, acquarelle ritratti dal naturale da vinti in circa; altri paesi dissegnati di chiaro oscuro, di acquarella, di lapis, tutti visti dal vero, circa cento. Altri pezzi di paesi schizzati visti dal naturale, tutti di mano del S.or Barocci circa a cinquanta.*[2] With the notable exception of the pen and wash drawing in Hamburg, most of them appear to have been done in the late 1570s and 1580s when landscape backgrounds play a critical role in the artist's compositions and the artist develops greater interest in effects of natural light and atmosphere. The sheet from the Lugt Collection might have served for any number of paintings which employ a landscape with a pair of isolated trees. Such a motif appears as a principal feature of the foreground in the Fossombrone *Stigmata* and the British Museum and Scholz *bozzetti* (Cats. 30–31) of the same subject and as a less conspicuous, but nonetheless important, background element in the Senigallia *Entombment* and Brussels *Calling of St. Andrew*.[3]

Although the Lugt drawing has less color than some of Barocci's other landscape studies, it is one of the most imposing in size and refined in technique in the oeuvre and can only be fully appreciated in the light of the more impressionistic studies of the artist's admirers, like Rubens, of the following century. No doubt it was this aspect of the drawing which led Skippe to inscribe on the mount the name of the French painter, Poussin. Such landscape studies were made on the artist's trips to the countryside and served as a means of creating a familiar setting for the sacred events depicted in his altarpieces.

1. A brief summary of Barocci's surviving landscape studies is given by Olsen, 1965, pp. 26–32.
2. Calzini, 1898, p. 107, reprinted in *Studie e notizie*, 1913, pp. 73–85.
3. Repr. Olsen, 1962, figs. 41b, 50, and 51.

## 33  *Flowering Bush above an Eroded Bank*

ILLUSTRATED ON FRONT COVER

Black chalk, brush and light and dark brown washes, heightened with white and pink, on pale tan paper, 198 x 132 mm. Annotated in pen and brown ink at lower right: *del Barocci*; on reverse: *Originale del Barocci*. Laid down; paper faded; vertical creases in upper left and lower right; black spot at upper right.

Cleveland, The Cleveland Museum of Art, Purchase from the J. H. Wade Fund, no. 73.171

Provenance: Camuccini Collection, Rome (sold Sotheby's of London, Florence, Palazzo Capponi, 18 Oct. 1969, lot D71, bt. Tan Bunzl); acquired from P. & D. Colnaghi and Co., Ltd., London in 1973. Exhibited: London, Faerber and Maison Ltd., 36 New Bond Street, April 1970, no. 7.

This small drawing showing the side of an eroded bank with a flowering plant on the summit is a characteristic and very delicate example of Barocci's landscape style. Although no painted composition to which the sheet can be connected exists, the subject matter and the treatment are closely related to those of other drawings, in particular the large landscape study of an eroded hillside in the British Museum.[1] The primary difference between the Cleveland drawing and other Barocci landscape studies lies in the use of gouache. Whereas in the London drawing bodycolor is added to several different colors, here it is used alone, with a little pink, strictly to highlight the scene and outline the foliage. The result has the effect of an Oriental screen painted in monochromatic tones over a gold ground. Barocci's use of mixed media in this and other landscape studies finds a precedent in Federico Zuccaro's modello for the *Vision of St. Eustace* in the Metropolitan Museum of Art, a work Barocci may have seen in Rome in the early 1560s.[2]

1. British Museum, no. Pp. 3–202 (repr. Olsen, 1962, fig. 402).
2. As noted by J. Gere, *Burlington Magazine*, CV, 1963, p. 394 n. 12.

## 34  *Head of a Boy*

Black and red chalks, on white paper, 90 x 70 mm. Annotated in pen and ink at lower right: *Barocci* (partly erased). Laid down; abraded; repaired losses at lower right and at lower left.

New Haven, Yale University Art Gallery, Maitland F. Griggs, B.A. 1896, Fund, no. 1976.37

Provenance: Camuccini Collection, Rome (sold Sotheby's of London, Florence, Palazzo Capponi, 18 Oct. 1969, lot D77); acquired from Thos. Agnew and Sons, Ltd. in 1976. Exhibited: London, Thos. Agnew and Sons, Ltd., *Master Drawings and Prints*, p. 21, no. 46.

34

Barocci's favored medium for small-scale portrait studies was red and black chalk on white paper. Like the preparatory sketch in the Uffizi for the *Portrait of Francesco Maria II della Rovere* in Weimar, this type of drawing records the likeness of the sitter in the most economical and direct terms and provides only a rough definition of the costume.[1] The painting for which the drawing served may, in fact, be the small *Portrait of a Boy* in the Doria Gallery in Rome, which represents a youth of about the same age, full-face, and similarly lit from the upper left, and dressed in a high-ruff collar. Both figures share the same large, round eyes, broad nose, and thick lips.[2] The abrasion which the painting has suffered makes it difficult to vouch for the design of the hairline and ears, but even in these areas the two likenesses are not dissimilar. Although the Doria painting bears a traditional attribution to Barocci which would appear to be correct, in recent catalogues of the collection the work is assigned to Santi di Tito, and Olsen considers the work to be by a pupil of the artist.[3] If one compares the treatment of flesh—veined in blue and rose—and other features of the execution with aspects of Barocci's Infant St. John in the *Madonna del Gatto* or of the cherubims in the Urbino *Immaculate Conception*, the validity of the traditional attribution becomes more apparent. The Doria painting may even be identifiable with the untraced portrait Barocci executed of Carlo Felice Malatesta in 1577–78;[4] it is difficult to determine the exact age of the sitter in the Doria painting, but a fair guess might be ten, Carlo Felice's age at the time of the sitting.[5]

1. Uffizi 1393F (repr. Emiliani, 1975, no. 320).
2. Repr. Venturi, 1934, fig. 510.
3. Olsen, 1962, p. 245.
4. *Ibid.*, pp. 162–163.
5. Carlo was born in 1567 and died in 1634.

**35** *Madonna del Popolo*

Black chalk, with some red chalk (for draperies of Christ and Virgin), pen and brown ink, light and dark brown washes, heightened and corrected in white, squared in black chalk, 551 x 384 mm. including 255 x 120 mm. correction pasted to original in lower right corner. Laid down; trace of horizontal center fold; gray stain at upper left.

Chatsworth, The Trustees of the Chatsworth Settlement, no. 357

Provenance: William, Second Duke of Devonshire (L.718).
Exhibited: London, Royal Academy, *Drawings by Old Masters*, 1953, no. 106; Washington, National Gallery of Art, *et al*, *Old Master Drawings from Chatsworth*, 1969–70, cat. by J. Byam Shaw, no. 16; Bologna, 1975, no. 87.
Published: Schmarsow, IIIb, pp. 39–40; di Pietro, 1913, pp. 38–40, fig. 45; Olsen, 1955, pp. 49–50, 130; Olsen, 1962, pp. 64–65, 167, fig. 432; Emiliani, 1975, p. 117; Bertelà, 1975, pp. 46–47.

The Fraternità dei Laici of Arezzo, a brotherhood of laymen dedicated to caring for the sick and poor, invited their native son, the famed architect and painter and author of the first history of art, Giorgio Vasari, to design a new chapel for the Fraternity in S. Maria della Pieve in Arezzo and to paint its altarpiece. At Vasari's death, on June 27, 1574, the chapel was complete, except for its altarpiece. The Fraternity, eager to see work go forward, wrote immediately to their ambassador at the court of Cosimo I in Florence for advice on the selection of a new artist. Quite remarkably—instead of one of Vasari's followers and colleagues—the brotherhood chose Federico Barocci, who was relatively unknown outside the Marches at the time and who had only completed one major work, the *Deposition* in Perugia. Although initially unhappy with the choice of subject, Barocci was quick to accept the commission, and in the spring of 1575 traveled to Arezzo to discuss a contract and inspect the site. After signing the contract, it took the artist four years to complete the work.

From the long series of letters exchanged between the rectors and the artist during the course of the painting's execution, the majority of which were published by Gualandi in the last century,[1] we know that the artist had trouble locating the wood to construct the panel, that the rectors delayed in paying him because he had not finished it within a year as promised, and that, when the picture was finally done and delivered to Arezzo in 1579, the panel began to crack and the rectors were generally displeased with it. In a letter dated June 30, 1579, they declared: "La tavola . . . non riesca di quella bona qualità che si aspetteva."

Barocci's difficulties with the Fraternity were the result of many factors, not least of which must have been the artist's unwillingness to rush the completion of the work and the Fraternity's impatience with the seemingly endless delays. The chief cause of problems, though, lay in the contract itself which, according to the correspondence, placed obligations upon the artist he had been unwilling to accept in the first place and could not meet. A hitherto unknown copy of this document survives in the Fraternity's private archive in Arezzo; it is of particular interest since it spells out the precise terms of the agreement and thereby helps to explain the causes of the subsequent difficulties that arose.[2] In the accord, dated June 18, 1575, the artist obliged himself to six principal conditions: first, that he execute the work himself (in "manu propria")—a common requirement of artists' contracts; second, that the artist employ fine colors and wood that was aged, firm, and stable—this latter being one of the conditions that delayed the beginning of work and made the painting expensive and difficult to ship to Arezzo in 1579, and served as a pretext for the Fraternity's dissatisfaction with the finished work when, shortly after the painting's arrival in Arezzo, a crack in the panel appeared; third, that Barocci place the finished work into a gilt wood frame paid for by the Fraternity; fourth, and most critical, the artist represent in the picture the Virgin interceding and praying to Her Son on behalf of the populace, shown with the particular qualities and conditions appropriate to each individual figure ("Historia ipsius tabulae sit gloriosissimae Mariae Deiparae semper Virginis intercedentis et orantes ad Dominum Yesum Christum filium eius benedictum pro populo ibi similiter picto et representato in dicta tabula cum decoro et venustate et gratia secundum conditionem et qualitatem figurarum ibi pingendarum, singula singulis congrue et respective referendo")—a stipulation that may explain the presence in the lower part of the painting of the variety of social classes, but does not specifically account for the portrayal of acts of misericordia (almsgiving, visiting prisoners, etc.) or the inclusion of the rectors of the Fraternity itself (the half-circle of eight men with prayerbooks on the right); fifth, that the artist execute a small tondo for the space in the frame above the altarpiece representing a subject of his own choice—this panel, though severely damaged, survives in the Pinacoteca Communale in Arezzo and represents God the Father Blessing;[2a] and lastly, that the painting itself be delivered within the period of a single year, in other words no later than June 18, 1576—a condition the artist later claimed was inserted into the agreement only to appease the general membership and was not binding. On the Fraternity's side, the rectors promised the following: to allow the artist to execute the picture in Urbino, rather than in Arezzo which they would have preferred; to bear the full costs of packing and shipping of the finished work; and finally, to pay the artist a total of 400 scudi in three installments—200 upon signing the contract, another 100 within eight months thereafter, and the final 100 upon the painting's installation in Arezzo.

Although the Fraternity's offer was generous in comparison to the 100 scudi the artist initially agreed to accept for the altarpiece of the *Perdono* of a few years earlier, there arose considerable misunderstanding about the schedule of payments. In the correspondence Barocci requested the second installment of his fee only after work on the painting had advanced to near completion, which was not until October of 1578, more

than two years past the date the painting was to have been installed.[3] The artist contended that he had not asked for the payment sooner because he had not needed it and because the painting had not progressed sufficiently. While the contract itself bore no penalty clause for late delivery of the painting, the rectors refused to make the payment on the grounds that the artist had not finished the painting.

After several letters the matter was resolved, and the artist received his money. The completion of the painting followed within a matter of months, although when the emissary of the Fraternity arrived after Easter in Urbino to arrange for packing and shipping of the painting to Arezzo, he discovered that the artist had not begun the small tondo, which caused a further small delay.[4] The final installation of the whole ensemble in the Fraternity's chapel, which the artist supervised at the expense of the rectors, took place in June.

Although Barocci may not have begun painting the altarpiece of the *Madonna del Popolo* until the summer of 1576, in his letters he states that he began making drawings for the proposed work immediately after returning from Arezzo, and by February had completed all the drawings and a portion of a small cartoon—"il Cartone . . . che é parte del hopera." The cartoon on which the artist was working while he looked for suitable wood to make the panel may have been a large-scale cartoon such as the one half the size of the finished work which he mentions in a letter to the Confraternity the following June, but it might also have been no more than the large modello or, in Bellori's terms, the *disegno compito,* for the composition which is preserved in Chatsworth. This drawing represents the result of preliminary sketching from studio models and served as the basis for more careful studies of the individual parts of the composition. The general outline of the composition accords with that of the final work, but some of the critical features of the final work are absent. For example, in the final painting the spectator becomes an actual witness to the miraculous intercession occurring in the upper part of the composition through the disposition of the foreground figures around a circle that includes the viewer[5] and through the outward glances of the angel beside Christ and the sympathetic dog in the lower right corner. In the Chatsworth drawing there is also a greater emphasis upon the recession into depth and the division between heavenly and earthly spheres, which recalls the *Perdono* altarpiece upon which the artist was working when he signed the contract. In addition, the references to charitable acts, the function of the lay brotherhood, are

more explicit in the representation in the drawing than in the one in the painting. While in the drawing one of the eight rectors leans forward from the right side of the foreground to place a coin in the hand of the crippled beggar reclining on the ground— for which he becomes the direct beneficiary of Christ's bestowal of the gift of the Holy Spirit in the form of the dove in the center— in the painting the dove descends upon the charity group (the mother and two children) at the right, while a young prince, almost totally obscured behind the edge of the painting on the right, makes an inconspicuous offering of alms to a gypsy woman who stands with a child and basket on the right. Similarly, while the drawing shows various acts of misericordia in the background, the painting contains only a single episode, the visiting of prisoners. Moreover, the artist may have originally intended to show more than one beggar in the right foreground of the drawing since the musician in the Chatsworth sheet represents a correction which was drawn on a separate piece of paper and then affixed to the surface of the drawing. And there is a drawing in Berlin of a kneeling beggar who looks backwards to the left which may have served for this part of the composition.[6] All these changes suggest that the Chatsworth drawing was finished early in the development of the composition.

1. M. Gualandi, *Nuova raccolta di lettere,* I, Bologna, 1844, pp. 133–192. For summaries of the contents of the letters, see Olsen, 1962, pp. 163–165 and Emiliani, 1975, pp. 112–117.
2. I wish to express my thanks to Dr. Leon Satkowski of Syracuse University and Professor Dott. Luigi Borgia, formerly Director of the Archivio di Stato in Arezzo, for facilitating my access to the private archive of the Fraternity. The transcription of the contract published in this catalogue (p. 26) was made with the generous assistance of Dr. Gino Corti.
2a. A drawing in chalk for the head of God the Father is in the van Altena Collection in Amsterdam (repr. Amsterdam, 1970, no. 48, pl. 29).
3. Gualandi's publication of the correspondence between Barocci and the rectors of the Fraternity omits the artist's first request for funds, dated October 26, 1578, and the Fraternity's reply of four days later. These letters are transcribed on p. 27.
4. A new date *ante quem* for the finishing of the principal panel can be established from a previously unpublished entry in the *Deliberazioni dal 1577 al 1579 BB 88* (Arezzo, Archivio della Fraternità dei Laici, filza 1487, c.211 recto); it states that on March 31, 1579, the rectors deliberated sending a letter to Barocci congratulating him on the painting's completion and advising him on the matter of framing and shipment. In this regard one should mention that the letters, "Iosep," which appear on the opened missal of the kneeling woman at the left in the painting, allude possibly to the actual day upon which the artist finished the painting; in the church calendar St. Joseph is celebrated on March 19.
5. This interpretation of the painting was first suggested by Sydney Freedberg (*Painting in Italy: 1500–1600,* Penguin Books, Middlesex, 1971, p. 439). For further remarks on the composition see Olsen, 1962, pp. 63–68; E. K. Waterhouse, "Some Painters and the Counter-Reformation Before 1600," *Transactions of the Royal Historical Society,*

5th Ser., XXII, 1972, p. 107; and Emiliani, 1975, pp. 112–118.
6. Berlin KK 20415 (3726), related by Olsen (1962, p. 162) to the *Madonna del Popolo* as "probably for the beggar."

**36** *Head and Arm of Sleeping Child; Separate Study of Hand*

Black, red, and white chalk, colored in pale pink pastels, on light greenish-gray paper, 257 x 265 mm., including ca. 15 mm. strip added by artist at top. Annotated in pen and brown ink at upper left: *6*. Laid down; paper faded from original blue; 25 x 35 mm. restoration on blue paper at upper left; lightly rubbed; brown stains in forehead and in center of drawing.

London, Trustees of the British Museum, no. 1901–4–17–32

Published: Schmarsow, IIIA, p. 21; Olsen, 1955, p. 131; Olsen, 1962, p. 168.

The greatest change between the Chatsworth modello and the final painting took place in the lower right corner of the composition, where the artist replaced the figure giving alms to a seated cripple with a gypsy woman and her baby and converted the figure playing the hurdy-gurdy instrument and looking upwards at the miraculous appearance of Christ into a blind musician whose head lies shrouded in shadow. There are numerous figure studies and a small compositional study which document the transition between the two versions. In this latter work, in Berlin, all the elements of the final composition appear, although the poses and lighting were submitted to further refinement.[1] For example, the Berlin sketch shows the gypsy's infant reclining backwards as if asleep, whereas in the painting the child stares, in awe, at the coin being placed in his mother's hand and holds a morsel of bread to his mouth.

The impressive chalk drawing in the British Museum exhibited here, a characteristic life study done in the final stages of planning, shows the child still asleep. In a further drawing for the same figure in the Uffizi, which is similar in scale and may have been traced from the London sheet, the head appears again, this time without pentimenti and juxtaposed to the head of a man whose expression of fear and awe became the model for the child's face in the final work.[2] In the lower half of this sheet in Florence is a developed study for the lower legs of the child and a small sketch of the bottom of the foot of the boy kneeling in the lower left side of the composition. Olsen and Bertelà have maintained that the Uffizi drawing served for the mother and child group in the right background of the Urbino *Last Supper*, completed in 1599,[3] yet because

36

of the connections with the London drawing and the small foot study, this proposal is improbable. It is, nonetheless, fair to say that when the artist conceived of the group for the *Last Supper* and began to paint it, he would have relied on the drawings for the *Madonna del Popolo* in Florence rather than undertake a new study. Accordingly, while in the small grisaille cartoon for the *Last Supper* in the Uffizi the child assumes a pose that is nearly identical to the one of the child in the *Madonna del Popolo*, in the final work the child places his right hand on his mother's chest, away from his mouth.[4] The artist may also have made use of the London and Florence drawings when he began painting the *Albani Madonna*—left unfinished at his death—which shows a sleeping baby similar to the one in the British Museum drawing, but in reverse.

1. Among these are Berlin KK 20419 (3728), 20413 (4237), 20420 verso (4290), and 20438 (4153) for the beggar and 20431 (4137) for the musician and Amsterdam, van Altena Collection, no. 47 (Amsterdam, 1970, repr. 33), recto and verso, for the gypsy woman. The sketch is Berlin KK 20414 (4115).
2. Uffizi 11426 (repr. Bertelà, 1975, fig. 104).
3. Olsen, 1962, p. 202 and Bertelà, 1975, no. 95.
4. Uffizi 819E (repr. Emiliani, 1975, no. 239).

**37** *Head of a Young Woman, Turned Three-Quarters to the Right and Looking Downwards*

Black and red chalks, with traces of white chalk on flesh parts, colored in ochre pastel on hair, stumped, on blue-gray paper, 252 x 191 mm. Annotated in pen and brown ink at lower right: *162*; in pencil on reverse: *Di Fedrico Barogia'* [?]. Severely abraded; paper faded from original blue.

New Haven, Yale University Art Gallery, Maitland F. Griggs, B.A. 1896, Fund, 1973.141

Provenance: D. D. Campbell (sold Sotheby's, 26 Nov. 1970, lot 27, bt. Duncan, £250); acquired from Wm. H. Schab Gallery, Inc., New York, in 1973.
Exhibited: New York, William H. Schab Gallery, Inc., *Old Master Drawings: XVth to the XVIIIth Centuries*, 1973, cat. no. 53, pl. VII; New Haven, Yale University Art Gallery, *Sixteenth Century Italian Drawings: Form and Function*, May–June 1974, cat. by E. Pillsbury and J. Caldwell, no. 28, repr.

Between the Chatsworth modello and the final painting, Barocci made fewer changes on the left side of the composition. The most important of these was the deletion of the boy on the far left side, for which the artist had already made two detail studies.[1] The poses of the three figures in the Charity group of the mother with her two children also underwent modification. For example, the mother's left arm rather than embracing the young girl beside her points upward to draw the viewer's attention to the heavenly

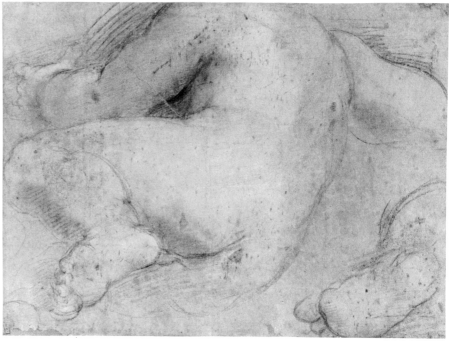

vision. In addition, the young girl kneels on one leg with her hands clasped in prayer and leans backward to admire her smiling brother on her right, rather than kneeling in an erect position with her arms at her side viewing the beggar who receives alms. A drawing in the Uffizi, with detail studies of the girl's hands and head, contains a brief sketch made from a studio model at an intermediate stage.[2] Another drawing documenting this change is the colored chalk drawing of a head of a young girl acquired recently by the Yale Art Gallery. This drawing was initially done to establish the correct angle of the head and the position of the eyes. In the black chalk underdrawing one notices that the head was originally turned further to the left, as in the above-mentioned Uffizi sheet, and the eyes were shown wide-open. In the margin is a separate study of the left eye half-closed as in the final painting. The drawing also served to study the modelling and coloring of the figure. Ochre pastel was added to the hair, and pale red chalk was softly rubbed on the right cheek. The shaded areas under the chin and round the outer areas were the last to be applied, and in this the artist made subtle adjustments in the final work, moving, for example, the shadow on the neck further to the left.

1. Berlin KK 7705 (4184) and 20138 (4152); the former repr. Emiliani, 1975, fig. 89.
2. Uffizi 812E (repr. Bertelà, 1975, no. 38, fig. 44).

**38** *Naked Angel Seen in Foreshortened View with Left Leg Raised, Left Arm Pointing to Left, and Right Arm Extended to Right; Separate Study of Right Foot.* VERSO (on separate piece of paper): *Small Sketch of an Angel*

Black, red, and white chalks, colored in buff-pink pastel, stumped, over traces of squaring in black chalk, incised for transfer, on bluish-gray paper, 240 x 336 mm. Laid down; small tears at lower left corner, lower center edge and upper right corner; scattered brown and gray spots in upper center and lower right; some small stains; rubbed. Verso (in another hand): black chalk on separate piece of white paper attached to reverse, 83 x 86 mm. Annotated in black chalk: *Barocci at Anversa.*

London, Trustees of the British Museum, no. Pp. 3–200

Provenance: Sir Joshua Reynolds, London (Lugt 2364); bequeathed by Richard Payne Knight in 1824.
Published: Schmarsow, IIIA, p. 19; L. Grassi, *Storia del disegno*, 1947, p. 137, pl. LII; Olsen, 1955, p. 131; Olsen, 1962, p. 168.

Among the didactic elements which Barocci employed to link the upper and lower zones of the composition in the Chatsworth modello for the *Madonna del Popolo* was an angel shown under the Virgin who holds an open scroll bearing a message for the half-circle of standing rectors. Like the dove sent to the alms-giving rector in the lower right, this figure underlines the role of the Virgin as the intermediary between the members of the Fraternity and Divine Grace. In the final work the artist abandoned this literal device of a single message-bearing angel in favor of a grouping of three plastically rendered angels who bear the Virgin upward and who, through their gestures, make contact with other events in the scene. The one at the far right smiles beguilingly and extends an open hand for alms; the one in profile at the left stares at the passing dove of the Holy Ghost; while the central one looks longingly over its shoulder at the viewer outside the scene. The rapport in scale and gesture with figures in the lower part of the scene establishes an effective transition between the lower and upper parts of the composition.

To give the three angels the same degree of corporeality and realism as the individual figures in the lower part of the scene Barocci submitted each figure to careful study. For the foreshortened angel in the center, there survive the cartoon fragment in the Biblioteca Ambrosiana, this colored chalk drawing of the whole torso in the British Museum and two detail studies of the left leg, again in colored chalks, in Berlin.[1] These drawings served to refine the pose and lighting. The most difficult problem was the degree of foreshortening in the raised left leg and the position of the left hand pointing in the direction of the left background. The Milan cartoon fragment shows that the artist was

39

### 39 Full-length Draped Male Figure Holding a Cloth

Pen and brown ink, brown wash, heightened with white, over incised contours of nude, squared in black and red chalks, on light brown prepared paper, 293 x 195 mm. Laid down; whites partially oxidized; severely abraded in upper central section; diagonal streak in center.

New York, The Pierpont Morgan Library, no. IV, 155A

Provenance: Earl of Warwick (Lugt 2600); Sir Charles Greville (Lugt 549); C. Fairfax Murray; J. Pierpont Morgan.
Published: Olsen, 1955, p. 134; Olsen, 1962, p. 172; Bertelà, 1975, p. 52.

On July 2, 1579, only a few weeks after completing the *Madonna del Popolo,* Barocci signed a contract with representatives of the Confraternità della Croce e Sagramento in Senigallia to execute an altarpiece;[1] evidently Barocci was prevented from entering into any kind of formal agreement until after discharging his obligation to the Fraternity of the Misericordia in Arezzo. On February 3, 1578, the Confraternity made their initial approach to the artist. Their first thought was for a simple heraldic representation of the "impresa della Croce et Sacramento." We do not know Barocci's reaction to this suggestion, but we can assume that it was negative, as had been his first response to the suggestion of doing the mystery of the Misercordia for Arezzo. The Senigallia brotherhood agreed to allow the artist two years to finish the painting—an allowance that turned out to be insufficient by almost a year—but refused to pay him six hundred scudi as the artist originally wanted and persuaded him to accept three hundred.

Due to the popularity of the composition and the availability of prints after the painting, it is not surprising that in the first edition of his monograph, published in 1955, Harald Olsen (*loc. cit.*) believed that the Morgan Library's drawing of a full-length draped figure shown here might be a copy from a print rather than an original preparatory study. The design, in fact, reverses that of the St. John the Evangelist in the painting. Olsen's conclusion, however, does not take into consideration the most critical factor in the preparation of the Senigallia *Entombment,* which is that the artist developed the composition with the principal figures facing one direction and only in the final stages, after executing numerous detailed studies from life for the draperies and individual parts of the composition, reversed the design. In the cases of many figures, moreover, he accomplished this change without altering any details. In fact, there are as many surviving studies for the com-

unsure of the location of the final contours, and he used the Berlin and London color studies to resolve the pose and make the necessary adjustments in the fall of light, while endowing the individual parts of the figure with the desired effects of breadth and monumentality.

The British Museum drawing belonged at one time to the English painter, Sir Joshua Reynolds, who may have executed the small chalk sketch of the finished angel appended to the reverse of the mount. An early annotation on the mount records: "Painted in a church at Anversa. The Virgin Mary interceding with Christ, in the clouds with angels, in favour of many people below,

amongst which is the Portrait of the Patrons of the Picture. The little sketch is taken from Sir Joshua Reynolds pocket book, which he selected as the most interesting part of perhaps the best Picture that Barocci ever painted." Schmarsow has suggested that instead of "Anversa" one should read "Arezzo," where the painting was until 1787 and where Reynolds might have stopped on his way from Rome to Florence in 1749–52.[3]

1. Ambrosiana no. F.261, Inf. p. 120 (Codice Resta) (repr. Grassi, 1947, p. 137, pl. 137) and Berlin KK 20425 (4370) and 20442 (4393).
2. Transcribed in Schmarsow, IIIA, pp. 19–20.
3. *Ibid.,* p. 20.

position in its initial, reversed, state as in the final one.[2] These begin with brief outline sketches and lead to finished torso and drapery studies. Through them we know that the artist first intended the Magdalene and the tomb to occupy the left foreground, with the Virgin and the sepulcre on the right side and Christ borne toward the right in the center—as in Raphael's altarpiece of the same subject, at that time in Perugia and now in the Borghese Gallery. The only earlier case of Barocci's developing a composition to an advanced stage and then reversing it in the final work is the *Moses and the Serpent* fresco of 1561–63 in the Belvedere apartments of the Vatican.[3]

The way the Morgan drawing itself was made sheds light on the artist's working method and the role of drapery studies in his creative process. Executed in pen, ink and wash, with white highlights, the drawing is begun not with a preliminary drawing in black chalk but with the transfer of incised outlines of a nude figure from another sheet. The nude study from which the transfer was made, in fact, can be identified with a drawing in the Uffizi.[4] With the stylus outlines of the nude as guide, the artist then sketched the design of the mantle and skirt adding whites to emphasize the highlights and brown wash, and a few hatched lines, to indicate shaded areas. The beige-tinted color of the paper acts as a middle tone, or ground, unifying and softening the overall lighting effect and creating a play of light and shade similar to that used in painting.[5] After completing his sketch of the draperies and adding and refining the lights, the artist then squared the design with chalk in order to transfer the design to another surface. By this means the drawing may have served to make a large-scale cartoon and to do more detailed studies from life for individual parts of the drapery, like the beautiful large black and white chalk drapery study formerly in the Boymans Museum in Rotterdam.[6] When the artist eventually reversed the composition, he may also have made a further set of detail studies, but if he did, he would probably have based them on the pen and wash modello of the overall design. A copy of the Morgan Library drawing, evidently done by a studio assistant or close follower, is preserved in Berlin; on its verso is a black chalk sketch of the first conception, evidently based upon a lost drawing.[7]

1. For the surviving documents for the commission, see E. Vecchioni, "La Chiesa della Croce e Sagramento in Sinigallia e la 'Deposizione' di Federico Barocci," *Rassegna marchigiana*, V, 1926–27, pp. 497–503.
2. Among the sketches are Berlin KK 20445 verso (4414) (Olsen, 1962, fig. 48b), Uffizi 1417E recto and verso (Bertelà, 1975, figs. 49–50), and British Museum 1966-7-23-1. Figure studies: Rotterdam Museum, Boymans-van Beuningen, Inv. no I–428, Berlin KK 20357 (4292) recto

and verso, and Uffizi 11401F verso for Christ; Uffizi 11536F and 11411F and Berlin KK 20228 (4441) verso for the three figures bearing Christ; Wurzburg, Inv. 7173 and Berlin KK 20361 (4267) for the Virgin. And drapery studies: Berlin KK 20363 (4308) and formerly Rotterdam, Museum Boymans (repr. *Kersttentoonstelling*, Museum Boymans, 1938–39, cat. no. 34, fig. 13).
3. See drawing in the Louvre, no. 2841 (repr. Emiliani, 1975, fig. 19).
4. Uffizi 11536F, black and white chalk, stumped, executed over black chalk squared lines, incised for transfer, on greenish paper, 197 x 110 mm. (repr. Emiliani, 1975, fig. 111).
5. Barocci's use of colored and tinted paper to establish a tonal and coloristic effect approaching that of the finished painting is discussed by M. Lavin, 1956, pp. 435–439.
6. See n. 2 above and Olsen, 1962, p. 172.
7. Berlin KK 20310, as a copy or from Barocci's school; not in Olsen.

## 40 *Entombment*

EXHIBITED IN NEW HAVEN ONLY

Pen and brown ink, with touch of gray wash on head of Christ, over a preliminary drawing in black chalk, squared in red chalk, on white paper, 485 x 342 mm. Laid down; trace of horizontal crease in center; stain from reverse at lower center.

England, Mr. and Mrs. H. M. Calmann

Provenance: J. Richardson, Jr. (Lugt 2170); Sir Charles Oakley (sold Sotheby's, 13 Feb. 1896, possibly lot 32, bt. Walker); W. Maxwell Bolten, Larchfield (Cheshire) (sold Sotheby's, 8 July 1964, lot 23, bt. Y. ffrench).
Published: Pillsbury, *M.D.*, 1976, p. 62.

According to Bellori, Barocci's customary way of preparing a composition involved the making of separate studies of the lighting and coloring. In the case of the Senigallia *Entombment* we are fortunate to have a fairly complete record of this process. For this composition there survive not only a black and white chalk cartoon and a color sketch in oils based upon it, both of which are a little less than half of the size of the finished work,[1] but also a pen and ink modello (Cat. 40) and a related chiaroscuro study (Cat. 41). Although Bellori would lead one to believe that the artist would make the colored bozzetto as the final step in the process, a comparison of the sketch in the Galleria Nazionale in Urbino with the finished work would suggest that the color study preceded the chiaroscuro modello in Chatsworth (Cat. 41).

The newly re-discovered pen modello in an English private collection is the least well-known of the group. In style it may be compared with that of the developed compositional studies for the *Martyrdom of St. Vitalis* and the *Visitation* of the same time (Cat. 45 and 51). The degree of finish, however, is greater in the *Entombment* modello than in the others. This fact may find a possible explanation from two circumstances

particular to the commission: the first is that, when the artist made the drawing, the composition had already been fully elaborated in reverse, in another set of drawings; the second is that at the time, in the early 1580s, the artist was experimenting with reproductive prints (his *Perdono* print dates from 1581), an experience that must have given him greater control of the graphic media. In this regard, the modello in England is not unlike a dry point whose lines are drawn directly on a copper plate with an etching needle. One other aspect of the modello which is of interest is the method of squaring, which does not rely on a simple grid but also employs several diagonal lines which subdivide the individual squares into smaller geometric units. These lines may have aided the artist to obtain greater precision in establishing the correct position of the heads and other parts of the figure in the final design or have been of use when he made the full-scale pastel or oil studies of the individual heads, which were executed while the artist worked on the actual painting.

1. Both works are reproduced by Emiliani, 1975, figs. 116–117.
2. While doubt has been expressed in the past in regard to the authenticity of both the Chatsworth and Urbino works, the documentary and stylistic evidence supporting the attributions is considerable and when they are viewed in correct sequence and from the point of view of their function in the creative process, the plausibility of their having been executed by anyone other than Barocci, or for any other purpose, is slight. A comparison of any of the above four works with the drawings that were made as copies from the painting underline this point (Louvre 2852 and 2853 and Rome, Gabinetto Nazionale delle Stampe, Inv. 4201 and 12006).

## 41 *Entombment*

Pen and point of brush, brown ink, brown wash, developed in white and gray gouache, with touches of pink, over a preliminary drawing in black chalk, on buff-colored paper, 475 x 355 mm. Laid down; repaired tears at lower right and across center; generally stained and darkened.

Chatsworth, The Trustees of the Chatsworth Settlement, no. 365A

Provenance: William, 2nd Duke of Devonshire (Lugt 718).
Exhibited: London, Royal Academy, *Italian Drawings*, 1930, no. 290; Amsterdam, Stadelijk Museum, *Italiaansche Kunst in Nederlandsch Bezit*, 1934, cat. by J. Q. van Regteren Altena and R. V. Marle, p. 133, no. 470; Bristol, Bristol University, 1936, no. 892; Bologna, 1975, no. 113.
Published: S. A. Strong, *Reproductions of Drawings by Old Masters in the Collection of the Duke of Devonshire at Chatsworth*, London, 1902, pl. 63; Schmarsow, IIIB, p. 41; Olsen, 1955, p. 133; Olsen, 1962, p. 171.

While Schmarsow published this compositional model for the Senigallia *Entombment* as a school-piece—an opinion accepted by Olsen in 1962—this drawing bears a traditional attribution to the artist and has been published as an original by Strong, Popham, Olsen himself (in 1955), and more recently Emiliani and Bertelà. The fine quality of the Chatsworth drawing is nowhere better seen than in the landscape where the morning light emerges from behind the hill in the left background in diaphanous rays which bathe the figures in the foreground. As has already been noted, the drawing is based upon a finished pen modello in an English private collection (Cat. 40). This drawing provided a guide for the initial black chalk underdrawing to which the artist applied the rich combination of colored washes and gouaches. The artist's intention was to refine the tonal values (i.e. the lights) in the final work; and the only local colors in the drawing are the pink flesh tints on the faces. When the drawing was nearing completion, the artist put it aside to study the colors in the canvas in Urbino, which is based upon the chalk cartoon in the Hague done on a slightly larger scale. It is of interest to note that in the Chatsworth drawing the artist left parts of the Magdalene in the foreground unfinished. This in itself would tend to undermine the argument that says the drawing is a copy. The reason that the artist left this part unfinished may, in fact, have been that he intended to execute a developed study of this figure in colored oils; this important, and still unpublished, "auxiliary cartoon"—on the same scale as the finished work—survives in an English private collection.

**42** *Study of Chest and Right Arm of Nude Male Figure Reclining to Right; Separate Studies of the Lower Arms (4) and of Right Knee (1); Study of Eyes Looking Downwards to Right*

Black and white chalks, with red chalk on arm and shoulder of principal study, stumped, on light blue paper, 275 x 414 mm.

Princeton, The Art Museum, Princeton University, Bequest of Dan Fellows Platt, no. 48–595

Provenance: Sir Charles Greville (Lugt 549); Earl of Warwick (Lugt 26–0); Charles Fairfax Murray (sold, New York, Anderson Galleries, 6–7 Nov. 1924, no. 214); Dan Fellows Platt.
Exhibited: New York, Metropolitan Museum of Art, *et al, Italian Drawings in the Art Museum of Princeton University*, 1966, cat. by J. Bean, p. 22, no. 13, repr.
Published: Baird, 1950, pp. 11–16, fig. 2; Olsen, 1955, p. 134; Olsen, 1962, p. 172; J. Scholz, "Italian Drawings in the Art Museum of Princeton University," *Burlington Magazine*, CIX, 1967, p. 293; Bertelà, 1975, p. 52; Gibbons, 1977, p. 9, no. 23, repr.

40

Barocci made a long series of drawings for the reclining figure of Christ in the Senigallia *Entombment*. The purpose of these was to refine the lighting and the pose of the torso. The earliest among these—preserved in Berlin, Florence, and Rotterdam—show the figure turned to the left as in the first scheme for the composition. [1] The drawing from Princeton exhibited here, which was first published by Thomas Baird in 1950, contains studies for various individual parts of the figure. These studies are based upon the four earlier drawings, but show the figure reclining to the right as in the final painting; hence they probably follow the pen modello in an English private collection and the chiaroscuro study in Chatsworth (Cat. 40–41). In the upper right is a study for the chest, shoulders, and right arm of the figure; in the left margin the lower arm and hand are drawn again, but on a larger scale; and in the lower margin are four further detail studies—three for the figure's arm and elbow and one for his right knee. The artist's chief concern appears to have been in the light reflection from the flesh (and for this the black and white chalk has been smoothed by rubbing) and in the anatomical

41

Oil paint on light brown paper, 400 x 278 mm. Lined on canvas; abraded, especially in margins.

New York, The Metropolitan Museum of Art, no. 1976.87.1

Provenance: London, Private Collection; acquired from Thomas Agnew and Sons, London, Ltd., in 1976.
Exhibited: Bologna, 1975, no. 115.
Published: Emiliani, 1975, no. 115; Borea, 1976, p. 60; Shearman, 1976, pp. 51–52; Pillsbury, *M.D.*, 1976, p. 56.

In the description of the contents of Barocci's studio taken shortly after his death one reads: "Vi sono da quatordici teste colorite a olio di mano del S.ᵒʳ Baroccio, di vecchi, di donne, di giovani."[1] A more detailed account of one of these fourteen drawings appears in a letter written in 1658 to the secretary of Leopoldo de'Medici: "Una testa di un vecchio, fatta a olio in carta di grandezza poco più di mezzo piede, et è conservata bene la testa, solo lese dal tempo la carta da un lato."[2] Until recently, the only known drawing of this kind was the study for the head of St. Jude in the *Madonna di S. Simone* in the Doria Collection in Rome—a drawing executed in gray and brown oils with pink and white highlights and red accents (on the lips and nose), over a preliminary drawing in red chalk, on brownish paper lined with canvas.[3] If we exclude the heads which Barocci painted on paper and then actually applied to the surface of his finished paintings—for example, the female donor in the *Madonna di S. Simone* and the St. Francis in the *Perdono,* which were, in fact, painted in a different technique and for a different purpose—the Doria study was the sole survivor among the artist's oil studies of heads. All of this changed in 1975. Among the few important discoveries made on the occasion of the Barocci exhibition in Bologna was that of two hitherto unknown oil studies of this type in an English private collection, subsequently acquired by the Metropolitan Museum: one head is for the Senigallia *Entombment* and the other for the Chiesa Nuova *Visitation.* Undoubtedly these two works, like the one in the Doria Collection, belong to the group of fourteen head studies which the artist left in his studio at his death. All three works are executed in a similar oil technique, although the proportion of medium to pigment varies in each case (in the present work for the head of the bearer of Christ in the *Entombment* the grays and browns dominate the local tints); they are done on light brown paper lined with canvas; and they are closely related to the respective heads in the finished work. Like the

accuracy of the various parts of the figure; in two further drawings the various poses and lighting for the two hands of the figure are explored.[2]

A final element in the Princeton drawing, and one which has escaped the notice of former writers, is the pair of eyes drawn in the upper center. To read this physiognomical feature, the sheet must be rotated 180 degrees, which reveals the outline of a head shown near full-face, inclined slightly to the left, with its eyes directed downwards and its right one in shadow. Although the light-

ing and design do not exactly match the painting, this study may possibly have been done for the head of the standing Virgin in the background. This kind of detail study may be compared with the pastel study for the head of a girl at Yale, which has a detail study for one eye in the margin (Cat. 37).

1. Berlin, KK 20357 (4292), recto and verso (repr. Emiliani, 1975, no. 107); Rotterdam, Museum Boymans-van Beuningen, Inv. no. I–428 (repr. Emiliani, 1975, no. 108); and Uffizi 11401F verso.
2. Berlin KK 20358 (4386) and 20359 (4294).

large-scale drawings of heads, done in colored chalks and pastels, which share a similar range of hues, the oil studies served as auxiliary cartoons made after the artist had started working on the painting in order to establish the exact effects of tone and color for the faces in the painting. The oil studies, far from being life studies, represent the distillation of all the preparatory work and culminate the creative process. John Shearman (*loc. cit.*) has quite correctly observed that they illustrate the "indivisibility of the drawing-process from that of painting" in Barocci's work. It is difficult to know why the artist preferred the medium of oil to pastels in some cases, but it seems that he may have regarded them as an equally satisfactory means to the same end, for neither in the case of this drawing nor in that of its companion, the St. Elizabeth, nor in the St. Jude, does there exist a comparable drawing in colored chalks.[4]

1. Calzini, 1898, p. 105.
2. Baldinucci-Barocchi, VI, p. 77.
3. Repr. Emiliani, 1975, fig. 35.
4. As an example, one might compare the oil study here with the large pastel study for the head of the bearded man in the Institut Néerlandais which is related to another figure in the Senigallia *Entombment* (Inv. 5681; repr. Emiliani, 1975, fig. 114).

**44** *Head of Man with Mustache, Short Beard, and Long Brown Hair, in Profile to Right, Looking Downwards*

Oil paint on brownish paper, 300 x 235 mm. (sight). Mounted on board; flattened and abraded in process of lining; scattered tears inpainted.

Sacramento (California), E. B. Crocker Art Gallery, no. 1872.681

Published: (F. Kent), *E. B. Crocker Art Gallery Catalogue of Collections*, 1964, p. 15, illus. p. 50; B. Fredericksen and F. Zeri, *Census of Pre-Nineteenth Century Italian Paintings in North American Public Collections*, 1972.

Although catalogued by Federico Zeri as a copy after Barocci, this painted head has many of the characteristics of a preparatory study for one of the artist's compositions. As in the Metropolitan and Doria head studies, it is executed in gray and brown oils with a few red accents (for the mouth, eyelids, and ear) and pink and white highlights, all on paper mounted to another surface. The buildup of the forms begins with the priming in gray and continues with the addition of the brown (for the hair), pale pink (for the flesh tones), and red (for particular features). The overall concern lies in the coloration of the face rather than in the establishment of the pose or expression. In style, there is a close relationship between this work and that of the Senigallia *Entombment*

43

44

figures and still-life details in one corner of the foreground.[4] Moreover, the pose for the Christ in the Allendale version derives from that of the St. John in the Senigallia *Entombment,* and his left arm which rests on the fence is directly adapted from studies for the young man cleaning the sepulcre in the earlier work.[5] In view of these relations, it is plausible that the Allendale painting was completed at the same time as the above-mentioned three works and also the Vatican *Annunciation* and Chiesa Nuova *Visitation*— that is in the early or middle 1580s—but sometime before the *Flight from Troy* (the first version of which was finished by 1589), the Louvre *Circumcision* of 1590, and the Munich altarpiece, also of 1590.

1. Repr. Olsen, 1962, fig. 82a.
2. The Ciamberlano print is reproduced by Olsen, 1962, fig. 122c. Neither of the other two works has been fully discussed in the literature, although each is critical in reconstructing the development of the composition. The Dresden drawing (Inv. C1914–62), which Olsen dismissed as a copy (1962, p. 278), is a fresh pen, wash, and white gouache compositional sketch that differs from the final work in many respects. The second drawing is a finished modello executed in colored chalks, which is similar in function, scale, and medium to the modello for the *Christ Appearing to the Magdalene* (Munich picture) in the Uffizi (no. 11425F, repr. Bertelà, 1975, no. 59, fig. 68).
3. di Pietro, 1913, pp. 78–82, fig. 103 and Olsen, 1962, pp. 75–76, 183–184.
4. In the case of the *Calling of St. Andrew,* the *Noli me tangere* may be compared not only with the finished design but also with a preliminary one, recorded by a drawing in the Uffizi (no. 11331F), in which the two protagonists are organized along a diagonal rising from the lower left to the upper right as in the Allendale picture.
5. Berlin KK 20357 (4292) and 20361 (4267).

## 45 *Martyrdom of St. Vitalis*

Pen and brown ink, brown wash, over a preliminary drawing in black chalk, squared in red and black chalks and in pen and brown ink, on light beige paper, 442 x 323 mm. Laid down; badly torn, abraded, and waterstained; numerous repairs and restored losses, especially on sides.

Private Collection

Provenance: Benjamin West (Lugt 419); unidentified armorial stamp, lower center (not in Lugt).

On June 20, 1580, Barocci signed a contract with the Casentine monks of Ravenna to paint an altarpiece for their church of San Vitale.[1] According to the contract, Barocci had previously submitted a drawing *(disignum)* which the abbot and superiors of the monastery had examined and which had received five favorable votes and one unfavorable. Out of deference to the one dissenting member, Barocci was asked to increase the number of figures *(pluribus figuris augere et accrescere).* The agreed price was six hundred gold ducats *(scudi d'oro),* of which one hundred were to be paid immediately and the rest upon request; this fee, which even-

study in the Metropolitan (Cat. 43), which has a similar tonal range based on grays and browns set off by a few rose-colored flesh tints.

If the Sacramento head was done as a study for a painting, there are two works for which it may have served. The first, in the Alte Pinacothek in Munich, represents *Christ Appearing to Saint Mary Magdalene;* it was done for Giuliano della Rovere and is signed and dated 1590.[1] The second, of the *Noli me tangere,* survives in the collection of Viscount Allendale, Bywell Hall, but in a state of almost total ruin; the composition is best known through Luca Ciamberlano's engraving published in 1609 and the cartoon fragments in a private collection in Oslo and compositional studies in the Kupferstichkabinett in Dresden and in an English private collection.[2] The only information we have on the commission of the second picture comes from Bellori, who maintained that the picture was ordered from the Buonvisi family and installed by them in a church in Lucca. The Sacramento oil is likely to have

been done for the earliest of the two works as the Christ's head is represented in a nearly identical pose in both works.

On the matter of precedence, however, there is no agreement between scholars. While di Pietro identified a drawing for Christ's face in the Uffizi as a study for the Allendale picture and concluded that the latter picture, because of its dramatic qualities, preceded the Munich work, Olsen has argued the reverse and suggested that the work in England was done some years later than its counterpart in Germany.[3] Both agree that the two works must be separated by at least a few years. In view of this, the choice lies in dating the Allendale *Noli me tangere* to the early or middle 1580s or a decade later. Of the two possibilities, the more plausible would seem to be the first. The Allendale *Noli me tangere* shares with the Senigallia *Entombment, Martyrdom of St. Vitalis,* and *Calling of St. Andrew,* all of which were finished before 1583, a scheme of organizing the composition along crossing diagonals supported by, dramatically posed

45

able revision before the final design. The earliest drawing—which may possibly be identifiable as the project shown to the priors in 1580—is preserved in the Louvre.[2] This drawing shows a group of soldiers gathered around an opening in the ground outside a city into which they cast the naked torso of the young saint, witnessed by a circle of women and children. While the general design of the composition anticipates the final work, the individual figures underwent many changes, and various elements were either added or deleted. For example, in the Paris drawing there are a pair of mounted knights entering the scene from the right which do not appear in the final design. Conversely the Paris modello fails to include the figure of the magistrate at the upper right, the agent of the Saint's martyrdom.

The transition from the Paris drawing to the final work is documented not only by numerous studies of the individual figures but also by a hitherto unknown pen and wash modello in a private collection. This drawing, which is unfortunately quite damaged, but which retains traces of a freshly conceived sketch in black chalk, documents an intermediate stage in the revision of the composition. Already many of the poses have assumed the form they will take in the final work: the magistrate sits on a raised dais at the upper right; the athletic stone-thrower in the center draws his arms to the right rather than holding them over his head; and a young figure rushes forward in the act of pushing the martyred figure into the opening in the ground, replacing the soldier who stabs at the feet of the saint with the end of his lance. Yet many discrepancies with the final work remain. The most important of these is the man on horseback in the middle distance on the left. This figure, which gives way to a single standing knight in the final work, harks back to the Paris drawing which had included two riders entering the scene from the opposite side. Other differences include: the kneeling woman holding out her hands in exclamation on the left side, who is subsequently replaced by a pair of boys in conversation; the seated girl in the foreground who in the drawing turns her back to the viewer and in the painting rotates her shoulders in the opposite direction; and, finally, the dog in the right foreground who in the drawing lies on the ground asleep and in the painting sits up alertly on one leg. One could enumerate many other alterations and refinements, especially in the accessories and small details, but the critical point is that this modello represents a definitive stage in the development of the composition from which the artist made a large group of further detailed studies to elaborate the poses and cos-

tually rose to 640, represents a substantial increase over that of his earlier works (400 for the *Madonna del Popolo* and 300 for the *Entombment*). There was no time limit specified in the contract, but from payments made to the artist, framemaker, and those who finally brought the work to Ravenna when it was done, we can establish the following schedule: the artist probably finished a preliminary set of drawings by August 1581, when he requested his second payment; he began painting sometime after December 1581, when the *tavalone* was ready and a

third payment was demanded; he continued working on the picture through the following year, receiving two further payments in September 1582 and February 1583; and finally he finished the painting and consigned it to Ravenna in April 1583—the date the artist inscribed on the work itself. It would seem that the artist's major period of activity in executing the altarpiece came in late 1582, after he had delivered the *Entombment* for Senigallia.

As one might conclude from the agreement, the composition underwent consider-

tumes of the individual figures. To the existing number of these can be added a beautiful drapery study for the seated girl in the foreground—wrongly identified by Olsen, who did not know of the drawing, as a study for an entirely different work.[3]

1. The documents are published by S. Muratori in: "Il Martirio di San Vitale del Barocci: Notizie, documenti, aneddoti," *Felix Ravenna,* fasc. 5, 1912, pp. 244–264.
2. No. 2858 (repr. Olsen, 1962, fig. 46).
3. Berlin KK 20139 (4401), which Olsen mistakenly related to the Virgin in the *Madonna della Gatta* (1962, p. 189). Among other studies based directly on the new modello, but incorrectly identified in the literature, is Berlin KK 20237 (4349) verso which contains three studies for the head and straw hat of the man pushing the martyred figure into the opening and an individual study for his shirt. Formerly this group of studies was related to the boy with the shovel on the right (Olsen, 1962, p. 173).

**46** *Head of a Young Man Inclined Downwards to Right, Viewed from Behind; Nude Figure Leaning to Left with Right Leg on Step*

Black chalk over stylus underdrawing, squared in black and red chalks, on blue paper (nude study); black and red chalks, colored with brownish and pink pastels, stumped (head study), 266 x 232 mm. Annotated in pen and brown ink on mount: *Fed. Barocci.* Laid down; small repaired tear at upper right.

Edinburgh, National Gallery of Scotland, no. D1589

Provenance: J. Richardson, Jr. (Lugt 2170); Sir Joshua Reynolds (Lugt 2364); David Laing; Royal Scottish Academy; transferred 1910.
Published: Olsen, 1955, p. 136; Olsen, 1962, p. 174; Andrews, 1968, p. 12, fig. 112.

The most important difference between the Louvre sketch for the *Martyrdom of St. Vitalis* and the finished work lies in the treatment of the central section. Whereas in the former the figures and architectural elements encircle a central void set back into space, in the final painting the right foreground is cleared of architectural elements and the figures form a diagonal rising from the left corner. This change has two effects: it draws the scene of the martyrdom nearer to the viewer and creates an accelerated recession into depth—which is both accentuated and counteracted by the gesture of the seated magistrate at the upper right.

A critical aspect of this revision occurs in the two principal figures of the martyred saint and the stonebearer. For instance, in the Louvre drawing, the saint's body twists from one side to the other in an exaggerated contrapposto that emphasizes the conjunction of two diagonals and the movement into depth, whereas, in the final work, the saint's torso comes forward and supports the diagonal that rises across the foreground. Similarly, the stonebearer, who is at

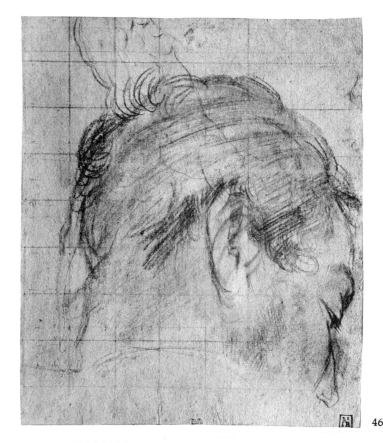

46

first depicted stepping into the background in a vertical position, assumes a broader stance that continues the dominant movement from left to right, while at the same time redirecting the eye in the opposite direction. The volumetric structure imposed upon this figure becomes nearly pyramidal.

To achieve this, the artist submitted the figure to a long series of individual studies, most of which were done from youths posed in the artist's studio. The first of these, a double-sided sheet in Urbino, reveals the artist moving away from the vertical pose shown in the Louvre sheet: the position of the feet widen and the arms extend more to the sides.[1] Further drawings in Florence and Berlin have detail studies for the draperies, for the right arm and for the right leg which are related to this revised conception.[2] In time, however, the artist became dissatisfied with this pose—possibly because it lacked the required balance and stability—and at this point he made the very spirited pen and wash sketch in Adelaide, showing the arms of the figure drawn further back to the right and the weight more evenly distributed between both legs.[3] Although this drawing represents a significant advance over the earlier formulation, it still follows the Louvre drawing in the placement of the legs on the

same level, with the right one slightly behind the left one. To effect this further change, the artist made a chalk drawing of the whole figure and with a stylus incised the contours to a new sheet to work on the bend of the left knee.

The first of the two, which shows numerous pentimenti, is preserved in the Uffizi.[4] The second, exhibited here, is in Edinburgh. Because of the colored chalk study executed over the figure, the pose is difficult to read. Upon careful inspection it becomes clear that the artist began the drawing by incising the contours of the nude from the Uffizi sheet. He then lightly drew in the figure in black chalk, modifying the straight position of the left leg to show the figure bending slightly at the knee. Having made this change, the artist executed a pair of drawings to refine the lighting and anatomical details of both legs.[5]

Since the artist only needed to make the single modification to the incised design of the figure, he left the greater part of the figure unfinished and was able to use the sheet for an altogether different purpose. The second study contained on the Edinburgh sheet represents the head of a young boy seen from behind. Executed in colored chalks, this drawing lies between the artist's regular head studies and those he did to study the color and texture of the hair alone. In his studio at his death the artist left as many as ninety drawings of this latter type (compared with about 180 of the normal kind); they are described as: "Teste abozzate grosso modo, ove sono capelli finiti e non altro, orecchie, gole, barbe, fronti lassate così che altro non li serviva."[6] The study shows the side of the face and the hair of a male figure looking towards the right background and downwards. Although the pose does not correspond with that of any of the figures in the *Martyrdom of Saint Vitalis,* it is possible the study was done for the head of one of the young spectators on the left side at a preliminary stage in the planning. As has already been pointed out (see Cat. 45), this group was among the last parts of the composition to reach its final form. Moreover, a drawing in Berlin for this section shows a variety of alternative poses for the standing spectators.[7] A drawing in colored chalks of a similar subject exists in Würzburg which has been identified as another study for the head of the boy spectator in the *Martyrdom of St. Vitalis* but which may possibly be for another composition entirely.[7]

1. Galleria Nazionale, Inv. 1664 (recto repr. Emiliani, 1975, fig. 120).
2. Uffizi 11623F (repr. di Pietro, 1913, fig. 67) and Berlin KK 20242 (4432).
3. Acquired at Sotheby's, London, 25 June 1970, lot 27, repr. in sale catalogue and published by B. Smith, "A Drawing by Barocci," *Bulletin of the Art Gallery of South Australia,* XXXII, no. 2, Oct. 1970, n.p., repr. in color.
4. Uffizi 11285F, red and black chalk, over black chalk squaring, incised and squared in red chalk for transfer, on white paper, 299 x 191 mm.
5. Berlin KK 20032 (4271) and 20243 (4282).
6. Calzini, 1898, p. 106. Examples of pure "hair" studies are Würzburg Inv. 7186 and Urbino, Galleria Nazionale, Inv. 1670.
7. Berlin KK 20186 (4201), which Olsen fails to identify as a study for the hands and general poses of the two young male spectators on left in the *Martyrdom of St. Vitalis.*
8. Martin von Wagner Museum, Inv. 7186 (repr. Emiliani, 1975, fig. 126). One possible connection is with the kneeling apostle on the left in the *Institution of the Eucharist* in S. Maria sopra Minerva, Rome.

**47** *Figure Studies: Man on Horseback; Kneeling Bearded Man Looking Upwards with Arms Outstretched; Two Old Men in Left Profile*

Pen and brown ink, brown wash, over black chalk, heightened with white (kneeling figure only), on light buff-colored paper, 180 x 201 mm. Laid down; rubbed; scattered glue stains and holes, particularly along edges.

Old Bennington (Vermont), Mr. and Mrs. Julius S. Held

Provenance: M. Marignane, Paris (Lugt 1872). Exhibited: Binghamton, State University of New York at Binghamton, University Art Gallery, *et al,* "Selections from the Drawing Collection of Mr.

47

and Mrs. Julius S. Held," 1970, cat. by M. Milkovich, p. 23, no. 107, repr.

The traditional attribution of this sheet of figure studies to Barocci finds support from stylistic links with the artist's works of the 1580s. The nervous, rather abbreviated contours which produce spiky fingers and angular drapery patterns; the parallel hatching in the shaded areas; the summary profiles of the two men at the right and of the horse; the delicate, but seemingly random washes; and the touches of white highlights broadly applied with the brush: all find a parallel among the artist's drawings for the Vatican *Annunciation,* Chiesa Nuova *Visitation* and other works of the same period.[1] The poses of the individual figures also are related to documented works. For example, the kneeling figure, with the two bearded men behind, recalls the principal figure in the *Calling of St. Andrew,* while the horseback rider bears a resemblance with the mounted knight depicted in the modello for the *Martyrdom of St. Vitalis* (Cat. 45). In this case the appearance of studies for figures in two different altarpieces may be the result of the coincidence of the two commissions. The *Calling of St. Andrew* in Brussels is dated 1583 and, according to Bellori, was ordered from Lucrezia d'Este, the sister of the Duke of Ur-

bino, in 1580. Therefore, Barocci was probably working on it at precisely the same period of time as the *Vitalis*—1580–83. Although neither of the figures fully corresponds with an element in the painted altarpiece, the artist normally made pen sketches to explore radically different solutions to compositional or figural situations, and the degree of divergence from the related work is, in this case, much less than in the sketches for the slightly later Chiesa Nuova *Visitation.* Moreover, it should be pointed out that the kneeling figure's relationship with the *Calling of St. Andrew* is even closer in the drawing in the Uffizi showing an early, and quite different, idea for organizing the two protagonists in the foreground; in the latter St. Andrew faces outward, with his legs back into space and his arms extended to the sides in a cross-like configuration.[2]

1. For example, the pen modello for the Vatican *Annunciation* formerly in the Ellesmere Collection and now in the National Gallery of Victoria in Melbourne (repr. sale catalogue, Sotheby's, London, 5 Dec. 1972, lot 100); the sheet of pen studies for St. Zacharias in the *Visitation* in the collection of the Earl of Plymouth, Oakly Park (Courtauld Institute neg. no. 364/1/8); or the finished compositional study for the *Calling of St. Andrew* at Windsor Castle (Inv. 6830; repr. Emiliani, 1975, fig. 138).
2. Uffizi 11331F (repr. Bertelà, 1975, fig. 59).

**48** *Two Compositional Sketches of the Visitation; Separate Sketches of Joseph, Zacharias, and the Architectural Background.* VERSO: *Compositional Sketch of the Visitation; Separate Sketch of a Bearded Figure (Zacharias) Seated at a Table*

Pen and brown ink, brown wash, with traces of black chalk, on buff-white paper, 327 x 219 mm. Annotated in pen and brown ink at lower right: *373*. Paper weakened along contours from iron-gall ink burns; lightly foxed and soiled. Verso: pen and brown ink, and brown wash.

Paris, Foundation Custodia (Coll. F. Lugt), Institut Néerlandais, no. 5483

Provenance: Sir Joshua Reynolds, London (Lugt 2364); Charles Fairfax Murray (sold London, Christie's, 30 Jan. 1920, lot 251); C. R. Rudolf (Lugt 2811B); Frits Lugt (Lugt 1028), acquired in 1938.
Exhibited: Paris, Institut Néerlandais, *et al, Le Dessin Italien dans les Collections Hollandaises*, 1962, p. 86, no. 127; Bologna, 1975, no. 153.
Published: C. Fairfax Murray, *Collection of Drawings*, V (ca. 1913), nos. 66–67; Olsen, 1955, p. 141; Olsen, 1962, p. 180, figs. 60, 61a; M. Jaffé, "Italian Drawings from Dutch Collections," *Burlington Magazine*, CIV, 1962, p. 231, fig. 5; J. Byam Shaw,

"Two Drawings by Barocci," *Miscellanea J. Q. van Regteren Altena,* Amsterdam, 1969, p. 89, n. 8; Jaffé, 1977, p. 52, no. 72, repr.

As early as 1582 the priests of the Oratory in Rome had applied to the minister of the Duke of Urbino for assistance in obtaining an altarpiece by Barocci.[1] For this work they had reserved the Chapel of the Visitation whose patronage had been assumed earlier in the same year by Francesco Pizzamiglio. Inquiries were made about price and other matters, and on June 19, 1583, the artist gave his consent to the proposal. Work on the painting itself, however, went forward slowly, and the secretary of the Duke of Urbino was forced to write the minister in Rome in August of 1584 to remind Cardinal Cesi, the protector of the Oratorians, of the impossibility of pressuring the artist to finish the work soon. The actual date of completion can be established from a series of letters recording the shipment of the painting to Rome, its installation in the Chiesa Nuova, and its favorable reception from artists as well as religious persons, which were written in May and June of 1586.

Judging from the number and range of surviving drawings the artist valued the commission and spared no effort to produce a work that would satisfy the Oratorians. The initial task was the arrangement of the composition, which the artist explored in a long series of pen sketches. Among the earliest of these is a brief pen drawing in the Rijksmuseum in Amsterdam,[2] which shows the two protagonists, Mary and Elizabeth, meeting in the open air outside the latter's house, flanked by Joseph and Zacharias; in this early stage there is a recollection of Andrea del Sarto's fresco in the Chiostro dello Scalzo in Florence which Barocci may have seen in 1579 when he visited Tuscany.[3] The next formulation of the subject, preserved in a drawing in Copenhagen,[4] relocates the scene in an interior and shows Saint Elizabeth in the doorway of her house receiving the Virgin who enters from the piazza in front of the actual Cathedral of Urbino. In the distance is the Palazzo Ducale and the Church of San Domenico; and in the foreground, beside a table, is Saint Zacharias. The double-sided sheet in the Institut Néerlandais, which we exhibit here, takes its inspiration from this model. In fact,

48 verso

which reveal that at this stage the artist already considered introducing into the background the view of a vaulted loggia. On the opposite side of the sheet, in fact, there are two sketches for this aspect of the composition, accompanied by a further sketch of the whole scene. The latter is important since it shows, for the first time, the architectural elements in reverse. The house of Elizabeth is still on the left, but the Virgin ascends a set of steps from the foreground rather than from the background, and the space the viewer occupies in front of the scene is now the street. This new scheme also shows Joseph bending forward in the left foreground, as he does in the final painting. While from this general scheme, the artist quickly developed the final design, he went on to make a further thumbnail sketch of the whole composition and detail studies of the arched loggia in the background and of the female protagonists.[6] All of these pen sketches, as well as a sheet of chalk sketches for the pose of St. Joseph in the Uffizi[7] and several drapery studies (e.g. Cat. 50), served to make the *disegno compito* in Edinburgh (Cat. 51) which became the basis for the full-scale cartoon, whose central portion survives in the Uffizi.[8]

1. The documentation for the altarpiece may be found in L. Ponnelle and L. Bordet, *Saint Phillippe Neri et la société romaine de son temps (1515–1596)*, Paris, 1928, pp. 363ff and G. Gronau, *Documenti artistici urbinati*, Florence, 1936, pp. 156ff; summaries are published by Olsen, 1962, p. 179 and Emiliani, 1975, pp. 146–148.
2. Inv. 1964–79 (repr. Emiliani, 1975, fig. 152).
3. The influence of Sarto's fresco on the *Visitation* has been pointed out by John Shearman (1976, p. 53).
4. Statens Museum for Kunst, Inv. 7404 recto (repr. Olsen, 1962, fig. 58).
5. Pen and brown ink, brown wash, on white paper, 196 x 265 mm. (Courtauld Institute of Art negative no. 364/1/ 8).
6. Uffizi 11398F verso and Stockholm NMH 412–413 (repr. Olsen, 1962, figs. 62a–b).
7. Uffizi 11622F (repr. Emiliani, 1975, fig. 158).
8. Uffizi 1784E (repr. Bertelà, 1975, fig. 64).

**49** *Head and Bodice of an Elderly Woman with Veil, Turned Three-Quarters to Right and Inclined Downwards.* VERSO: *Schematic Profile of a Face, Turned to Left*

Black and red chalks, incised, on white paper, 135 x 95 mm. Annotated in pencil at lower right: *F. Barotius*. Lightly foxed; trace of crease down center. Verso: black chalk. Annotated in red chalk at lower left: *F. Barotius*.

Paris, Fondation Custodia (coll. F. Lugt), Institut Néerlandais, Inv. 3459

Provenance: John Kerr-Lawson, London; F. Lugt (Lugt 1028), acquired in 1928.
Exhibited: Rotterdam, *Meesterwerke*, 1938, no. 455.
Published: Olsen, 1962, p. 180, fig. 63a.

the first marks on the sheet, located in the upper right corner of the verso, show a seated bearded man recalling the St. Zacharias in the Copenhagen design. The principal sketch on the same side of the drawing shows Elizabeth greeting the Virgin as in the Copenhagen drawing, but now the background has become a hillside with a group of common structures and the positions of Joseph and Zacharias have been turned to the right by 90°. The recto of the same sheet bears further revisions. In a developed sketch on the right side of the sheet, Elizabeth's house appears on the left, Zacharias emerges from the house behind his wife, and Joseph lays his luggage on the ground in the right foreground. Individual sketches for Zacharias depicted in this way appear on the left side of the same drawing and in a little-known drawing belonging to the Earl of Plymouth, Oakly Park, Ludlow.[5] There are also pentimenti in the background

49

50 recto

After Barocci established the general outlines of the composition of the Chiesa Nuova
*Visitation* and the poses of the individual
figures, he began making chalk drawings of
the draperies.[1] Among these early drapery
studies, the small red and black chalk drawing in the Lugt Collection shows the artist's
direct response to the model, recording first
the face and then the mantle and blouse of
Saint Elizabeth. Drawings like this one have
the immediacy and simplicity of portrait
sketches, and no doubt served a function
similar to that of the artist's small chalk
sketches done for portrait commissions (e.g.
Cat. 34). In this case, the description of the
figure, by means of a few lines and broadly
faceted contours, has an immediacy and response to observation that recalls the drawings of Andrea del Sarto—an artist whose
influence is apparent in Barocci's painted
works of the same time.[2] The drawing differs from Barocci's portrait studies in that it
is based upon a figure whose pose and
drapery were already formulated in a compositional structure. When Barocci finished
his drawing, he put it aside to do other
drapery studies and returned to it when he
came to make the modello in Edinburgh (Cat.
51), at which time he incised the contours to
transfer the design to the larger sheet. In the
Edinburgh drawing the artist made slight
alterations in the drapery but retained the
physiognomy, pose, and expression of the
figure.

On the reverse of the drawing is a schematic rendering of the profile of a face turned to

the left and seen slightly from behind. Although this may have been added by a subsequent owner of the drawing, it is possible
that Barocci did it as a preliminary idea for
the revised, final pose of the young handmaiden in the right foreground.

1. These drawings include: East Berlin, Staatliche Museen, no. 4–1974 (for Elizabeth's mantle and left hand);
Uffizi 11622F, Berlin KK 20527 and 20531 (4130), for the
pose and draperies of Joseph; Uffizi 11400F for Zacharias;
three drawings for the overall draperies of the Virgin and
Elizabeth discussed in the succeeding entry; and Berlin
KK 20515 (4437) for the clinched hands of the Virgin and
Elizabeth.
2. One should compare the Allendale *Noli me tangere*
with Sarto's painting of the same subject in the Uffizi, the
Vatican *Annunciation* with the San Gallo *Annunciation* in
the Pitti, and the Chiesa Nuova *Visitation* with the Scalzo
fresco of that subject. The general architectural setting
and some of the individual figural motifs in the *Tribute to
Caesar* fresco at Poggio a Caiano also seem to be reflected
in the *Martyrdom of St. Vitalis* and its preparatory studies.

**50** *Two Draped Female Figures Embracing on
Steps; Separate Drapery Fragments.* VERSO:
*Draped Female Figure Climbing Steps to
Left, in Profile*

Black and white chalks, stumped, over black chalk
squared lines, partially incised for transfer, on
grayish paper, 382 x 253 mm. Annotated in black
chalk at lower center: *F. Barotsius Urbino.* Paper
discolored from original blue; light spots at upper
right. Verso: black and white chalks, on buff-
colored paper. Annotated in black chalk at lower
left: *8;* in pen and brown ink along lower edge: *F.
Barocci portf. G. N.º 8.*

Chatsworth, The Trustees of the Chatsworth Settlement, no. 918

Provenance: N. A. Flinck (Lugt 959); William,
Second Duke of Devonshire (Lugt 718).
Exhibited: Washington, National Gallery of Art, *et
al, Old Master Drawings from Chatsworth*, 1969–
1970, cat. by J. Byam Shaw, p. 19, no. 17; Bologna,
1975, no. 154.
Published: Schmarsow, IIIB, p. 40; Olsen, 1955,
pp. 140–141; Olsen, 1962, p. 180, fig. 63b.

50 verso

Pen and brown ink, light and dark brown washes, heightened with white and beige-colored gouache, with red chalk marks for stairs, with the aid of a straight-edge and compass, over incised lines and a preliminary drawing in black chalk which was squared in black chalk, re-squared for transfer in black chalk, on blue paper, 462 x 316 mm. Annotated in red chalk on reverse: *N.° 436.1;* in pen and brown ink on piece of paper pasted to reverse: *N.° 70. 1559: Frederico Baroccio.* Gouaches partially oxidized; trace of horizontal fold in center; small brown oil stains over Elizabeth; small brown oil stain at upper left; repaired loss at lower right.

Edinburgh, National Gallery of Scotland, no. RSA 216

Provenance: Sir Thomas Lawrence, London (Lugt 2445); David Laing; Royal Scottish Academy (Lugt 2188); on deposit from the Royal Scottish Academy since 1966.
Exhibited: Bologna, 1975, no. 161.
Published: Andrews, 1968, p. 12; II, fig. 108.

The appearance of this drawing confirms its function as the synthesis of the artist's early pen sketches for the figures (Cat. 48) and chalk studies for the draperies (Cat. 49–50). The artist began by setting down in black chalk the limbs of the principal figures. For this he relied upon transferred stylus lines. The artist then squared the whole sheet in black chalk and used this grid as a guide in sketching, with the pen, the draperies of the five figures. After doing this, he brought the drawing to a finish by establishing with a pen, straight-edge, and compass the architecture and with a brush, light and dark brown washes and white and beige gouaches, the lighting. As a final correction, the artist relocated the foreground steps in red chalk. The parts left unfinished were essentially the inanimate elements—the donkey on the left, Joseph's saddle-bags, and the handmaiden's basket—which the artist later submitted to independent study. In the modello the heads, which were also the subject of further study, were of secondary interest. In fact, only that of the Virgin and Elizabeth were brought to any degree of finish or characterization, no doubt because of the existence of preliminary studies like the Lugt drawing for Elizabeth (Cat. 49). Evidently Barocci's principal purpose in making the Edinburgh drawing was to work out the final relationship of the figures and their draperies to the architectural setting. It comes as no surprise that the final cartoon, a large fragment of which is preserved in the Uffizi,[1] follows the design of the Edinburgh modello in all respects, including the poses of the St. Zacharias and handmaiden which were significantly altered in the final work. As we shall see, Barocci made these alterations at

One of the final drapery studies which Barocci made before the modello*(disegno compito)* in Edinburgh is this double-sided chalk drawing in the Devonshire Collections. Executed in black and white chalks which were carefully rubbed to soften the contrasts of light and shade, the recto establishes the folds of the Virgin's and Elizabeth's draperies, with studies in the margin for individual parts of the Virgin's mantle. A set of squared lines in black chalk evidently served as a guide not only in drawing from the model but also later in transferring the design to the Edinburgh sheet. A further drawing of the same two figures, formerly in the Benno Geiger Collection in Vienna, served a similar function and uses a related black chalk grid, but on a smaller scale.[1] In this drawing the drapery of Elizabeth is de-

veloped more fully than in the Chatsworth drawing; as a result it was probably done subsequently to the Chatsworth one. For the Virgin Barocci made two further studies: one is on the reverse of the Chatsworth drawing itself and another is in the Uffizi.[2] In both cases the artist has abandoned the grid and freely sketched the folds of the mantle from the draped lay model. These drawings represent an attempt to endow the design of the Virgin's mantle with simplicity and amplitude. Upon examination of the Edinburgh drawing, we can see that both works influenced the formulation of the figure in the Edinburgh drawing and later in the cartoon (in the Uffizi).

1. B. Geiger, *Handzeichnungen alter Meister*, 1948, no. 30, repr.
2. Uffizi 11420F (repr. Emiliani, 1975, fig. 157).

51

the last minute, only after scrutinizing the individual parts of the two figures in large scale chalk drawings (see Cat. 52).

1. Uffizi 1784E (repr. Bertelà, 1975, fig. 65).

## 52 *Neck and Head of Young Woman with White Cap, in Left Profile*

Black, red, and white chalks, colored in flesh-pink pastel, stumped (in shadows), on blue paper, 388 x 270 mm.

New York, Private Collection

Provenance: Peter Lely, London (Lugt 2092); Jonathan Richardson, Sr. (Lugt 2184).

One of the critical changes that took place in the design of the Chiesa Nuova *Visitation* between the cartoon and final work occurred in the pose of the handmaiden in the right foreground. In the Edinburgh modello and Uffizi cartoon fragment, this figure stands with her shoulders turned slightly outwards to the viewer and her head held in an erect position facing in the direction of the Virgin, while in the final work, her arm and shoulder are rotated to the left and her head placed further back into space and slightly more forward toward the Virgin. This change not only brings the figure into closer rapport with the central protagonists (Elizabeth and the Virgin), thereby helping to unite the scene, but it also accentuates the recession into depth and provides a stronger, more emphatic counterpoint to Joseph's forward and downward movement on the left side. As we shall see, the idea for the change may, in fact, have arisen from the Loreto *Annunciation*, finished in 1584, which shows a similarly posed figure in the right foreground (Gabriel).

Before making the change in the design, however, the artist executed a full-scale drawing of the head in colored chalks. Hitherto unpublished, this drawing, in a New York private collection, establishes the lighting and coloring of the figure as it would have been painted if the artist had never revised the composition. The large expanse of exposed flesh on the face and neck is colored in a light pink pastel, set off against soft shadows around the back of the neck and in front of the face. However, in contrast to the delicately finished flesh parts, the front contour of the face has numerous pentimenti suggesting that the artist was, at this point, still searching for the correct angle of the head. With this problem in mind, he took a small piece of plain white paper and, in red and black chalks only, redrew the head and shoulders. In this drawing, in the Uffizi, which was done with the aim of revising the pose—not to study ef-

52

*Head of Woman with Veil, Turned Three Quarters to Right, Inclined Downwards*

Oil paint on brownish paper, 397 x 278. Lined with canvas.

New York, The Metropolitan Museum of Art, no. 1976.87.2

Provenance: London, Private Collection; acquired from Thomas Agnew and Sons, London, Ltd., in 1976.
Exhibited: Bologna, 1975, no. 160.
Published: Emiliani, 1975, no. 160; Borea, 1976, p. 60; Shearman, 1976, pp. 51–52; Pillsbury, *M.D.,* 1976, p. 56.

As has been mentioned in regard to other works in the exhibition (Cat. 43–44), Barocci occasionally made studies of individual heads in oils rather than in pastels. The purpose of these drawings seems to have been similar to that of the pastels—to blend the colors and refine the tonal qualities—and like the pastels, they can probably be considered as a class of auxiliary cartoon, executed after the composition had already been incised on the picture surface and when the artist was in the process of coloring the forms.

For the Chiesa Nuova *Visitation* a beautifully preserved pastel for the head of St. Zacharias exists in the Albertina.[1] Comparable to it, in both chromatic and tonal richness, is the oil study for the head of St. Elizabeth recently acquired by The Metropolitan Museum of Art. This study defines the form in terms of color. And the tone of the paper itself—brown—plays a part in the formulation of the design. The artist began the study by establishing the general outlines in a brownish oil, mixed with little pigment. He then applied a ground of transparent gray-blue to the area around the head and the flesh parts of the figure. With this preparation as a basic structure—recalling the initial black chalk sketch on blue paper in his pastels—Barocci proceeded to indicate in a reddish pigment (like his red chalk) the principal features—the eyes, cheek, nose, lips, and ear—and to finish the study by strengthening the shadows and highlights and by adding local tints in specific areas—for example, a coral pink on the collar and rusty brown on the left shoulder (as in his pastels). One interesting feature of this work is the absence of a brown or ochre tint in the hair. The latter element, because of the sitter's age, is executed solely in grays and blacks; and the actual brownish hue of the veil is achieved by exposing the original paper rather than by adding a separate color.

1. Albertina Inv. 556 (Cat. R.383).

fects of lighting or color—we see the neck extended and the head moved forward.[1] In addition, the V-neck of the dress has now become continuous to emphasize the breadth of the figure's shoulders. The final rotation of the left shoulder and arm, the repositioning of the head, and the introduction of the straw hat on the figure's back, which Bellori says was included to denote the time of year, was only accomplished in a subsequent sketch in Berlin.[2] Executed on a small scale in pen, wash, and gouache on blue paper—as if the artist were planning a small pentimento, or correction, to paste over the figure in the Edinburgh modello (something Barocci actually did in the case of the musician in the Chatsworth modello for the *Madonna del Popolo* [Cat. 35])—the drawing shows the entire figure as it was finally painted. Having altered the position of the head of the handmaiden, the artist executed a new study of the head in colored chalks, with particular emphasis on the neck and chin. This same drawing in the Uffizi also bears a compositional sketch for the

*Annunciation*—the possible source of the revised pose—and a study for the head of the Virgin in the Chiesa Nuova *Presentation* completed more than fifteen years later. The presence of the latter on a sheet with drawings for the other two heads suggests that the artist may have relied on the *Annunciation* and also the *Visitation* to formulate the design of the Virgin in the *Presentation*. It is tempting to speculate that the artist's adaptation of a figure from the *Visitation* for his second altarpiece in the same church was intentional.

1. Uffizi 11355F (repr. Emiliani, 1975, fig. 155).
2. Berlin KK 20522 (4159) (repr. Emiliani, 1975, fig. 156). Another sketch for the figure, executed in black chalk, is in the Accademia di S. Fernando in Madrid (Velasco, no. 257, repr.).
3. Uffizi 11391F verso. Both Olsen (1962, p. 178) and Bertelà (1975, p. 59) have proposed that the head in the center of the verso of Uffizi 11391F is a study, in reverse, for Gabriel in the Vatican *Annunciation*. This suggestion is not only implausible but also fails to take into account the two additional neck studies on the same sheet which are unquestionably related to the handmaiden in the *Visitation*.

**54** *Aeneas' Flight from Troy: Compositional Sketch and Separate Sketches for Creusa and for Aeneas and Anchises*

Pen and brown ink, light and dark brown washes, heightened in pale yellow gouache, with touches of white gouache, over a preliminary drawing in black chalk, on light blue paper, 275 x 421 mm. Annotated in pen and brown ink at lower left: *17;* in pen and brown ink at lower right: *55.* Annotated in pen and brown ink on reverse: *Intagliato da Agostino Caracci Il quadro è in Casa Borghese.* Laid down; tears, abrasion, and water stains in lower half.

Cleveland, The Cleveland Museum of Art, L. E. Holden Fund, no. 60.26

Provenance: E. Aeschlimann, Milan; acquired in 1960.
Exhibited: Los Angeles, L.A. County Museum of Art, *Old Master Drawings from American Collections*, 1976, cat. by E. Feinblatt, no. 112.
Published: Richards, 1961, pp. 63–65, fig. 64; Olsen, 1962, pp. 77–78, 182, fig. 64.

As we have seen in the Chiesa Nuova *Visitation* (Cat. 51), Barocci was often disposed to rethink or modify his design after preparing a full-scale cartoon. A further example of this practice is the *Aeneas' Flight from Troy*, a commission the artist undertook in 1586 for Emperor Rudolf II and finished in 1589. Although the painting sent to Prague no

53          54

longer survives, the composition is known through Agostino Carracci's engraving of 1595 (Cat. 79) and a replica painted by the artist himself for Giuliano della Rovere and dated 1598 which is now in the Borghese Collection in Rome. The final cartoon for the painting, which was in the artist's studio at his death, is preserved in the Louvre.[1] Rediscovered in 1974 by Roseline Bacou, this work diverges from the final painting in the handling of the architectural setting and background cityscape.

Whereas in the cartoon a large staircase rises to a portal in the middle ground and a view of massive buildings, rooftops, and a belvedere can be seen in the distance, the final work employs a vaulted portal flanked on the left by a flaming window and staircase and on the right by a view of a piazza with recognizable Roman monuments—Bramante's Tempietto, Trajan's Column, and the Theatre of Marcellus—evidently copies from engravings published in Serlio's *Antichità di Roma*.[2] In addition to these changes, there are minor modifications in the poses and draperies. For example, in the final work Creusa and Anchises hold their heads slightly higher than they do in the drawing, and in the former's draperies the right leg is exposed and the right arm covered.

As in the *Visitation*, Barocci accomplished the revision of the composition by making a pen, wash, and gouache sketch. Whereas in the case of the former this sketch represented a single figure (the handmaiden), for the *Aeneas* the artist executed a sketch of the whole composition, the underdrawing of which bears traces of the scheme in the cartoon (e.g. the staircase). In this drawing, which is preserved in the Cleveland Museum and which, in style, may be compared to other large-scale compositional studies by Barocci,[3] the attention is as much upon the setting as upon the poses of the individual figures; in both respects the drawing makes innovations. The most obvious of these is the introduction of the staircase and the open window, the vaulted portal, and a view of a cityscape with the Tempietto and triumphal column which appear in the final work. In addition, the drawing served to revise the poses and draperies of Creusa and Anchises and to experiment, in the right margin, with alternative ideas for the two figures. The drawing also includes certain compositional elements which the artist abandoned in the final work. In the Cleveland drawing, Ascanius jumps back in fright at the appearance of a small dog on the staircase—an anecdotal detail suppressed in the final version. In addition, the Cleveland drawing calls for a sculpted decoration on the inside of the portal (above Aeneas)

which the artist failed to include in the final work.

We may conclude that both the Cleveland drawing and the Louvre cartoon were executed for the first version of the subject and that the later version in the Borghese faithfully reproduces the original composition and probably derives from the same set of drawings. A similar sequence of events took place in the case of two earlier commissions: the *Return from Egypt* and the *Calling of St. Andrew*. Like *Aeneas' Flight from Troy*, which the Duke of Urbino heralded upon its completion as Barocci's greatest work to date, the other two achieved immediate popularity and the artist executed replicas from an existing, rather than new, set of drawings.

The question then arises: upon what was Agostino's print based? It was issued in Rome three years before the completion of the Borghese replica. Wittkower proposed that Agostino used the artist's cartoon for the second version, which he believed could have been done by 1595.[4] It is more likely, as first Bacou and more recently Emiliani have suggested, however, that a lost modello for the first version served as Agostino's guide.[5] In view of Barocci's dissatisfaction with Carracci's print, it was probably not a chiaroscuro study, as Emiliani proposed, but a pen drawing like the one in an English private collection for the Senigallia *Entombment* (Cat. 40).

1. Louvre 35774, repr. Bacou, 1974, p. 19, no. 14, pl. IX.
2. Barocci's drawing for the Tempietto in the painting is preserved in the Uffizi (no. 135A). For a discussion of this drawing and of the sources for the architectural elements, see Günther, 1969, pp. 239–246 and Malmstrom, 1969, pp. 43–47.
3. Cf. the *Noli me tangere* sketch in the Staatliche Kunstsammlungen in Dresden (Inv. C1914–62) and the *Annunciation* sketch in the National Gallery of Victoria, Melbourne, Australia (formerly Ellesmere Collection, repr. sale catalogue, Sotheby's 5 Dec. 1972, lot 100).
4. R. Wittkower, *Carracci Drawings at Windsor Castle*, London, 1952, p. 113, no. 99.
5. Bacou, 1974, p. 19, no. 14, pl. IX and Emiliani, 1975, p. 152.

**55** *Young Boy Resting Head on His Right Arm: Study for Head, Arm and Sleeve*

Black and white chalks, stumped, on greenish paper, 359 x 243 mm. Annotated in pen and brown ink at lower left: *Le Baroche*; in pen and brown ink on reverse of mount: *Studio del Barrocci per la testa d'Ascanio nel Quadro d'Anchise portato da Enea che è in Casa Borghese a Roma, e che fu inciso da Agostino Carracci*. Bordered in red chalk; laid down; abraded; small tears on right and lower edges; scattered small black flecks.

Princeton, The Art Museum, Princeton University, no. 47–119

Provenance: Frank Jewett Mather.
Published: Pillsbury, *M.D.*, 1976, p. 63; Gibbons, 1977, p. 10, no. 28.

Among the studies for *Aeneas' Flight from Troy* should be counted this hitherto little known black and white chalk drawing of Ascanius in Princeton. It depicts the young boy with the same broad features, short hair, and serious demeanor as he bears in the Louvre cartoon. Further detail studies for the arm and hand preserved in Berlin and one of the head alone at the Musée Bonnat, Bayonne, are related in style and technique.[1] All these drawings share a similar concern for smooth modelling and plastic definition. Although it has recently been suggested that the Princeton drawing derives from the painting,[2] this possibility is unlikely for several reasons. On internal evidence, one can see pentimenti on the hand and in the drapery folds. Moreover, we know from the three other drawings for the same arm, none of which has ever been questioned as an original, that the artist was unsure of the exact placement of the fingers and experimented with various alternatives. The media too—black and white chalks on natural blue (now discolored to greenish) paper—and the technique—employing the stump to achieve a smooth, almost polished, surface in places and to erase or soften contours in others—is characteristic of the artist and finds a comparison with numerous other, fully accepted, preparatory works (e.g. Cat. 64). A second reason which argues against the drawing's being a copy of the Borghese, or even the lost, version of the *Aeneas*, is the characterization of the face, which as I have noted above is close to that in the cartoon. In the painting itself, the head has curly hair and there is a more youthful smile on the boy's face. The artist's desire to animate the attitude of the figure in the Louvre cartoon is already evident in the Cleveland sheet, and it is not implausible that the Princeton sheet, which was done after the cartoon, contributed to the artist's conviction that the figure needed some of the vitality and character which the Cleveland sheet attempted to provide the youth.

1. Berlin KK 20220 (4232), 20293 (4240), and 20353 (4421) and Bayonne, Musée Bonnat, N.I. 1590 (J. Bean, *Les dessins italiens de la Collection Bonnat*, Paris, 1960, no. 5).
2. Although the drawing fails to receive a mention in Olsen's monograph and Felton Gibbons (*loc. cit.*) has recently catalogued the work as a copy derived from the painting, a note on the mount of the drawing written by John Gere gives a more favorable assessment. It reads: "Is this necessarily a copy? The drawing, of the arm and hand especially, seems to me good enough for Barocci himself."

55

56

**56** *Drapery Study for Woman Kneeling in Profile to left; Separate Studies of Mantle over Left Arm and Hem of Dress*

Black and white chalk, stumped, incised, on light blue paper, 400 x 257 mm. Laid down; paper lightly faded; small repaired tear, center of upper edge.

Hamburg, Hamburger Kunsthalle, no. 21055

Provenance: E. G. Harzen, Hamburg.
Exhibited: Hamburg, Kunsthalle, *Italienische Zeichnungen 1500–1800*, 1957, cat. by K. Hentzen, p. 23, no. 108; Hamburg, Kunsthalle, *Hundert Meisterzeichunnungen aus der Hamburger Kunsthalle*, 1967, cat. by B. Wolf Stubbe and H. Hohl, p. 25, no. 21; Bologna, 1975, no. 204.
Published: Olsen, 1955, p. 177; Olsen, 1962, p. 226.

In the latter part of his career Barocci accepted more commissions than he had time to execute and was forced to rely on assist-ants who worked from his designs. The best of these executants were Alessandro Vitali (1580–1640) and Antonio Viviani il Sordo (1560–1620); others included Ventura Mazzi (1560–after 1635), Francesco Baldelli (died 1591?) and Antonio Cimatori. These artists executed replicas of the artist's works (the Brera *Nativity* by Vitali), restored damages on his paintings (the Oratorio della Morte *Crucifixion*), and were entrusted to complete paintings left unfinished at his death (the Bologna *Lamentation* finished by Mazzi).

Among the earliest examples of this kind of studio collaboration is the *Madonna of St. Lucy* in the Louvre, commissioned for the Danzetta Chapel in S. Agostino, Perugia, and ascribed in seventeenth-century sources to Francesco Baldelli, the artist's nephew.[1] For this work Barocci did numerous compo-sitional sketches, a developed chiaroscuro model (Uffizi 817E), and various life studies for the individual figures and their

draperies, incorporating ideas which he had already developed in earlier works, espe-cially the *Perdono, Madonna del Gatto,* and the *Visitation.* The appearance of a perspective sketch for Bramante's Tempietto on the re-verse of one of the early compositional sketches (Urbania, Biblioteca Communale, no. II, 137) suggests that Barocci started work on the commission at the time he was preparing *Aeneas' Flight from Troy* (1586–89). In support of this, the exhibited drapery study for St. Lucy in Hamburg has a close stylistic connection with the Chatsworth drawing for Elizabeth and Mary from 1583–86 (Cat. 50). Although Barocci adopted a traditional *sacra conversazione* grouping for the figures which recalls his altarpieces of the sixties like the *Madonna di S. Simone,* he experimented with various different loca-tions and poses for each figure. For example, in the earliest drawings the Virgin appears seated on a throne and St. Lucy occupies a

57

position on the left.[2] When he finally decided to move the saint to the right side, he made an elaborate pen sketch for the saint's mantle.[3] This drawing, in the Uffizi (11311F), served as the model for the Hamburg drawing which shows the entire mantle and dress and contains separate studies of the sections of drapery over the left arm and left foot. The detail studies seemed to have been done to explore alternate light effects. The one at the upper right, for example, lightens the shaded area under the left arm and gives the forms greater simplicity and breadth. Further detail studies for the saint's drapery are contained on a sheet in Berlin (KK 20178 [4429]), which also alters the overall lighting scheme. The Hamburg drawing and the one in Berlin assisted the artist in making the small cartoon in the Uffizi, which is actually made up from separate pieces of paper as if the composition were the sum total of different parts.[4]

1. For the documentation and other information see Olsen, 1962, pp. 224–225.
2. Urbania, Biblioteca Communale, no. II, 137 recto (Bianchi, 1959, pl. 5), Uffizi 11311 verso (di Pietro, 1913, fig. 82) and 11537F (Emiliani, 1975, fig. 205).
3. Repr. Emiliani, 1975, fig. 206.
4. Uffizi 817E (Bertelà, 1975, fig. 143).

**57** *Head of Bearded Man, Turned to Left and Inclined to the Side*

Black, red, and white chalks, with charcoal, colored with touches of light pink and ochre pastels, stumped, on light blue paper, 252 x 204 mm. Annotated in pen and brown ink at upper left: *43;* in pen and brown ink at lower right: *Baroche Ecole Romaine 8965* [?]

Sacramento (California), E. B. Crocker Art Gallery, no. 1871.234

Provenance: Probably Weigl Collection; acquired by E. B. Crocker in Dresden in 1869–70.
Exhibited: Regina, Norman Mackenzie Art Gallery and Montreal, Montreal Museum of Fine Arts, *A Selection of Italian Drawings from North American Collections,* 1970, cat. by W. Vitzthum, no. 9, repr.; Sacramento, E. B. Crocker Art Gallery, *et al, Master Drawings from Sacramento,* 1971, cat. by J. Mahey, no. 25, repr.

This very bold and characteristic chalk drawing for the head of a bearded man, although traditionally ascribed to the artist, has for no apparent reason failed to find its way into the literature. Correctly identified as a study for the head of St. Joseph in the *Circumcision* in the Louvre by Walter Vitzthum in 1970 (*loc. cit.*), the drawing documents Barocci's debt to Venetian art, particularly to Jacopo

Bassano's similar pastel studies.[1] As in Bassano's works, the outlines are vigorously established in broad strokes of black and brownish-red chalks, and local color is applied in painterly applications of pastels—in this case rose and ochre, with the final addition of white chalk to highlight and harmonize the colors. Like Bassano, Barocci has used the stump (or his fingers) to produce smoothness and continuity between the various hues. Although less purely pictorial in its conception than similar heads in colored chalks by Bassano, it shows a concern for the material quality of color which is unlike that of the drawings of any Central Italian artist of the time. A telling comparison may be made between this particular Barocci head and Bassano's *Head of a Bearded Old Man* in the Scholz Collection, which Roger Rearick connects with a painting of ca. 1563–64 in the Galleria Estense, Modena.[1]

From a document discovered only after the recent exhibition of Barocci's work in Bologna, we know that the artist contracted to paint the altarpiece of the *Circumcision* for the Compagnia del Nome di Gesú in Pesaro as early as 1583. According to the *ricordo,* it was agreed on October 2nd of that year that Barocci would execute the painting for the high altar of the Company's church for 550 scudi. On the basis of this information, it is plausible to conclude that although the artist finished the painting only in 1590—the date inscribed on the picture itself—he began work on the commission in the mid-1580s, at the same time as he was finishing the Loreto *Annunciation* (1582–84) and Chiesa Nuova *Visitation* (1583–86). This circumstance would help to explain the close stylistic relationship between the first drawings for the *Circumcision* and both of these pictures.[4] In fact, an early study for the head of Saint Joseph, a black and white chalk drawing in the Uffizi (11399F), bears on its reverse a pen and ink compositional sketch for the *Visitation*.

The Uffizi drawing, and the Sacramento drawing, appear to have been done on the basis of the figure represented in the full-scale cartoon preserved in the Uffizi,[5] In the chiaroscuro modello, executed later to study the lighting, which is also in the Uffizi, the physiognomy and pose of the saint take on their final form.[6] Two colored chalk drawings, a small one in the Rasini Collection in Milan and a larger, more developed one in the Albertina, document the figure's transformation from a balding man with a round face and stubble beard to a white-haired, slightly older man with a thin face and long, flowing beard.[7] It is rare for Barocci to make so many drawings of the same head, particularly large-scaled colored ones like those for Joseph, but the importance of the figure in the overall composition as the concluding link in the informal movement into space along a serpentine path may have justified the attention devoted to the head in this case.

1. For example, Albertina Inv. 1553 (V. 72) for the *Pentecost* of 1570 in the Bassano Museum (repr. W. Koschatzky, K. Oberhuber, and E. Knab, *Italian Drawings in the Albertina*, Greenwich, Conn., 1971, no. 64) and New York, Janos Scholz Collection for *St. Peter and St. Paul* of ca. 1563–64 in the Galleria Estense, Modena (repr. K. Oberhuber and D. Walker, *Sixteenth Century Italian Drawings from the Collection of Janos Scholz*, National Gallery of Art, Washington and Pierpont Morgan Library, New York, 1973–74, no. 108).
2. See n. 1 above.
3. Published and reproduced in a review of the Bologna exhibition written by Floriano De Santi which appeared in the Nov. 8, 1975, issue of *Brescia Oggi*. I wish to acknowledge my gratitude to Dr. John Shearman for bringing this publication to my attention.
4. In Uffizi 11551F (repr. Bertelà, 1975, fig. 69), one of the artist's *primi pensieri* for the *Circumcision*. The setting and various individual figures derive from the *Visitation* and the sketches for the latter while the kneeling Virgin on the left comes directly from the *Annunciation*.
5. Uffizi 91459F (repr. Bertelà, 1975, fig. 72).
6. Uffizi 818E (repr. Bertelà, 1975, fig. 71).
7. Albertina Inv. 555 (cat. III, no. 388) (repr. Emiliani, 1975, fig. 187), and Milan, Rasini Collection (repr. Morassi, 1937, p. 39, pl. XLIV).

**58** *Holy Family with Sts. Elizabeth, Zacharias, and John the Baptist; Superimposed Sketch of St. Elizabeth*

Black chalk, on white paper, 227 x 200 mm. Annotated in pen and brown ink on mount: *F. Barochius.*

Edinburgh, Dr. Keith Andrews

Provenance: Sir Joshua Reynolds (Lugt 2364); J. Richardson, Jr. (Lugt 2170).
Exhibited: Bologna, 1975, no. 209.
Published: Shearman, 1976, p. 51, n. 11; Borea, 1976, p. 60; Pillsbury, *M.D.*, 1976, p. 56.

In his biography of the artist Bellori states that Barocci executed for Duke Francesco Maria II della Rovere a picture of the Visitation in which the Virgin rocks the newborn in a cradle, a book in one hand and a cat feeding its kittens at her side, while Saint Elizabeth arrives at the door. Bellori's careful description of the composition and his remark that the figures were no bigger than three *palmi* (ca. 67 cm.) suggest that the picture which he saw in Rome at the Noviziato dei Gesuiti was a reduced version of the artist's *Madonna della Gatta*, sent to Florence in 1631 with the inheritance of Vittoria della Rovere and now in almost total ruin in the depot of the Palazzo Pitti (inv. 5375). The composition is known through a small (70 x 67 cm.) copy—conceivably the one seen by Bellori—which belonged to the Orleans Collection in the eighteenth century, later passed to the Metropolitan Museum of Art in New York (from which it was "de-accessioned" at Sotheby Parke-Bernet in New York on Feb. 15, 1973, no. 22), and is now in a private collection in Florence.[1] Although the 1623 inventory of the ducal collection in Pesaro says that the painting was done for the Chapel of Pope Clement VII when he visited Urbino (in 1598), Olsen has correctly identified the painting with the *quadro della Madonna* for which the artist received 635 scudi from the ducal treasury in the years 1588–1593 and which may have been initially planned as gift to the Spanish Infanta.[2] Both the relatively large amount of money and the proposed dates would seem compatible with the picture. Not only was the painting carefully planned but it was executed on a large scale and in a style that is closely related to that of the *Aeneas, Circumcision,* and *Christ Appearing to Mary Magdalene* (Munich), all finished in 1589 and 1590. The combination of simple domesticity—the Virgin rocking Christ's cradle, the large cat at her side feeding its kittens, and Joseph's carpentry tools laid down at random in the foreground—and grandiloquent gestures, chiefly the Atlantis-like figure of Saint Joseph who

draws back the *portiera* to expose the interior drama to the arriving visitors, make this work a "pezzo di teatro" performed on a domestic scale. Its closest parallel, both in mood and in informality of figural construction, is the Louvre *Circumcision.*

Barocci's inspiration for the composition as well as some of the individual poses seems to have come from his genre drawings showing women seated in simple interiors engaged in sewing and other domestic activities.[3] These drawings are relatively rare in Barocci's work, and one of the best known and most beautiful, the drawing of *Three Seated Women* in the van Altena Collection in Amsterdam, appears on a drawing which also has studies for the *Nativity* of ca. 1597 in Madrid.[4] The preferred medium for these genre sketches of the 1590s was red and black chalk.

It is in simple black chalk that the artist executed his only surviving sketch for the *Madonna della Gatta*. This work, in the collection of Keith Andrews, employs a shorthand drawing style that is closely related to that of a sheet in the Uffizi which served a similar function in regard to the Chiesa Nuova *Presentation*.[5] Like the Andrews drawing, this work is executed in black chalk on white paper and relies upon low diagonal hatching and summary contours to lay out the scene. Although most of the elements depicted in the final work appear in the Andrews drawing, including Joseph's donkey in the garden in the background, the poses were refined and altered through an extended series of life studies.[6] Joseph, for example, who leans backwards rather precariously in the drawing, steps forward emphatically in the painting and lifts his right hand directly upwards rather than letting it curl round his head. Since in the compositional sketch the artist ran out of space on the right side, he did a separate study for St. Elizabeth on a larger scale, which he superimposed in the window opening above St. John. All of these qualities would seem to suggest that the Andrews sheet was a working drawing rather than "a ricordo of the painting by an artist trained in quite a different culture," as was recently suggested by John Shearman (*loc. cit.*) without justification.

1. Emiliani, 1975, no. 216, reproduced.
2. Olsen, 1962, p. 188.
3. Cf. especially Uffizi 1394F and 11495F.
4. Repr. Olsen, 1962, fig. 69b.
5. Uffizi 11434F (repr. Bertelà, 1975, fig. 78).
6. To those listed in Olsen, 1962, pp. 189–190, can be added several further ones (for which see Pillsbury *M.D.*, 1975, p. 63).

59

60 recto    60 verso

82

**59** *Upper Half of Standing Donkey, Turned Three-Quarters to Right*

Black chalk, with traces of red chalk, heightened with white (over donkey's eyes), on white paper, 110 x 219 mm. Unevenly cut down on lower edge; laid down; lightly foxed on left; some abrasion.

Geneva, Miss Natalie Koerfer

Provenance: Sir Thomas Lawrence, London (Lugt 2445); William Esdaile, London (Lugt 2617); Charles Sackville Bale, London (Lugt 640); James Knowles and Dr. J. Paul Richter (sold Amsterdam, F. Muller, 27–28 May 1913, lot 373, pl. 58, att. to Titian); [Higgons] (sold London, Sotheby's 25 Nov. 1971, no. 73).
Published: Olsen, 1962, p. 234.

Although Barocci made various studies for the donkey and cat which he depicted in the *Return from Egypt* and the *Madonna del Gatto* in the 1570s (see Cat. 25), he executed fresh drawings for those animals shown in the *Madonna della Gatta* and other later works. For the large mother cat—by which the painting has come to be known—there are two general studies, one in reverse, and a detail study of the head in Berlin and Florence.[1] For Joseph's donkey shown grazing in the small garden in the background there survive two drawings, neither of which has hitherto been connected to the painting.[2] The first, formerly in the collection of J. Paul Richter and now in a private collection in Switzerland, shows the entire animal, its head held up as in the Andrews sketch rather than turned forward and downwards to the ground as in the reduced copy of the final work. When the artist decided to alter the position of the head, he executed the separate study of the head preserved in the Uffizi.[3] These and other carefully observed details in the painting create a feeling of familiarity and intimacy which gives as much meaning to the work as does the religious narrative in which they play a part.

1. Uffizi 922 Orn–923 Orn and Berlin KK 20216 (4343).
2. The present work and Uffizi 919 Orn are both listed by Olsen (1962, pp. 232, 234) among the drawings unrelated to known compositions.
3. The replica, now in a private collection in Florence, is reproduced by Emiliani, 1975, no. 216.

**60** *Incredulity of Saint Thomas.* VERSO: *Flock of Grazing Sheep*

Black chalk, stumped, on white paper, 204 x 273 mm. Abrasion and water damage; gray spots. Verso: black chalk.

Amsterdam, Professor J. Q. van Regteren Altena

Exhibited: Amsterdam, 1970, no. 49.
Published: Olsen, 1955, p. 151; Olsen, 1962, p. 193.

As Harald Olsen was the first to observe (*loc. cit.*), the sketch on the verso of this sheet served as a study for the grazing and sleeping sheep represented in the background of the *Stigmatization of St. Francis* done ca. 1594–95 for the high altar of the Chiesa dei Cappucini in Urbino and now in the Galleria Nazionale. The animals are observed in a variety of attitudes, and the seeming informality of the grouping—no doubt the result of the artist's observation of an actual herd of grazing sheep in the vicinity of Urbino—belies the drawing's function as a working compositional study. The row of the three sleeping sheep in the right center appears in the painting with practically no modification, and the other individual sheep in the drawing inspired the poses of the other animals shown in the painting. The notational quality of this kind of drawing, rapidly executed in black chalk for the purpose of capturing the haphazard gestures and movements of animals in a group, brings to mind nineteenth-century French artists, like Troyen, who specialized in rural scenes with this type of animal life.

The sketch of the *Incredulity of St. Thomas* on the recto, although unidentified with a known work, can probably also be dated to the same period. There is a clear recollection of the Allendale *Noli me tangere* of the 1580s in the pose and placement of both Christ and St. Thomas, but the compact grouping of figures in the foreground and strong chiaroscuro effects evident in the handling of the chalk itself suggest a closer parallel with some of the artist's works of the 1590s. A particular point of reference exists with the Madrid *Nativity* completed by the artist in 1597 and the series of drawings done in preparation for it, like Uffizi 11432F.[1]

1. Repr. di Pietro, 1913, fig. 152.

**61** *Full-length Male Nude Viewed from the Front; Two Separate Studies of the Right Leg*

Black and white chalk, with some red chalk in legs, stumped, on beige-tinted paper, 424 x 264 mm., spotted in brown oil at lower right and upper left; light stains on edges; some abrasion; right edge worn.

Princeton, The Art Museum, Princeton University, no. 48–598

Provenance: Jonathan Richardson, Sr. (Lugt 2183); Sir Charles Rogers (Lugt 624); Sir Charles Greville (Lugt 549); Earl of Warwick (Lugt 2600); Charles Fairfax Murray (sold New York, Anderson Galleries, 6–7 Nov. 1924, no. 214); Dan Fellows Platt (Lugt 750a).
Exhibited: Chicago, The Art Institute, *Drawings from the Collection of Dan Fellows Platt Loaned to the College Art Association*, 1932, no. 15 or 16; New York, Metropolitan Museum of Art, *Italian Drawings in the Art Museum, Princeton University*, 1966, cat. by J. Bean, no. 14, repr.; Providence, Rhode Island School of Design Museum of Art, *Visions and Revisions*, 1968, cat. by S. Ostrow, no. VII, 1, repr.
Published: Mongan, 1932, pp. 5–6, pl. 12; *idem*, "Drawings in the Platt Collection," *American Magazine of Art*, XXV, 1932, p. 53; Olsen, 1955, p. 153; Olsen, 1962, p. 196; J. Scholz, "Italian Drawings in the Art Museum of Princeton University," *Burlington Magazine*, CIX, 1967, p. 293; Gibbons, 1977, pp. 9–10, no. 24, repr.

See entry for Cat. 62 below.

**62** *Studies for Legs of a Male Nude: Thigh of Left Leg; Whole Right Leg with Separate Studies for Thigh, Lower Leg, and Foot*

Black and white chalk, with some red chalk on full leg-study, stumped, on beige-tinted paper, 417 x 274 mm. Brownish stains on edges; creased at lower right and upper right; small tear at lower right corner; abrasion in upper right; reddish mark at lower right.

Princeton, The Art Museum, Princeton University, no. 48–599

Provenance: same as Cat. 61 (sold New York, Anderson Galleries, 6–7 Nov. 1924, in lot 213, preceding Cat. 61).
Exhibited and published: same as Cat. 61.

These two drawings at Princeton belong to a series of life studies for the figure of St. Sebastian in the *Crucifixion* in the Cathedral of Genoa. Barocci accepted the commission in 1590 from Senator (and later Doge) Matteo Senarega—largely due to the considerable sum (1000 scudi) offered him for the work—and finished the painting in 1596.[1] The work itself—one of the artist's most accomplished—inspired the admiration of a host of artists of the following century, including Van Dyck, Rubens and Reni. The scene is set in a moonlit landscape with the Palazzo Ducale in the distance; Christ hangs from the cross surrounded by a circle of mourning angels and turns slightly to the right in the direction of the Virgin Mary and Saint John the Evangelist who react to the event with expressions of pathos and anguish. The figure of St. Sebastian on the opposite side conveys a different impression. His heroic pose, with its upward serpentine movement and sublime facial expression, radiates a feeling of triumph. By no chance, the source for this figure is a fresco of Mars painted by Giulio Romano in the Palazzo del Té in Mantua, a figure in turn derived from the *Apollo Belvedere*.[2]

Barocci's first intentions for this figure are revealed in a sheet in Berlin.[3] On this draw-

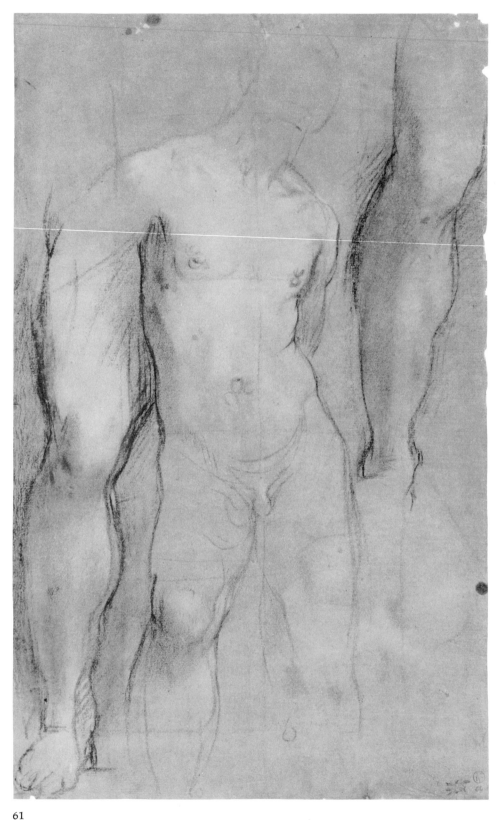

ing, but partially obscured by the figure study and unrecognized by former Barocci scholars, is a chalk copy of the head and raised right arm of the left-hand figure in the second-century B.C. *Laocoön* group. This antique sculpture provided the general model for the sublime expression and serpentine pose of the figure. In the Berlin drawing the upper part of Sebastian's body leans awkwardly to the left, but in the next known drawing for the figure, in Florence, the artist rotated the shoulders and head in the reverse direction, recalling the *Laocoön* group.[4]

The artist then drew the whole figure on another sheet in Berlin.[5] It was at this point that the artist made the first of the two Princeton sheets, which deals with the chest and right leg. Two further studies in Florence and Berlin refine the lighting in the specific areas of the figure's neck and shoulders.[6] As we see in the first Princeton drawing, the figure's legs—the part of the design most indebted to Giulio's model—underwent its own independent study. In addition to the two studies for Sebastian's right leg in the first Princeton drawing, there are detail studies for the knees, hips, thighs, and feet contained in the second drawing in Princeton and two further ones in drawings in Berlin and Florence.[7]

A salient feature of these detailed life studies for the St. Sebastian is their modelling. As has already been mentioned, the painted figure stands in a nocturnal setting. To approximate the tones of the evening light, Barocci executed the majority of pastel studies for the figure's limbs on paper prepared in a light brownish wash. This tinted ground creates an overall tonal effect recalling a mezzotint, where the artist defines form by adding light to a dark ground. Barocci used this technique as early as the 1580s (see Cat. 39), but it was only with his numerous large paintings of the nineties which employ dark or evening settings that this medium is fully developed. The artist's "night" pictures include, in addition to the *Crucifixion* in Genoa, the *Stigmatization of St. Francis*, *Nativity* (in Madrid), *Last Supper* (Urbino Cathedral), *St. Jerome* (Borghese), *Madonna of the Rosary* (Senigallia), and *Beata Michelina* (Vatican).

1. A summary of the letters related to the commission is given by Emiliani, 1975, p. 186.
2. The figure by Giulio appears in the fresco of the *Bath of Mars and Venus* in the Sala di Psiche (repr. F. Hartt, *Giulio Romano*, II, New Haven, 1958, fig. 259).
3. Berlin KK 20269 (4140).
4. Uffizi 11370F (repr. Bertelà, 1975, fig. 91).
5. Berlin KK 20267 (4175).
6. Berlin KK 20261 (4204) and Uffizi 11350F (repr. Bertelà, 1975, fig. 92).
7. Uffizi 11671F and Berlin KK 20285 (4426).

61

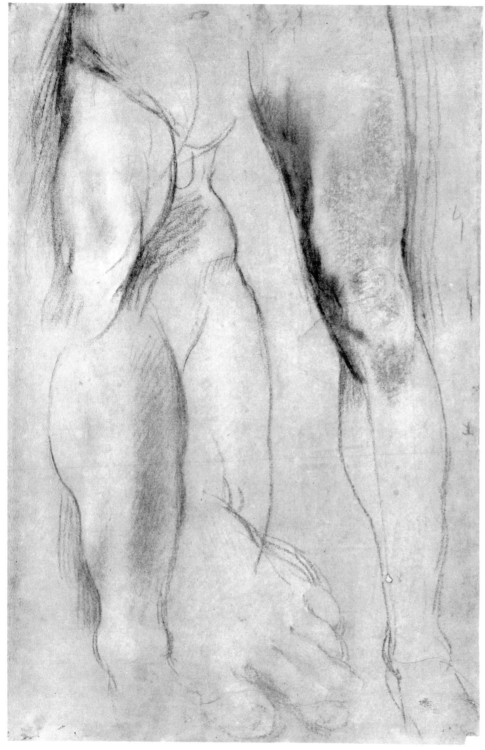

62

**63** *Virgin Kneeling Forward to Right, Adoring the Sleeping Christ Child*

Black and white chalks, over incised outline of naked figure, squared in black chalk, on pale gray paper, 200 x 170 mm. Laid down; discoloration of paper; small repairs at upper right and lower right corners and at lower center edge; light brown stains at upper and lower right.

Detroit, The Detroit Institute of Arts, William H. Murphy Fund, no. 34.139

Provenance: Hermann Voss, Berlin; acquired in 1934.
Published: H. Voss, *Zeichnungen der italienischen Spätrenaissance*, Munich, 1928, p. 55, pl. 20; E. Scheyer, *Drawings and Miniatures from the XII. to the XX. Century*, Detroit, 1937, p. 17, no. 41; Olsen, 1962, p. 197; Smith, 1973, pp. 88–91, fig. 9.

In August 1597 Barocci received from the Duke of Urbino nearly 275 scudi in payment for a painting of the *Nativity* which was later sent as a gift to the Queen of Spain for her chapel. This painting, now in the Prado, underwent four stages of development.[1] The *primo pensiero* for the composition—Uffizi 11485F—called for a representation of the Virgin and Saint Joseph engaged in making up the crib for the Christ Child.[2] In the second version, recorded by Uffizi 11432F, the artist converted the domestic scene into a more traditional Adoration of the Shepherds: in it Joseph gives up his bed-making activities to open the door in the background to shepherds and the Virgin kneels in a motherly embrace with her arms round the Christ Child.[3] The third stage is recorded in an unfinished canvas in the Rasini Collection in Milan, which is the same size as the finished work and which was executed over a set of traced outlines of the second scheme.[4] This version follows the Virgin's pose and those of the foreground animals and Christ Child established at the second stage but recalls the initial idea by including the bed-making incident of Joseph in the foreground. This version also introduces angels in the sky, recalling Correggio's *Notte*. The final design places the emphasis upon the Virgin's contemplation of the Christ Child and the supernatural light emanating from the crib. She kneels in adoration in front of the divine Christ with her arms extended to either side and Joseph stands partially obscured at the door in the background and opens it slightly for two shepherds who view, but do not enter, the scene.

One of the interesting aspects of this development is that the artist gave careful consideration to each phase before abandoning it in favor of the succeeding one. For each stage, in fact, including the first one recorded in the Uffizi pen sketch, life studies

63

64

for the individual figures exist. The participant that occupied the artist's greatest attention was the Virgin; for her there are by far the greatest number of surviving drawings. The example exhibited here, a black and white chalk drapery study, belongs to the series of studies which the artist made for the Virgin as she appears in the second version (Uffizi 11432F). Like a similar drawing in the Uffizi, which concentrates upon the pleats and folds in the sleeve and upper part of the dress, it follows an incised drawing of the limbs and employs the same squared module as the Uffizi modello.[5] A slightly larger scale served for two further drapery studies of the whole figure which are in the Fitzwilliam Museum in Cambridge and in the Uffizi.[6] The artist completed his study of the Virgin's drapery—before changing the Virgin's pose and embarking upon a new set of life studies—with two drawings in Berlin executed for individual parts of the sleeve and skirt.[7] All of these drawings were done from nature—probably from clothed statuettes as Bellori would have us believe. Their probable sequence, based on scale and degree of finish, begins with the Detroit and related Uffizi drawing which were executed before Uffizi 11432F and follow with the Cambridge study and other works done after the Florentine modello.

1. The development of the composition suggested here follows that of di Pietro in 1913 (pp. 122ff). This account would seem to be essentially correct despite recent doubts raised—in my view incorrectly—by Emiliani in

regard to the authenticity of the Rasini painting (Emiliani, 1975, p. 193).
2. Repr. Bertelà, 1975, fig. 97.
3. Repr. *ibid.*, fig. 95.
4. Repr. Olsen, 1962, fig. 89.
5. Repr. Bertelà, 1975, fig. 100.
6. Repr. Emiliani, 1975, fig. 226 and Bertelà, 1975, fig. 99 respectively.
7. KK 20321 (4425) and 20336 (4326).

**64** *Half-length Male Figure, with Head Turned to Right and Hands Clasped, Seen from the Front; Separate Studies of Head and Hands*

Black and white chalks, with touches of red chalk on hands and head at left and of light buff pastel on left hand at lower left, stumped, on light blue paper, 278 x 413 mm. Soiled on edges; paper slightly faded; lower right corner repaired; small water stain at upper center edge.

New York, The Metropolitan Museum of Art, Rogers Fund, no. 50.143

Provenance: The Earls Spencer (Lugt 1530; Spencer sale, 10 June 1811, no. 22); Lionel Lucas (Lugt 1733a; sold London, Christie's, 9 Dec. 1949, lot 54); Thomas Agnew and Sons, Ltd., London; acquired in 1950.
Exhibited: New York, The Metropolitan Museum of Art and The Pierpont Morgan Library, *Drawings from New York Collections: The Italian Renaissance,* 1965, cat. J. Bean and F. Stampfle, p. 70, no. 119, repr.
Published: M. Lavin, 1954–55, pp. 266–271; Olsen, 1955, p. 158; Olsen, 1962, p. 203; J. Bean, *100 European Drawings in the Metropolitan Museum of Art,* New York, 1964, no. 24, repr.

The decorations for the Capella del SS. Sacramento in the Urbino Cathedral were commissioned to Barocci in 1590, after eight years of planning and construction and through the financial assistance of Duke Francesco Maria. The counsellors of the church originally wanted the artist to paint two large murals of subjects relevant to the Sacrament—the Fall of Manna and the Last Supper—and agreed to pay him 1600 scudi for the pair. However, after waiting until 1599 for the artist to finish the first of the two paintings, the *Last Supper,* the counsellors decided to look for another artist to execute the second mural. In 1605 they ordered the *Fall of Manna* from Barocci's pupil, Alessandro Vitali, stipulating he finish the painting during the master's lifetime; two years later the second work was installed.

For the *Last Supper* there survive the artist's chiaroscuro modello and his full-scale cartoon, both in the Uffizi.[1] As has been noted by Marilyn Lavin (*loc. cit.*), the artist made various changes of style as well as detail between the modello and finished work. In the final painting the figures not only grow in scale and plasticity but they become more intensely animated and their poses more fully integrated into the overall work. Drawings like this one in New York for the third apostle on Christ's right played a critical role in this transformation. Not only does this drawing reveal the artist in the process of establishing the final position of the hands and head, but it illustrates his use of

86

another artist's work as a model for the revised pose and physiognomy of the figure. The study of the head at the upper right, though lit in accord with Barocci's composition, is not drawn from life but from a recollection of the Michelangelo head of Adam in the *Creation of Man* in the Sistine ceiling. Michelangelo's fresco served as a means of recasting the narrow proportions and pointed features of the apostle as seen in the modello and cartoon into a more heroic figure and of adjusting the position from a simple profile view, with the head riveted upon Christ, to a three-quarter view, with the apostle's head turned slightly away from the center.

The position of the hands also became the subject of the Metropolitan study. In the modello in the Uffizi the apostle holds up his left hand in surprise and points with his other hand to the apostle across the table while in the cartoon the clasped hands are held vertically in front of the figure. In the final work, as reflected in the alternate studies on the New York sheet, the hands capture the divine light from above and are inclined away from the center, establishing a tension between the impulse of the head toward Christ and the movement of the rest of the figure to the left. This revision not only relieves the concentration of the narrative on the figure of Christ but also suggests that through Christ the apostles will receive the Holy Ghost, symbolized by the divine radiance that enters the room from above.

1. Uffizi 819E and 91458F (repr. Emiliani, 1975, fig. 239 and Bertelà, 1975, fig. 105).

65

**65** *Head of Man with Short Beard, Full-face, Inclined to Left, with Eyes Directed Upwards*

Black, red, and white chalks, colored with pale-pink and brown pastels, stumped, on grayish paper, 331 x 247 mm. Watermark similar to Briquet 749. Laid down; paper discolored from blue; small repaired tear at upper left.

Chatsworth, The Trustees of the Chatsworth Settlement, no. 354

Provenance: Sir Peter Lely (Lugt 2092); William, 2nd Duke of Devonshire (Lugt 718).
Exhibited: London, Royal Academy, *Drawings by Old Masters*, 1953, cat. by K. T. Parker and J. Byam Shaw, p. 31, no. 99; Washington, National Gallery of Art, *et al, Drawings from Chatsworth*, 1962–63, cat. by A. E. Popham, p. 16, no. 4; Bologna, 1975, no. 233.
Published: Schmarsow IIIB, p. 40; Olsen, 1955, p. 158; Olsen, 1962, p. 202.

Bellori informs us of the difficulty Barocci experienced in establishing the pose of the upward-looking St. Francis in the altarpiece of the *Perdono* and his eventual painting of the head on a separate piece of paper which he pasted to the surface of the canvas. The head of Christ in the Urbino *Last Supper* presented the artist with a similar problem of pose and expression.[1] Accordingly, Barocci executed several large-scale chalk drawings, the earliest of which would seem to be identifiable with one in the British Museum.[2] In this drawing the artist has drawn the head from life but endowed it with the particular facial features of Barocci's patron and the most important financial backer of the project, Francesco Maria II della Rovere.[3] In a second drawing in Chatsworth the artist elongated the head and gave it more vertical emphasis focusing the light on the expressive features and generalizing the appearance. These two drawings, in turn, served for a more finished pastel study in Lille which shows the head with the more perfectly ovoid, almost androgynous, features and long hair of the final work.[4] This latter work, incorrectly considered a copy by former writers, bears a set of incised contours which would suggest that its function was that of an auxiliary cartoon made to transfer the design to the final work for execution in paint.

As we see in the Chatsworth drawing, Barocci's main concern was to set the figure off from the others in the scene and at the same time to convey the drama of Christ's vision. He achieved this through the expression, through the countermovement of the head and eyes, and through the monumentalization of the neck and individual features of the head.

1. A diagram of the perspective of the scene is preserved in a drawing by the artist in the Uffizi (11660F).
2. Pp. 3–199 (repr. Emiliani, 1975, fig. 236).
3. Compare, for example, the portrait drawing in the Institut Néerlandais, Paris (no. 5061) (see Cat. 66). In this regard, it is of interest to note that Schmarsow (IIIB, p. 40) identified the subject of the Chatsworth drawing as Francesco Maria della Rovere as Christ and drew a comparison with the Uffizi portrait.
4. Lille, Musée des Beaux-Arts, Inv. 1912:32, black, red, and white chalks, colored with pink and ochre pastels, stumped, on buff-tinted blue paper, 412 x 268 mm. Krommes, 1912, p. 107 and Olsen, 1962, p. 288 list the drawing as a copy.

**66** *Portrait of Francesco Maria II della Rovere, Duke of Urbino*

Black and red chalks, with touches of white chalk and ochre pastel, on buff paper, 188 x 154 mm. Laid down; lightly foxed; somewhat abraded; diagonal cut in paper at lower right; small repaired holes in upper left and lower right corners.

Paris, Fondation Custodia (Coll. F. Lugt), Institut Néerlandais, no. 5061

Provenance: Sir Joshua Reynolds (Lugt 2364); J. P. Heseltine (Lugt 1507); H. Oppenheimer (sold London, Christie's, 10–14 July 1936, no. 21, bt. Lugt); F. Lugt (Lugt 1028).
Exhibited: Rotterdam, *Meesterwerken uit Vier Eeuwn*, 1938, no. 459; Paris, Institut Néerlandais, et al, *Le Dessin Italien dans les Collections Hollandaises*, 1962, no. 132, pl. C; Bologna, 1975, no. 321.
Published: Olsen, 1955, pp. 81, 182; Olsen, 1962, pp. 103, 234, fig. 99a.

In his life of the artist Bellori relates that Barocci not only painted numerous portraits of the ducal family and his friends but also made pastel portraits which possessed the greatest fidelity to nature: "Fece . . . molti altri [ritratti] così di colori, come di pastelli, che sono in perfettione di naturalezza." The fine chalk and pastel study in the Lugt Collection may have been done as either an independent portrait drawing of this kind or as a study for one of the artist's known

paintings of his chief patron. It represents Francesco Maria II della Rovere in a white ruff and black suit at an advanced age. The costume recalls that of the three-quarter length portrait done in 1583 at the request of Grand Duke Francesco de' Medici, now in Weimar, but in the drawing the face is older—the eye sockets have receded and the beard has thinned out. Harald Olsen (*loc. cit.*) has suggested the drawing was made when the Duke was about fifty, that is to say around 1600, and such a dating would coincide with the artist's closest working association with his patron, who not only supported his activities but also intervened on the artist's behalf with prospective patrons. [1]

1. See E. Calzini, "Federico Barocci e il suo mecenate," *Rassegna bibliografica*, XVI, 1913, pp. 54–65 and Gronau, 1936, pp. 23–33 and *passim*.

**67** *Presentation of the Virgin*

Brush and brown wash, heightened with white and gray gouache, with touches of pink on Joachim's drapery and face of girl with basket, over a preliminary drawing in black chalk, in part traced from another surface, on beige paper, 397 x 340 mm. Annotated in pen and brown ink at lower right: *Baro . . .*; in pencil on reverse of mount: *Baroccio*. Laid down on board; waterstained at lower right edge; restored losses along upper edge; scattered light stains.

New York, Mr. Ian Woodner

Provenance: Unidentified collector's mark (similar to Lugt 2883); New York, William H. Schab Gallery, Inc.
Exhibited: New York, William H. Schab Gallery, Inc., *Master Prints and Drawings from the Fifteenth to the Twentieth Centuries*, Cat. no. 54, 1974, pp. 2–3, no. 1, pl. 1, repr. in color.

On the strength of Bellori and a remittance to the artist dated 8 Mar. 1593—one of the rare new documents published by Olsen—it was formerly believed that the *Presentation of the Virgin* in the Cesi Chapel of the Chiesa Nuova in Rome was finished in the early 1590s. However, from the recent cleaning of the painting undertaken on the occasion of the Bologna exhibition, which has revealed a signature and date of 1603, and from documents published by Maria Bonadonna Russo, we know now that the painting was probably begun only in 1593 and actually finished in 1603. According to further documentary sources, we can establish that the Oratorian fathers of the Chiesa Nuova wanted Barocci to paint the *Coronation of the Virgin* for the right transept and a *Nativity of the Virgin* for the high altar, which would have brought the total of his works in the church to four. [1]

The development of the composition for the *Presentation* is documented by a small chalk sketch for the group of figures around the high priest in the background (Uffizi 11434F) and a long series of individual figure sketches and life studies. To this body of preparatory studies can now be added this important, and hitherto little-known, chiaroscuro study in a private collection. The drawing is identifiable as the artist's small cartoon executed, according to Bellori, to study the lighting. Like a similar drawing for the Senigallia *Entombment* in Chatsworth (Cat. 41), the work is executed with the point of the brush, brown washes, and a combination of white, gray and pink gouaches, over a preliminary drawing in black chalk traced from another sheet. Moreover, in each case a portion of the composition is left unfinished. In style the new drawing also shares qualities with the grisaille for the *Madonna del Rosario* in the Ashmolean Museum.[2] The major divergence from the final work appears in the unfinished section of the drawing: the shepherd, lightly sketched in the right center, holds his staff and looks towards the high priest while in the final painting he becomes a blind figure with his head turned to the side and placed in shadow. Alternate poses for this figure are actually explored in a drawing in the Galleria Nazionale in Urbino.[3] In the absence of any other autograph modelli or small cartoon for the composition, one is tempted to identify the drawing as the artist's "Cartone grande della Presentazione della Madonna" mentioned in a letter of 21 August 1673 to Leopoldo dei Medici—one of several Barocci drawings which were little bigger than a "foglio di carta assai belli" and which belonged to a local Urbino collector, Giovanni Lavalas.[4]

1. A summary of the documentation, with a full list of bibliographical references, appears in Emiliani, 1975, pp. 206–208.
2. Repr. Olsen, 1962, fig. 76b.
3. No. 1669: Rome, GFN negative no. F 8139.
4. Paola Barocchi, in an appendix volume to her new edition of F. Baldinucci, *Notizie dei professori del disegno* (Florence, Edizioni S.P.E.S., VI, 1975, pp. 172–173), publishes the text of the letter but omits the list of drawings in the Lavalas collection appended to the letter, which included some twenty Barocci drawings—several modelli, oil studies, and landscape drawings.

**68** *Heads of Two Angels Turned Downwards in Left and Right Profile; Separate Study of Head in Right Profile*

Black and white chalks (two studies on left only), black, red, and white chalks, colored with ochre and light pink pastels (head study on right), stumped, on greenish-blue paper, 241 x 272 mm. Laid down; foxed; paper stained light brown except for 35 mm. strip at top; abrasion.

67

New York, The Pierpont Morgan Library, no. IV, 155

Provenance: Unidentified collector (partially effaced mark with double circle in black ink at lower right); possibly J. Bailey (cf. pencil inscription on back of lining with Lugt 1412); C. Fairfax Murray; J. Pierpont Morgan.
Published: *J. Pierpont Morgan Collection of Drawings by the Old Masters Formed by C. Fairfax Murray*, IV, London, 1912, no. 155; Olsen, 1962, p. 192.

Harald Olsen (*loc. cit.*) correctly associated this sheet of head studies with the circle of cherubims depicted in the upper part of the artist's *Presentation of the Virgin* in the Chiesa Nuova, Rome. These cherubims surround the opening in the clouds through which, in a burst of heavenly light, the small angel bearing a garland wreath to crown the Virgin emerges. The Morgan sheet bears two studies for the head in the foremost left position and one for its counterpart on the right. The tentative black chalk outlines

suggest that the initial function of the sheet was to fix the angle of the head in profile or lost profile, and that once this was accomplished, the artist sought to work out the light reflections and lay in the coloring. In this drawing, however, only the study on the right is developed with red chalk and colored pastels. Therefore, the juxtaposition of single black and white chalk studies at the left and the colored one at the right provides a demonstration of the artist's transition from a light study to one in which color plays a part.[1] A similar colored study on blue paper for another of the cherubim is in the Koenig's collection in Fachsenfeld.[2]

1. A similar type of drawing belonged to Don Giovanni Antonio Vagnarelli, the brother-in-law of Barocci's nephew. In a letter to the secretary of Leopoldo de' Medici of 1658, it is described as: "Tre cherubini di lapis rosso et uno non finito di lapis negro; questi sono benissimo condizionati e sono in foglio reale" (Baldinucci-Barocchi, VI, p. 77).
2. Inv. no II/135 recto.

Although damaged, this pastel study of a bearded man would appear to be an autograph drawing dating from the latter part of the artist's career. The physiognomy and the beard may be compared with that of the head of the high priest in the *Presentation of the Virgin* finished in 1603. Characteristically the artist began the drawing with a black chalk outline of the head; after adjusting the angle of the head—e.g. moving the left contour of the face to the side and redrawing the ear—he developed the features in red chalk and then colored the flesh parts in a pale pink pastel and added white chalk for the beard and highlights. In his usual manner Barocci has softened the shadows and blended the colors by rubbing the chalks with the stump. The weak appearance of the drawing would seem attributable to the severe abrasion the drawing has suffered in the areas around the head and the discoloration of the paper (from its original rich blue) due to exposure to light. These factors help to explain the reservations expressed by modern writers about the drawing's authenticity.[1]

1. In a letter in the museum files Harald Olsen concluded the drawing dated from around 1600 and was a possible product of Barocci's school. More recently Christel Thiem (*loc. cit.*) has catalogued the drawings as "Federico Barocci?", noting the unpublished opinion of Olsen and a more favorable one given (orally) by this writer on a visit to Stuttgart in 1974.

**69** *Head of Old Man with Long White Beard, Inclined Slightly Forwards and to Left*

Black, red, and white chalks, colored in rose-pink pastel, stumped, on buff-colored paper, 423 x 285 mm. Annotated in black chalk on reverse: *Leonardo da Vinci.* Surface abraded; edges creased and damaged; paper discolored to yellowish-brown tone; small stain at lower right.

Stuttgart, Staatsgalerie Stuttgart, Graphische Sammlung, Inv. C63/1192

Provenance: sold Munich, Weinmuller, 13–14 Oct. 1938, no. 35, repr.
Published: C. Thiem, *Die italienischen Zeichnungen in der Graphischen Sammlung der Staatsgalerie Stuttgart*, Stuttgart, 1977, no. 370.

**70** *Assumption of the Virgin*

Pen and brown ink, brown and gray washes, heightened with white, with gray gouache on apostle in left foreground, over a preliminary drawing in black chalk and a black chalk squared grid, on buff paper, 522 x 368 mm. Watermark similar to Briquet no. 749. Laid down; trace of horizontal crease in center; lightly abraded across center.

Chatsworth, The Trustees of the Chatsworth Settlement, no. 364

Provenance: Sir Peter Lely (Lugt 2092); P. H. Lankrink (Lugt 2090); William, Second Duke of Devonshire (Lugt 718).
Exhibited: London, Royal Academy, *Drawings by Old Masters*, 1953, cat. by K. T. Parker and J. Byam Shaw, no. 106; Washington, National Gallery of Art, *et al*, *Old Master Drawings from Chatsworth*, 1969–70, cat. by J. Byam Shaw, p. 19, no. 16; Bologna, 1975, no. 287.
Published: Schmarsow, IIIB, p. 41; Olsen, 1955, p. 167; Olsen, 1962, p. 212, fig. 110.

Among the most important works left in the artist's studio at his death was a large unfinished painting of the *Assumption of the*

69

*Virgin.*[1] Offered unsuccessfully to Leopoldo de' Medici in 1658, the painting subsequently passed into the Albani Collection in Urbino and by descent to the present owner, a private collector in Milan. Although the destination of the picture is unknown, its large scale suggests a commission for an altarpiece, and Emiliani has conjectured, on the basis of subject matter, that it may have been intended for the high altar of the Chiesa Nuova in Rome—an hypothesis, unfortunately, for which no corroborating evidence exists.[2]

When the painting was exhibited in Bologna in 1975, which was the first time it had been exposed to wide public view, it offered a number of significant insights into the manner in which the artist prepared his paintings. The artist evidently began work on the canvas by applying an overall ground in brown. His next step was to transfer the design from the cartoon to the canvas by means of a stylus. Having established the design and the ground color, the artist then blocked in the lights and darks and, in chiaroscuro tones of gray and ochre, sketched the figures and draperies, adjusting and correcting the original design (e.g. the large angel at the left). The next stage involved the coloring. For this, the artist applied very bright, transparent hues of royal blue (for the Virgin's mantel), tomato-red (for her skirt and the draperies of several apostles), golden orange and a spearmint green (for other draperies)—with the intention of strengthening the colors and design through the subsequent addition of pigment. The artist's pictorial approach is underlined by his use of the colored ground as a middle tone between the blacks which establish the shadows and the yellow light introduced to define the forms, and the subsequent modelling of the scene in pure color rather than chiaroscuro tones. Had the *Assumption* been completed, we can imagine that its rich palette would have approached that of the recently cleaned *Presentation of the Virgin* of 1603 in the Chiesa Nuova, Rome.

The beautiful *cartoncino* in Chatsworth served as the artist's model in reaching the final stage of the unfinished altarpiece. It shows not only all the elements of the final design, including one or two angels around the Virgin which the artist failed to sketch on the canvas, but also the lighting scheme. In the oil painting the artist relied upon this drawing to block in the lights in the early stages. As in the canvas, the artist employs a brownish paper as the ground color, freely sketching the design in black chalk over a grid of squared lines and then adding the lights with brown and gray washes. To strengthen the light effects—the abstract play of light, in fact, creates the real drama

70

in the scene—the artist added white and gray gouaches. The gray, which is limited to the back of the robe of the apostle kneeling in the foreground, establishes the darkest spot in the composition, thereby intensifying the contrast to the light-filled space above.

1. Repr. in color in Emiliani, 1975, after page LVI.
2. *Ibid.*, p. 234.

71

at his death.[1] Completed by Ventura Mazzi in 1635, the work is now preserved in the Biblioteca Communale of the Archiginnasio in Bologna. The state of the painting before Mazzi's intervention can be established from a description prepared in 1630 by Marchese Pietro Antonio Lonati: "Sono tredici figure, compreso un puttino et un diavolo sotto alli piedi di S. Michele, cioè il Christo morto nudo finito, la Maddalena parte finita et parte abozzata, il vescovo è finito ed il restante delle 10 figure sono abozate solamente." Numerous individual figure studies by Barocci and a small cartoon in the Hague served Mazzi as a guide in the completion of the painting, although Mazzi himself executed "un poco di saggio" to show the deputies what he intended to do.[3]

The present sketch is one of the largest and most broadly conceived compositional studies in the artist's oeuvre. The welter of black chalk lines—repeated and elaborated in wash and gouache—reveal numerous pentimenti. The figure of Christ, for example, appears in the center of the sheet with his legs projecting toward the viewer, and, in a second study at the lower left executed almost solely with the point of the brush, wash and gouache, he is seen with his feet extended to the side. The figures who crowd round Christ have been redrawn so many times their individual poses are practically indecipherable. The basic elements of the scene are, nonetheless, similar to those used in the final painting. The drawing already shows the vaulted architecture in the background, the prominent tomb slab in the center bearing Christ's body and a circle of mourners, the kneeling Magdalene in the right foreground, and a figure in the right background whose outstretched hands may be compared with those of St. Michael in the final work. While the kneeling bishop on the left does not appear to be present in the scene, there are other individual studies by the artist which document an initial stage in which Christ reclined to the left as in this sketch.[4]

1. A summary of the documentation, with full bibliographical references, appears in Emiliani, 1975, pp. 228ff.
2. *Annali della fabbrica del Duomo di Milano*, V, Milan, 1883, p. 159.
3. E. Arslan, *Le pitture del Duomo di Milano*, Milan, 1960, p. 35, n. 81.
4. E.g. the study for Christ in Berlin KK 20360 (4144). Uffizi 11403F (Emiliani, 1975, no. 276) also shows Christ reclining to the left, but this drawing does not appear to have been done by Barocci, as Olsen proposed. Two further drawings related to this composition—large-scale studies in colored chalks for the bishop's head and for the youth behind Christ—were sold at the Skippe sale (London, Christie's 20–21 Nov. 1958, nos. 14a–b) and are now in a New York private collection. Skippe ascribed them to Luti, but they seem to be by Ventura Mazzi or some close follower of the artist.

**71** *Lamentation of Christ*

Black chalk, brush and brown wash, gray and white gouache, on grayish paper, 352 x 275 mm. Annotated in pencil on reverse: *56/C;* in pen and brown ink on reverse in an old hand: *Federico Baroccio/Questo quadro ora è in Bologna posseduto dal Sig.*re *Antonio Magnani/Bibliotecario del Instituto Delle Scienze;* in pen and brown ink on reverse in an earlier hand: *Disegno originale di Federico Barozzi, a cercata per il Quadro/fatto al Cardinale Federico Borromeo, che lo pose nel Duomo di Milano, del quale ho parlato nella Guida di quella Cittá impresa/nel 1787 —Carlo Bianconi Seg.*rio *perp.*o *della G:*1a [?] *Accad.*a *Mil:*o *delle B.*e *A.*ti. Laid down; paper discolored from blue; repaired loss at lower left corner.

England, Private Collection

Provenance: Benno Geiger, Vienna.
Exhibited: London, Burlington Fine Arts Club, Winter 1923; London, Royal Academy, *Paul Oppé Collection*, 1958, no. 380; Edinburgh Festival, 1969, no. 7.
Published: B. Geiger, *Handzeichnungen alter Meister*, Zurich, et al, 1948, no. 31, repr.

The two early annotations on the reverse of this large sketch correctly relate it to the *Lamentation of Christ* which Barocci agreed to paint for the chapel of S. Giovanni Buono in Milan Cathedral in 1600 and left unfinished

# Federico Barocci as a Printmaker

The sequence in which Barocci made his four etchings cannot be determined with absolute certainty. Only one of the etchings is dated, the *Perdono* (Cat. 73) which has the copyright date of 1581.[1] The etched *Madonna in the Clouds* (Cat. 74) was completed by 1582 or before, as we know from the date on the engraved copy by Agostino Carracci (Cat. 78). And Barocci would not have etched the *Annunciation* (Cat. 75) earlier than the completion of his painting of the same subject in 1584.[2] The little *Stigmatization of St. Francis* (Cat. 72) has no documentary anchor, only its correspondence to the image of the saint in the *Perdono*. Indeed, the pictorial interrelationships of three of the four prints compound the difficulty of establishing a clear chronological sequence, because the two cherub heads in the upper corners of the *Madonna in the Clouds* are also to be found in the *Perdono*. As the shared motifs all come from the *Perdono* painting they suggest that the three prints were made at about the same time—but still reveal nothing about their sequence.

The determination of date is further complicated by the fact that this small oeuvre of four prints also divides in format and idiom between the two large etchings, in which Barocci sought the splendor and formal perfection of the paintings they reproduce, and the two little etchings, which by comparison are intimate and informal. Whereas Barocci's large etchings evoke the *colorito* of painting, the small prints convey the immediacy and directness of drawings. But the four prints are more etching than either drawing or painting, and therefore it is as etchings that they must be examined for a key to their chronology.

Not only is the dating made difficult by Barocci's use in the instance of the *Perdono* of a subject completed five years earlier, but also by the fact that he was a novice printmaker and at the same time a mature, confident, and innovative artist. The latter

has caused the greatest and most persistent misjudgment in the dating of the etchings. For all its boldness of concept and daring delineation, the *Stigmatization of St. Francis* (which was once considered the last of Barocci's etchings)[3] is, as Oberhuber pointed out,[4] considerably less accomplished technically than the *Madonna in the Clouds*, which has often been considered the earliest because of its correspondence to the Fossombrone *Madonna* (cf. Cat. 12), and because of the modesty of its dimensions and appearance.[5] However, the *Madonna in the Clouds* owes its simplicity and its directness to the artist's more skillful use of the etching medium and his mastery of an etching style.[6] The *Stigmatization*, even in the best impressions, shows an obvious duality between dark and light etched lines. The *Madonna in the Clouds* is completely integrated; the modulation of shading is controlled and the dark accents fall exactly where the artist intended. Even the technical flaw that caused the gray spots of overbite within the black accents testifies to a more frequent and bolder use of mordant than the artist had dared in the *Stigmatization*.

The more skillful use of mordant, the more uniform etched line, and the sparer use of engraving in the *Madonna* is evidence of the artist's expanded skill in the etching process. Taking these factors into consideration, but with the understanding that what appears to be a progressive development may result from the chance success of an early etching attempt, the following seems a reasonable chronology: the *Stigmatization of St. Francis* with its tentative, uncertain use of the etching process must be the earliest. The *Perdono* and the *Madonna in the Clouds* follow—possibly in that order, but the larger plate is so much more ambitious an undertaking that it cannot be compared fairly with the

---

1. The difficulty of arranging the four etchings chronologically was well described by Krommes (1912, p. 77) who also noted that the plate for *Il Perdono* might have been completed earlier than its publication date.
2. Schmarsow, 1909, p. 164, pointed out that Philippe Thomassin's 1588 engraved copy supplies a terminal date for Barocci's etching.

3. Schmarsow, 1909, p. 164; Krommes, 1912, p. 78.
4. Oberhuber, 1966, p. 168, cat. no. 284.
5. Schmarsow, 1909, p. 163; Olsen, 1962, pp. 106, 152; Petrucci, *Panorama*, 1964, p. 63; Emiliani, 1975, no. 51.
6. Krommes, 1912, pp. 77–78, recognized and described the technical and stylistic maturity of the etching and even, rather wishfully, wondered whether the date on Carracci's copy (which he had not seen) could be read 1592 instead of 1582!

more successful execution of the little *Madonna*. These three etchings may well have been made within months of each other, but at most, over no more than three years—the *Stigmatization* probably dates no earlier than 1579, and the *Madonna in the Clouds* cannot be later than early in 1582. Then after a gap of about three years Barocci etched the *Annunciation*, his final, most ambitious and most beautiful print.

From Karel van Mander in 1604[7] to Giovanni Gori Gandellini in 1771[8] to Adam Bartsch in 1818,[9] connoisseurs have remarked on the extraordinary beauty of Barocci's few etchings, and in this century Alfredo Petrucci has analyzed Barocci's remarkably innovative etching technique.[10] By the time Barocci tried his hand at etching, the process had been in use for over sixty years and was just at the point of an almost explosive growth that would bring it to full maturity in the seventeenth century. Barocci's brief practice of etching set an example for the future development of the medium.

Etching is a printmaking medium that appealed to the painter-printmaker from the first because it is practiced in a manner fairly comparable to the artist's accustomed practice of drawing on paper with pen. It is drawn with a sharp point in a pliant ground covering the metal plate. Its drawback, however, is that the necessary steps between the inscribing of the image in the ground and the printing of the image on paper involve variables that are not so readily controlled as is the image directly inscribed in the plate by the hand of the skilled engraver. Since the etched image must be "bitten" into the etched plate by the corrosive action of acid, a successful outcome depends on the composition of the ground that covers the plate, the action of the acid mordant (which can vary with the daily temperature), the length of time the plate surface is exposed to the mordant, and the composition of the metal plate itself. The part played by these variables is evident in the erratic development of the etching medium during the forty-odd years following its inception, sometime after 1510.

The ground used to cover the etching plate ideally should be pliable—easy to draw upon with the etching needle in order to expose the metal surface to the acid without chipping or flaking around the line—and it must be impervious to the acid elsewhere. As there is no recorded recipe from the sixteenth century, we can only guess that Barocci's etching ground somewhat resembled Abraham Bosse's *vernis mol* (a mixture of three parts wax, two parts resin, and one part asphalt)[11] and surmise that it may have originated as a variation of the recipe for painter's varnish. However, the most troublesome problem at the beginning was the interdependent working of acid and plate metal. Etching was first employed on a large scale for printmaking by Daniel Hopfer (ca. 1470–1536) of Augsburg and his brothers.[12] The Hopfers were metalworkers practiced in the use of etched decoration on armor, and it is logical that Daniel Hopfer printed from iron plates since that metal and its reaction to acid were familiar to him. Albrecht Dürer (1471–1528), in Nürnberg, evidently learned the Augsburg process: his five etchings, dated 1515, 1516, and 1518, were etched on iron plates, even though he was well aware of the superiority of copper over iron for printing. In fact, he used copper plates exclusively for engraving and for his three experiments with drypoint.

Sixteenth-century iron, though stronger than copper for the heavy work of implements and armor, contained undigested particles of dross that were easily loosened in the polishing of a printing plate, causing scattered pits in its surface. Copper was a purer metal that allowed a smooth surface from which to print as well as uniform resistance to the thrust of the engraving burin or bite of the etching mordant.[13] Lucas van Leyden (1489–1533) in Holland used a combination of etching and engraving in a few prints so well blended and with such fine detail that they must have been made on

7. "Van zijn eyghen handt sietmen oock eenighe Printen ghetetst daer men in soo cleen dingen soo grooten aerdt en welstandt siet dat het verwonderlijck en vermackelijck is te weten . . ." (Van Mander, 1604, fol. 187).
8. "Mostrò altresì eccellenza sopra gli altri professori nell' intagliare ad acqua forte . . .," Gandellini, 1771, p. 52.
9. "La perfection du dessein et la manière savante dont elles sont exécutées," Bartsch, vol. XVII, p. 2.
10. Petrucci, *Panorama*, 1964, pp. 63–65.
11. A. Bosse, *Traité des manières de graver en taille douce sur lairain* (originally published 1645), reprinted in Luigi Servolini, *Abraham Bosse e il suo trattato della calcografia*, Bologna, 1937. By the time Bosse wrote his manual the printmaker's esthetic had changed, and etching reverted to its early role as a fast, easy substitute for the burin, but was so disguised that the etched line in the finished print was indistinguishable from engraving. Bosse clearly considered the process of etching with the fragile *vernis mol* ground and nitric acid impractical—a method to be used only in extreme cases (Bosse, *op. cit.*, p. 126). Vasari, in his *Vite*, says ground may be either wax, varnish or oil paint (Vasari-Milanesi, V, p. 423).
12. Hind, 1923, p. 108–109. (The early date Hind assigns to an etched portrait has been disproved.) Wolfgang Wegner, "Eisenradierung," *Reallexikon zur Deutschen Kunstgeschichte*, IV, Stuttgart, 1957, columns 1145–1147.

copper plates.[14] Both Dürer's etchings and Lucas's etching-engravings are pictorial masterpieces, but Lucas's plates are superior technically—this is probably because the Dutch artist was able to use a mordant stronger than that required for iron. The acid most widely used since antiquity was the relatively weak acetic acid (of which vinegar is a common example) which worked as a mordant on iron but also attacked impurities in the plate surface more readily than the surrounding metal and therefore etched coarsely and unevenly.[15] But by mid-sixteenth century both nitric, and to a lesser degree, sulphuric acids were available in Europe. Indeed nitric acid (*aqua fortis,* which became the term in Italian for etching) was important in metallurgy to separate gold from silver.[16] Once the etcher was acquainted with nitric acid he could etch the more reliably uniform copper. And the strength of nitric acid allowed the etcher to vary the action of his mordant by dilution, and so permitted greater control over its action.[17]

Although a few sixteenth-century Italian etchings show, through signs of plate corrosion, that they were etched on iron, Italian printmakers had the materials and expertise for copperplate etching very early, among them Marcantonio Raimondi (ca. 1475–before 1534) who etched some small plates which he finished in engraving.[18] It is worth noting that the early Dutch and Italian etchers who etched on copper were slower than the Germans to develop an etching style distinct from their engraving style. They welcomed etching as a shortcut for fixing the basic design in the plate which

they then finished off with the engraving burin in their accustomed engraving style. Those who etched on iron, however—beginning with the Hopfer family, then Dürer, and including the etchers of the Danube school—had to depend for the finished print on etched lines alone and therefore were forced to accommodate their etching style to the overall uniformity of the etched line.

Francesco Mazzuoli of Parma, called Parmigianino (1503–1540), was the first Italian artist to develop a strong personal idiom in etching.[19] Instead of using the etched line for an underlying sketch to be completed in detail with the engraving burin, as had been the practice in Italy before, Parmigianino used etching as his principal medium—accented occasionally with the burin or with drypoint burr. The freedom of the etched line admirably suited Parmigianino's graphic style, and although he produced no more than sixteen plates, his sketch-like, vibrant, and widely spaced line became the model for Italian painter-printmakers through the eighteenth century.

Battista Franco (ca. 1510–1561) of Venice, Barocci's early mentor and himself a prolific printmaker,[20] must have been acquainted with the work of Andrea Meldolla, called Schiavone (1522–1563), who was active in Venice between about 1540 until his death in 1563.[21] Schiavone was strongly influenced by Parmigianino and his prints were instrumental in spreading Parmigianino's freer manner of etching. Barocci might have learned the fundamentals of etching from Franco, although Franco left Urbino by 1554—over twenty years before Barocci made his prints. It is one of the drawbacks of historical research that practical or technological knowledge is communicated anonymously. Whereas the ancestry of images and styles can be traced to the works of a known artist, practice and materials are transmitted by journeymen craftsmen whose names are unrecorded for, or unrecognizable by,[22] posterity. As for Barocci, we do not even know where or by whom his plates were printed. We know only that as a youth he was apprenticed to Franco who was a

13. Copper, with a lower melting point than iron, could be liquefied by heat, bringing the dross to the surface from which it could be in large part removed. But iron could not be heated to liquidity by sixteenth-century technology, only softened and imperfectly purified by forging and hammering. For a thorough and detailed article on early etching technology see Wegner (*op. cit.* in n.12 above, columns 1140–1151), from which I have drawn most of the information summarized here. I am indebted to Jane Peters for bringing this important article to my attention.
14. Notably the *Portrait of the Emperor Maximilian* (Bartsch VII, 432.172), dated 1520.
15. Another serious defect of iron plates, their susceptibility to corrosion, results from the fact that a weak acid will etch iron.
16. C. Singer, E. J. Holmyard, A. R. Hall, T. I. Williams, *A History of Technology,* vol. II, 1956, p. 356. It is interesting in this connection that Vasari (Milanesi, V, p. 423) in his description of the new printmaking process calls etching mordant "acqua da partire" (parting liquid) thus signifying that nitric acid was commonly used for etching in Italy. Bosse (*op. cit.* in n.11, p. 167) also identifies nitric acid as the parting agent for refining gold.
17. Although acetic acid at full strength is too weak to etch copper, undiluted nitric acid is much too active and etches a wide ragged line. In weaker solution nitric acid bites a fine, clean line.
18. Oberhuber, 1966, p. 23. Pittaluga, 1930, p. 332 n. 64.

19. Pittaluga, 1930, pp. 266–270, 331 n. 63. K. Oberhuber, *Parmigianino und sein Kreis*, Vienna, Albertina, exhibition catalogue, 1963.
20. Pittaluga, 1930, pp. 284–286, 333 n. 76. Oberhuber, 1966, pp. 24–25, 152, and *passim.*
21. Pittaluga, 1930, pp. 274–278, 332 n. 71. Oberhuber, 1966, pp. 145–146.

printmaker, and that he had also spent time in Rome, a printmaking center.

From the evidence of his prints, we may deduce that Barocci began with the copper plate and nitric acid technology which was in common use by the third quarter of the century. He had printers capable of handling plates the size of the *Perdono* and *Annunciation* (although early impressions of the former sometimes have printing folds or ink streaks, and both large prints sometimes show doubled lines from plate slippage). He had some trouble with his ground, at least on the plate for the *Madonna in the Clouds* (see Cat. 73). He took for granted the mixture of engraving with etching, and he knew the use of drypoint burr.

Battista Franco was as eclectic in his prints as in other media, and his prints run the gamut from engravings that use the orderly, volume-encompassing burin lines of Marcantonio, to etchings, usually augmented with engraving, that rather timidly imitate Parmigianino's flowing lines. Franco occasionally modelled form with stipple dots, a graphic device used by some North Italian engravers early in the century for a softer modulation than any line system provides.[23] Barocci adopted and expanded stipple modelling into an expressive tool especially suited to the delicacy and grace of his *Madonna in the Clouds* and the Virgin and angel of his *Annunciation* (Fig. A). However, in considering the communication of image and style in prints, it is important to remember that prints themselves traveled freely; in part they owed their popularity to their portability. An artist as dependent on the example of others as Franco was, would have been disposed to amassing a personal collection of prints, and such prints could have become familiar to Federico Barocci in his youth.

While Barocci needed a personal contact to learn the process of making an etching, he needed only

Fig. C. Detail of Cat. 73

the readily available products of the print commerce to absorb the graphic style of all Europe where an imaginative printmaker like Parmigianino could be seen alongside interpretations of Titian by the expert engraver Cornelis Cort. Parmigianino shows the flexibility of the new process, Cort offers the perfected vocabulary of the engraving style developed to reproduce the tonal range of painting. Whatever prints Barocci may have known, it was these two streams of printmaking that he combined.[24]

By the last quarter of the sixteenth century etching stood at the threshold of its evolution, whereas the long-established process of engraving had already reached a peak of formal perfection. Engraving plates were executed with the aim of the greatest possible duplicability. This goal was pursued by the print craftsman who achieved with skill, training, and much practice, a system of line engraving which was sufficiently uniform and regular to preserve the metal surface through repeated impressions and was also capable of producing a wide spectrum of tones between light and dark. Such plates normally reproduced images invented by others in another medium. The immediacy and subtlety of the creator's inspiration was therefore subdued by the translation into another medium and homogenized by the formal systemization of the engraver's technique. In return, the system yielded hundreds of impressions and a flood-tide of pictures. By the end of the sixteenth century there was a flourishing commerce in reproductive prints and a tradition for the role of

22. Lamberto Donati published a note concerning an otherwise unknown Leonardo Caccianimici (a descendant of the obscure painter-printmaker Vicenzo Caccianemici?) of Bologna who was granted a papal copyright on March 1, 1577, for a new method of printing engravings in silver ink ("Chi fu Leonardo Caccianimici?," *Maso Finiguerra*, I, 1936, pp. 248–249; I am indebted to Antony Griffiths for the interpretation of the Latin text). Even the introduction of the practice of etching by the Hopfer family, who remained in the craftsman-workshop tradition and were dependent on the designs of others, is a case in point.
23. Giulio Campagnola (c. 1482–1515/17) engraved one subject entirely in stipple, *Venus Reclining in a Landscape* (A. M. Hind, *Early Italian Engraving*, V, 1948, p. 202 no. 13).

24. Kristeller, 1921, p. 279, observed that Barocci had invented a novel etching system that rivaled the versatility of engraving while avoiding its coldness.

print publishers, who directed and underwrote that commerce.[25] Among the foremost engravers of Barocci's time, a man of nearly his own age, was Cornelis Cort. Among the many engravings after Barocci's designs, the earliest dated example is by Cornelis Cort, the *Rest on the Return from Egypt* (Cat. 76), dated 1575.

Cort was born in Hoorn, Holland, in 1533 and began his career in Antwerp as an engraver for Hieronymous Cock (ca. 1510–1570), whose "Four Winds"[26] was then the dominant publishing establishment in Europe. The "Four Winds" published prints after drawings both by Pieter Bruegel I, the greatest living Flemish master, and also by Titian, the grand old man of Venetian painting. Whatever his subject, the engraver worked from a drawing model made especially for the purpose. No matter whether the composition was created solely for use in an engraved edition, or whether a painting already existed as an independent work, engravings were executed from drawing models. In the case of the painting to be reproduced by engraving, the drawing model was commonly supplied by the painter himself. While he was working for Cock in Antwerp, Cornelis Cort engraved two subjects by Titian.[27] By 1565 Cort was himself living in Titian's household in Venice, engaged by the painter to make authorized engravings after Titian's designs and under his direction. In Venice Cort developed his characteristic system of engraving employing swelling parallel lines to define volume and variations in width and spacing to produce light and shadow. In 1566 Cort left Venice for Rome where he engraved designs by, among others, Federico and Taddeo Zuccaro, Giulio Clovio, and Girolamo Muziano. Except for another short term in Venice around 1572 Cort remained in Rome until his death.

The influence and the popularity of prints by Cornelis Cort and other reproductive engravers can hardly be overstated. They acquainted other artists with compositions by the most admired masters and they filled the needs of an image-hungry public whose chief interest was subject matter. It is well to remember, furthermore, that we do not see Cornelis Cort's engravings the way Barocci and his contemporaries saw them. To some extent they were the sixteenth-century equivalent of the twentieth century's photographic reproductions: as we have learned to interpret photographs in order to visualize paintings we have never seen, so Barocci and his contemporaries were able to "read" into engravings the appearance of otherwise inaccessible works of art. In the role of interpreter, Cort was an acknowledged master.

In a footnote to his chapter on Barocci's etchings,[28] Olsen pointed out that Cort could have gone through Urbino on his way from Rome to Venice in 1572. One may wonder whether the two men ever met. It is conceivable, whether or not the artists met face to face, that Cort's two engravings after paintings by Barocci were made according to an agreement by which Barocci supplied the engraver with a drawing model for a fee, or even shared in the profits from the sale of the engravings. Cort's relationship with Titian was one in which the engraver was employed by the painter. Titian decided what works should be reproduced; he supplied the drawing models, obtained the "privilege" (copyright) from the pertinent authority, and arranged for and profited by the eventual sale of the prints.[29] There were doubtless many possible arrangements between artist and engraver which gave more authority to the printmaker and probably the responsibility for and the receipts from the sale of the print edition. But it seems to have been common for the engraver at least to pay the painter for the drawing model, and there may have been other variations of the financial contract between artist and printmaker for dividing between them the costs and the profits from the sale of prints.[30] It is possible, then, that Barocci received some financial profit from Cort's reproduction of his pictures, as well as the growth of his reputation and influence by the dispersal of multiple replicas of his designs.

25. See Oberhuber, 1966, pp. 13–16. Oberhuber's introductory essay to the catalogue gives a superb overview of printmaking in sixteenth-century Italy and its relationship to European culture and commerce. For a detailed discussion of print publishing in the Netherlands see T. Riggs, *Hieronymous Cock (1510–1570): Printmaker and Publisher in Antwerp at the Sign of the Four Winds*, University Microfilms, Ann Arbor, Michigan, 1972, pp. 17–21, 203–226, and *passim*.

26. T. Riggs, *op. cit.* in n. 25 above.

27. J.C.J. Bierens de Haan (*L'Oeuvre gravé de Cornelis Cort*, The Hague, 1948, p. 4) suggests that Cort might have brought to Antwerp a stock of drawings by Italian masters on his return from his 1548 stay in Italy.

28. Olsen, 1962, p. 106 n. 222.

29. See Bierens de Haan (*op. cit.* in n. 27 above, p. 14 n. 1) for an important discussion of Cort's arrangement with Titian, and various other contracts between artists and engravers.

The Counter Reformation created a need for new images purged and purified of false myths and doctrines which could excite the private spiritual fervor of the true believer. The great popularity of Cort's engraving of the *Rest on the Return from Egypt* showed how well Barocci's mind and spirit were attuned to meet that need. Barocci's pictures invite the emotional participation of the worshipper by opening the spiritual world to the viewer. The onlooker is included in the circle of his Holy Family through a perspective viewpoint that moves downward and outward, widening in the foreground plane like the apron of a stage to draw him into the holy scene. Not only was another version of the subject reproduced in a large, contemporary chiaroscuro (Cat. 80), but no less than seventeen print copies of Cort's engraving are cited in the catalogue raisonné by Bierens de Haan,[31] one of them dated 1576.[32] When Cort's engraving of Barocci's *Madonna del Gatto* (Cat. 77) was published in 1577, it was protected for ten years with a papal copyright in anticipation of a similar popularity. Indeed, these two engravings inspired a whole genre of devotional subjects in the Netherlands.[33]

It has been suggested that Cort's success convinced Barocci to begin making prints himself.[34] It can also be argued that he did so because of Cort's untimely death in the spring of 1578,[35] which denied the painter a fruitful collaboration with one of the finest engravers of his time. That Cort's death was a factor in Barocci's decision to make his own prints is more probable than the theory sometimes expressed that Barocci was motivated by disapproval of Cort's reproductions of his work.[36] There

is no reason to think that Barocci did not share his contemporaries' high regard for Cort's skill. That Barocci succeeded in far surpassing Cort's accomplishment, by trying to produce with etching the appearance of Cort's engravings, is the happy consequence of Barocci's endeavor—evident only when the prints of both men exist for comparison. Furthermore, if Barocci was unusually hard-pressed financially by 1578 because of the terms of the contract for the *Madonna del Popolo,* or for other reasons (see Cat. 35), an additional motivation may have existed for his brief essay in printmaking. In any case, the evidence of the etchings themselves suggests that close to 1580 Barocci briefly turned to etching, and that he characteristically attacked the process with few preconceptions or inhibitions as to procedure or tools of the trade.

In his earliest etching, the *Stigmatization of St. Francis,* there is evidence of Barocci's boldest technical procedure—the immersion of the plate more than once in the acid in order to vary his etched lines. The process of submitting the plate to the mordant more than once had been used by a few earlier etchers.[37] Augustin Hirschvogel (1503–1553), one of the Danube school landscape etchers, occasionally exposed the lines of a selected foreground detail to a second bite after stopping out, or covering over, the rest of the initial etching, in order to deepen and widen the lines of the foreground detail and thereby emphasize the contrast between near and far.[38] Close examination of Barocci's etchings indicates that his method was to re-cover his whole plate after the first bite and add to the first image a new network of lines. This second network was exposed to the acid longer; the lines therefore hold more ink and are darker in the printed image. The small *St. Francis Receiving the Stigmata* most clearly shows the contrast between the dark lines of the second bite and the lighter lines of the first bite. But, since the artist aimed for

30. Such arrangements between the printmaker and the "inventor" of the design naturally pertained only to contemporaneous artists. But the idea of the inventor's right of ownership was quite strong—hence the "privilegio." Bierens de Haan (*op. cit.* in n. 27 above, appendix II, item 5, pp. 230–232) quotes a notary's statement of an agreement made July 16, 1578 between Girolamo Muziano and the printer Bonifazio Bregio for the division between them of a set of engraving plates, expenses and profits of the sale of an edition of prints, and seven Muziano drawings. Six of the plates, which were all of Muziano's designs, were engraved by Cort, and it is interesting that they were in Muziano's possession, evidently not yet published, after Cort's death. Further it should be noted that the inventory of Barocci's studio describes ten drawings by Barocci as "finished so one could issue prints" (Calzini, 1898, p. 107).
31. Bierens de Haan, *op. cit.,* in n. 27 above, p. 63.
32. *Ibid.*, p. 63, no. 43(h), by Giovanni Jacomo Valeggio.
33. Especially through the prints of Hendrik Goltzius, e.g. *The Holy Family under the Cherry Tree* of 1589 (Bartsch III. 18.24).
34. Laran, 1959, p. 77. Olsen, 1962, p. 106 n. 222.
35. The *post mortem* inventory of his possessions was notarized April 22. Bierens de Haan, *op. cit.* in n. 27 above, p. 15.

36. Emiliani, 1975, p. 99, no. 76. Schmarsow, 1909, p. 163, thought Barocci etched the *Perdono* because he perhaps wished to "publish a painting of such importance himself."
37. Hieronymous Cock (Riggs, *op. cit.* in n. 25 above, pp. 128–130), and possibly Battista Fontana (Oberhuber, 1966, p. 27). In both instances the printmaker sought the effect of atmospheric distance. A systematic examination of etchings before 1550 might reveal many further unnoticed examples of multiple bite.
38. Significantly Hirschvogel's use of a second bite appears to begin with his change from iron to copper plates. M. Forster, *Die Landschaftsradierungen des Augustin Hirschvogel,* unpublished dissertation, Vienna, 1973, p. 10.

a harmonious effect, he blended the two tones of etching by finishing the plate with the engraving burin. Strong engraved lines darken the lower half of the saint's robe; these lines capture ink in the manner of drypoint burr. The burr is seen in the shadow above and to the right of the forward foot and in a patch on the ground, left of the foot (Fig. B). Lightly engraved lines augment or complete pale, etched lines that did not quite "take" in the acid bath. There are indications that the artist worked over the plate more extensively than the simple image reveals at first glance. Furthermore, there are numerous indications of burnishing in the interrupted light lines of the background (the slightly curved parallels at the upper left in the enlarged detail). There is also evidence of tree forms originally drawn at the left and covered over. The initial etch was not always successful. Frequently where Barocci encircled a shaded area, such as a leaf, the acid spread across the enclosed surface obliterating lines and creating a shallow depression that retained only a thin layer of ink. Possibly the two small patches of overly black shading lines above the saint's head were added in the second bite.

There is no indication in the *St. Francis* of a problem that appears in Barocci's other etchings, one that was especially troublesome in the etching of the *Perdono*. In the three other etchings Barocci enhanced the shadows with accents of deepest black. Such accents were achieved by overlapping networks of etched lines that were so dense the ink in the lines spread over the miniscule areas left between. This etching style—which boldly pushes the etching technique to, and beyond, its limits—remained unmatched in yielding an unlimited spectrum of tone between light and dark until the time of Rembrandt. On occasion the etching process failed to meet the demands of the artist's intention and the plate surface would dissolve, with the result that where the darkest shadow was desired the impression takes on a dull gray tone instead (Fig. C).

While trying to produce effects in etching beyond the capacity of the process, Barocci succeeded in expanding the technique to accommodate the full, tonal spectrum of the reproductive engraver without sacrificing warmth and vitality. There were precedents for all his innovations—

Fig. A. Detail of Cat. 75

Fig. B. Detail of Cat. 72

multiple bite, the mixture of engraving and etching, the use of drypoint burr for deeper blacks. Barocci's graphic style gathers them together and bends them to serve his own characteristic vision. He used the soft modelling of clustered dots that had been used by Venetian engravers early in the century, the flickering half-shadows of Parmigianino's open hatchings as well as his fluid, uneven parallel strokes; and, where it suited his purpose, the oblique cross-hatchings with dots in their interstices, and finally the order and brilliance of evenly spaced parallel lines of the reproductive engravers.

Barocci's reason for abandoning etching after completing only four plates is as mysterious as his reason for taking up so arduous a process in the first place. He may have become discouraged because of the technical problems encountered in the large plates or because the plates could not withstand the wear of large editions.[39] However, he may have found he had little time for printmaking once his reputation as a painter was sufficient to attract more commissions than he could possibly

Fig. D. Jacques Bellange (1594-1638), *Annunciation*, etching

Fig. E. Philipp Uffenbach (1566-1636), *Resurrection*, etching, 1588

Fig. F. Rembrandt van Rijn (1606-1669), *Faust in his Study*, etching and drypoint, 1652

complete himself, which occurred in the 1580's (see Cat. 56). Indeed, one might wonder why as late as 1584 Barocci etched the *Annunciation;* but possibly Duke Francesco Maria II, who commissioned the altarpiece, asked Barocci to expand its fame by executing the print as well. In any event, it is the good fortune of posterity that Barocci was motivated to etch at all, and surely fortunate that he did not cease before attempting his lovely final plate of the *Annunciation,* the crowning achievement of his short career as a printmaker.

It is difficult to isolate the influence of Barocci's etching style on the work of later Italian printmakers since etching, more than any other print process before the invention of lithography, allows the artist freedom to work in his own individual style. The Sienese artists Francesco Vanni (1563–1610) and Ventura Salimbeni (1567/8–1613), whose paintings show their admiration for Barocci, also imitated his etching style without approaching the brilliance of Barocci's prints. Kristeller cites the portrait prints of Ottavio Leoni (Rome, 1574–1630) as the closest stylistic imitation of Barocci's etchings.[40] And it may have been in Barocci's example that Orazio Borgiani (1577–1620), the Roman follower of Caravaggio, found the etching style suited to his tenebrist chiaroscuro. Nevertheless, the outer boundaries of etching technique that Barocci explored did not engage the major etchers of the next generation in Italy. The prints of Annibale Carracci (1560–1609), Guido Reni (1575–1642), and Simone Cantarini (1612–1648), for example, reflect the style of the *Madonna in the Clouds* but do not approach the technical complexity of Barocci's two large plates. It awaited the innovative and highly original artist, Jacques Bellange (1594–1638) of Nancy,[41] to follow Barocci's laborious etching technique and vocabulary as a means of dramatizing form through strong patterns of light and shadow (Fig. D); or the lesser talent of Philipp Uffenbach (1566–1636) of Frankfort, whose 1588 print of the *Resurrection*[42] suggests that the artist found a model for etching his visionary subject in one, or both, of Barocci's large etchings (Fig. E).

It was in Rembrandt's work in Amsterdam in the mid-seventeenth century that Barocci's aims as a printmaker found their final and fullest expression. The 1656 inventory of Rembrandt's house included an album of prints by Vanni and Barocci.[43] Rembrandt's *Virgin in the Clouds* (Bartsch 61) of 1641 is clearly a Dutch version of Barocci's etching. However, it is not Rembrandt's little etching of 1641 that best represents Barocci's influence but rather the profound and mysterious print, *Faust in his Study* of 1652 (Fig. F). Rembrandt's strangely moving portrayal of the philosopher's vision might look quite different were it not for the precedent and example of Barocci's *Annunciation.* Rembrandt's *Faust* emulates the shadowed interior of Barocci's print with its half-glimpsed shapes and spaces. Above all Rembrandt studied and recreated in his own etching the otherworldly radiance that unexpectedly lights the foreground of Barocci's *Annunciation* and outshines the common daylight in the window behind. Rembrandt's manipulation of the etching, engraving, and drypoint tools for painterly effects; his overlapping networks of etched lines for warm, deep shadows; and his varied hatching for the glow of reflected light continued the course set by Barocci and developed the etching medium to the ultimate richness that Barocci's etchings anticipate.

41. A. M. Worthen and S. W. Reed, *The Etchings of Jacques Bellange,* Des Moines, Iowa, Des Moines Art Center, *et al.,* exhibition catalogue, 1975, pp. 11–12, 67 cat. no. 42. Bellange's exploration of the possibilities of the medium was similar to Barocci's.
42. Uffenbach evidently owned Grünewald drawings. He was the pupil of Abel Grimmer, pupil of Grünewald; he was the teacher of Adam Elsheimer.
43. Item 195. English translation of the inventory in K. Clark, *Rembrandt and the Classical Tradition,* paperback edition, New York, 1968, p. 201. Olsen, 1962, p. 132.

39. A worn impression of the *Perdono* in the New York Public Library collection shows white spots surrounding the corrective burin work where in the original state of the plate the etched hatching was too shallow to hold enough ink and the lines finally disappeared completely under the pressure of the press.
40. Kristeller, 1921, p. 279.

# Catalogue of Prints

**72** *Stigmatization of St. Francis* (Bartsch XVII.3.3)

Etching, engraving, and drypoint, 231 x 152 mm. (page). Signed in plate at lower center with the initials: •F•B•V•F•

New York, The Metropolitan Museum of Art, Harris Brisbane Dick Fund, no. 27–82–2

Published: Mayor, 1947, p. 163, repr. p. 162. Bibliography for the print: Van Mander, 1604, fol. 187a; Gandellini, 1771, p. 53; Heinecken, 1788, pp. 149–150; Huber, 1800, p. 179, no. 4; Bartsch XVII, p. 3; Le Blanc, 1854, p. 149, no. 3; Nagler, *Künstler-Lexikon*, 1885, p. 29, no. 3; Schmarsow, 1909, p. 164; Krommes, 1912, p. 78; Hermanin, 1913, p. 131; Pittaluga, 1930, pp. 315–317; Olsen, 1962, no. 28; Petrucci, *Panorama*, 1964, p. 64; Oberhuber, 1966, under no. 284; Emiliani, 1975, no. 79.

Gandellini and Bartsch related this print to the painting of the same subject of ca. 1594–95 formerly in the church of the Capuchins in Urbino and now in the Galleria Nazionale; Schmarsow, however, pointed out that the composition of the painting differed from that of the print and concluded that the etching was made for its own sake. Krommes, and later Olsen and Emiliani, have compared the etching to the unfinished painting of the late 1570's in the Museo Civico in Fossombrone, now on deposit in the Galleria Nazionale in Urbino. See also Cat. 30 and Cat. 31.

The principal figure in the print derives its pose from that of the St. Franris in the *Perdono*, which was finished in 1576. In order to transpose the figure from the dark interior to the sunlit landscape the artist burnished out part of the etched foliage behind the figure and covered the bank with engraved parallel lines. By doing this the artist was able to leave the modelling on the principal figure intact. In this new context the shadows which fall on the saint's left arm and hand and on the bank in the background appear to come from overhanging foliage or from a passing cloud.

The burr visible in this impression in the lower part of the saint's robe and on the ground near his feet was not produced by a special tool, such as the seventeenth-century drypoint needle, but was made by the same engraving burin employed in the rest of the robe. By leaving the edges of the grooves rough and unpolished, Barocci allowed the lines to capture extra ink, producing an effect similar to that of drypoint.

72

**73** *Il Perdono di S. Francesco d'Assisi* (Bartsch XVII.4.4)

Etching and engraving, 542 x 325 mm. (plate). Signed, copyrighted, inscribed in plate at lower right: *Fediricvs • Barocivs • Vrbinas | Inventor incidebat.1.5.8.1 | Gregorii • XIII • Privilegio | AD •X̄•*; at lower left: *Ostendit Christus se se Franciscus adorat, | Atque animae hic poscit sit sua cuique salus. | Annuit.· aeterno firmat sub faedere templum | O' ueré Aligerum nomine sancta domus.*

**A**
Cambridge (Massachusetts), Fogg Art Museum, Harvard University, Purchase by Exchange, Knapp Fund, no. M13, 655. Watermark: Unidentified, escutcheon enclosing stylized plant (?). Published: Rosenberg, 1963, pp. 10–12, repr. p. 11.

**B**
Philadelphia, Philadelphia Museum of Art, Pennsylvania Academy of the Fine Arts Collec-

tion, no. A–P–1263. Provenance: John S. Phillips. Cut at platemark, within platemark at bottom edge; indistinct watermark.

**C**
Philadelphia, Philadelphia Museum of Art, Gift of Lessing J. Rosenwald, no. 41–14–1. Provenance: Johann Wilhelm Nahl, Kassel (Lugt 1954); Gustav Seeligman, New York (Lugt 1215). Cut just within platemark; watermark: anchor in circle with star (?).

Bibliography for the print: Bellori, 1672, p. 220; Gandellini, 1771, p. 53; Heinecken, 1788, p. 149; Huber, 1800, p. 179, no. 5; Bartsch, XVII, p. 4; Le Blanc, 1854, p. 149, no. 4; Nagler, *Künstler-Lexikon*, 1885, p. 29; Schmarsow, 1909, p. 163; Krommes, 1912, p. 77; Hermanin, 1913, pp. 131–133; Pittaluga, 1930, p. 314; Olsen, 1962, pp. 107, 160; Petrucci, *Panorama*, 1964, p. 64; A. M. Petrioli Tofani, *Stampe italiane dalle origini all'ottocento*, Florence, Gabinetto Disegni e Stampe degli Uffizi, exhibition catalogue, 1975, no. 78; Emiliani, 1975, no. 76.

73A

The subject of the *Perdono* is the apparition of Christ to St. Francis who requested a plenary indulgence for all penitents who visited the chapel at Portiuncula, which is represented in the background. The etching reproduces the painting on the high altar of the church of S. Francesco in Urbino which Barocci finished in 1576. The inclusion of St. Nicholas in the upper part of the composition reflects the fact that the painting was commissioned from a Nicolò Ventura who died in 1574. Although Bellori states that the artist worked on the commission for seven years, it is conceivable that he mistook the date of the print (1581) for the date of the painting's completion and wrongly assumed that work on the painting extended through the latter part of the decade.

Barocci took pains with his etching to reproduce the quality and variety of light effects in the painting. As Bellori relates, there are several light sources: the supernatural il-lumination from Christ which falls upon St. Francis; the natural light which fills the heavenly sphere; and the candlelight on the altar in the chapel which lights the background. The lighting therefore both unites the upper and lower zones in the composition and supports the perspective system which establishes a different viewpoint for the two parts—a low one for the vision and a high one for the kneeling saint and church interior.

Because of the complexity of the design and technical weaknesses in the plate, the printing of the *Perdono* required special handling. The degree of improvisation in the inking and wiping of the plate can be measured by comparing the three early impressions exhibited here.

In the Fogg Museum impression (73A) the plate was heavily inked and then selectively wiped to create strong contrasts of light and shade. A film of plate tone can be seen by the candle flame in the chapel and in various places in the clouds. And the excessive inking produced several long streaks when the surface of the plate was wiped, which accounts for the diagonal lines on the lower face and base of the left baluster and on other parts of the composition.

The impression belonging to the Pennsylvania Academy (73B), which was also heavily inked, has a fine, even gray ink tone over the whole printed surface. A white rectangle between the third and fourth fingers of the saint's hand, left uninked in the press, was corrected by hand with the addition of small, fine ink strokes.

In the third impression in the exhibition, in the Philadelphia Museum of Art (73C), the plate was less heavily inked than in the case of the former two prints. This impression most clearly shows where Barocci found it necessary to supplement the etched crosshatching with engraving: for example, near the ball on the baluster at the right where rather coarse, vertical engraving strokes cover a patch of overly shallow etching.

As in the *Stigmatization of St. Francis* (Cat. 72), Barocci interspersed engraving and etching throughout the plate.[1] The purpose of the addition of engraving was not only to correct mis-bite but also to give sheen to drapery and to the rays of the nimbus. The artist also employed stipple modelling, although in a fashion that was still relatively restrained, to soften the transition between etched parallels and clear highlights and to support the linear modelling of faces and hands.

Impressions of the *Perdono* exist in great number, which would suggest there was a prolonged demand for the print. In the seventeenth century the plate came into the

73B

**74** *Madonna in the Clouds* (Bartsch XVII.3.2)

ILLUSTRATED ON BACK COVER

Etching and engraving, 155 x 107 mm. (page).
Signed in plate at lower left with the initials:
·F·B·V·F·

Cleveland, The Cleveland Museum of Art, Gift of
The Print Club of Cleveland, no. 25.1222.

Provenance: George Ambrose Cardew, London
(Lugt 1134); acquired from P. & D. Colnaghi &
Co., Ltd., London.

Bibliography for the print: Van Mander, 1604, fol.
187a; C. Malvasia, *Felsina pittrice: Vite dei pittori
bolognesi,* 1678 (ed. M. Brascaglia, Bologna, 1971),
p. 268; Gandellini, 1771, p. 53; Heinecken, 1788,
pp. 146, 148; Huber, 1800, p. 179; Bartsch, XVII, p.
3; Le Blanc, p. 149; Nagler, *Künstler-Lexikon,* 1885,
p. 29; Schmarsow, 1909, p. 163; Krommes, 1912,
p. 77; Hermanin, 1913, pp. 130–31; Pittaluga,
1930, p. 315; Laran, 1959, p. 98; Olsen, 1962, no.
20; Petrucci, *Panorama,* 1964, p. 63; Emiliani, 1975,
no. 51.

This etching reproduces the figures in the
upper portion of the altarpiece executed for
the Capuchins in Fossombrone in the 1560's
and now untraced (see Cat. 12). The Virgin
and Child are less remote from the viewer
than in the painting although they still appear on a pedestal of clouds. The etching
was copied by Agostino Carracci in 1582 (see
Cat. 78).

Barocci's use of loose, open parallels and
crosshatchings in the clouds and
background contrasts with the dense modelling of the figures and drapery. Stipple
modelling serves to soften the body of the
child, the faces, and a wing of the angel at
the upper right. In this impression the acid
overbite can be seen in almost all the dark
accents, and black patches appear along the
edges where the ground failed to protect the
metal plate. But neither these, nor the other
smudges and spots unintentionally etched
onto the plate, mar the harmony of Barocci's
print.

While the *Madonna in the Clouds* seems to
survive in a single state which bears the artist's initials at the lower left, as in the exhibited example, the existence of various
trimmed impressions have led former writers to conclude that the artist issued an early
edition of the print, without his signature, or
made more than one plate depicting the
Madonna and Child. The leading advocate
of the former view has been Schmarsow
who attempted to identify a trimmed impression as an early state, before the initials.
Although Bartsch carefully limited Barocci's
oeuvre of prints to four, various writers—
from Heinecken and Huber to Le Blanc—
have argued that he made five prints including two separate prints of the Madonna and
Child, an unfinished one and one bearing

possession of the Venetian publisher,
Stefano Scolari;[2] and at that time, or later, it
was extensively reworked for continued
publication. A mediocre engraved copy of
the *Perdono,* in the same direction and of
similar dimensions, bears inscriptions similar to those of the original, altered only in
the second line·on the right by the word,
"inventor," and by an additional line below
that reads: "Superioru permissu. 1594." Schmarsow erroneously identified the copy as a
second edition of Barocci's print.[3]

1. Petrucci's statement (*Panorama,* 1964, p. 63) that this
print is executed entirely in etching is incorrect; even a
cursory examination reveals engraving combined with
the etching.
2. Impressions published by Scolari carry the marginal
address: *Stefano Scolari forma in Venetia* (Nagler, 1885, p.
29, no. 4).
3. Schmarsow, 1909, p. 164. Repeated by Olsen (1962, p.
160) and Emiliani (1975, p. 94). Nagler (1885, p. 29, no. 4)
had already recorded the copy.

73C

**75** *Annunciation* (Bartsch XVII.2.1)

Etching, engraving, drypoint, 438 x 311 (plate).
Signed in plate at lower right: *Federicus. Barocius. Vrb. / inuentor excudit.* Watermark: fleur-de-lis in circle (similar to Briquet 7127).

Chicago, The Art Institute of Chicago, The Joseph Brooks Fair Collection, no. 1942.528.

Provenance: Acquired from Dr. H. Wallach, New York.

Bibliography for the print: Mariette, 1741, p. 22, lot 223; Mariette, *Abecedario*, ca. 1750–54, I, p. 69; Gandellini 1771, pp. 52–53; Heinecken, 1788, p. 141; Huber, 1800, p. 179, no. 3; Bartsch, XVII, p. 2; Le Blanc, p. 149; Nagler, *Künstler-Lexikon*, 1885, p. 29; Schmarsow, 1909, p. 164, no. 3; Krommes, 1912, pp. 76–79; Hermanin, 1913, pp. 130–132; Disertori, 1922, pp. 137–138; Pittaluga, 1930, pp. 314–315; Laran, 1959, pp. 77, 98; Olsen, 1962, pp. 107, 177, under no. 37; Petrucci, *Panorama*, 1964, p. 64; Winner, 1964, no. 2; Oberhuber, 1966, no. 283; Emiliani, 1975, no. 151.

This print reproduces the altarpiece commissioned by Francesco Maria II della Rovere for the ducal chapel in the basilica in Loreto in 1582. Replaced by a copy in mosaic in the eighteenth century, the painting now hangs in the Vatican Pinacoteca. The etching probably dates to the period between the completion of the picture in 1584 and the publication of Philippe Thomassin's engraved copy in 1588.[1] The print demonstrates Barocci's full mastery of the printed line. While the treatment of reflected light on the angel's back recalls reproductive engraving in its use of a line pattern with slightly curved hatchings which cross at an acute angle and leave varied lozenge-shaped white spaces, the etched hatchings elsewhere create a subtle pattern that becomes a shimmer of movement within the shaded areas. Barocci depicted the soft texture of the Virgin's cloak by using a mixture of etched and engraved parallel lines mingled with clustered dots; the crisp sheen of the angel's taffeta-like robe is described by patches of etched or engraved parallels, varied in weight each from the other, and bounded by white highlights. The drypoint accents which are prominent above the angel's foot and in a few dark accents elsewhere, seem to have been drawn with a thinner, sharper point than the tool Barocci previously used for burr in the little *St. Francis* (Cat. 72). But even in this advanced example of printing Barocci had difficulty controlling the acid and patches of overbite can be seen on the mouth of the cat and by the inkpot. An oblong patch of shading in the drapery behind the angel's head, which printed unevenly in the Chicago impression, wore out or printed incorrectly in later impressions.

his initials.[1] A certain amount of confusion regarding the original appearance of the print may still exist, in fact, because both Pittaluga and Olsen reproduce an impression in the Uffizi in which the composition ends just below the Virgin's sandal, where the print was cropped.

1. As recently as 1972 L. Moscone asserted that Barocci made four or five prints (*Dizionario enciclopedico bolaffi dei pittori e degl'incisori italiani*, I, 1972, p. 357).

75

CORNELIS CORT (Hoorn, Holland, 1533–Rome 1578)

**76** *Rest on the Return from Egypt*

Engraving, 437 x 285 mm. (plate). Engraved on stone at lower right: *Federicus Barotÿus Vrbinas inuentor;* and under leaves at lower right: *Cornelio cort fe.;* in bottom margin, three verses of two lines each: *Virgo quid hauris aquas; Natone datura petenti? / Ah sitit: vt nostro pellat ab ore' sitim. / Arboris vt fructus tibi dulces, Christe, videntur; / Sic tua Crux mundo dulcia poma dabit. / Virginis et pueri Custos, no' tecta subintras? / Hospitione, Orbis rector, in orbe, caret.?;* below verses: *Romae An. Iub 1575;* on cartouche at right: *AMPLmo Cardinali et ILLmo Domino / JACOBO SABELLO Snti VICARIO. / deuotionis ergo, / Laurentius Vaccarius, D.D.;* inscribed in pencil below plate mark: *from an original in the possession of Lord Grosvenor.*

New York, The Metropolitan Museum of Art, Harris Brisbane Dick Fund, no. 26.70.3 (12).

Barocci painted three versions of the Rest on the Return from Egypt between 1570 and 1573. According to Bellori, the earliest of the three, which is now lost, was ordered by Duke Guidobaldo della Rovere as a gift to Lucrezia d'Este, the Duchess of Ferrara and his future daughter-in-law. The second, a larger version executed in tempera and oils, was sent to Count Antonio Brancaleoni in Piobbico where it can be seen in the church of S. Stefano today. The third, and final, version, identifiable as the work in the Vatican Pinacoteca, was sent to a friend of the artist in Perugia in 1573. The three versions differ in several details. For example, the first version, whose appearance is known through Raffaello Schiaminossi's engraving of 1612[1] and the anonymous chiaroscuro print in the artist's possession at his death (Cat. 80), shows the Christ Child kneeling with his right hand held open to receive the cherry branch and the Virgin's hat face down in the lower left. The second version retains the position of the hat but alters the pose of the Child showing him now seated with his right hand grabbing the branch with a clenched fist. The third version follows the second in the pose of Christ but shows the Virgin's hat upside down.

Cort's engraving of 1575 reproduces the second version of the composition. The engraving is proportionately wider and less high than the painting and specific details, such as the blades of grass floating on the water, are rendered with an almost anecdotal clarity. The engraver placed particular emphasis upon the abstract play of light and shadow as seen in such passages as the water in the foreground and the large fruit tree behind Joseph.

Cort's engraving exists in three states. The exhibited impression is the third, and final,

Meyer's edition of Nagler's *Künstler-Lexikon* (1885) lists two states for this print: the first without, the second with, the text. Since no examples of Meyer's proposed first state have come to light, it is likely the print described by Meyer was less than a complete impression; the same mistake appears to have been made with a cut-down example of the *Madonna in the Clouds* (Cat. 74).

The *Annunciation* is the only one of Barocci's four prints for which the plate survives. Recorded among his possessions in his studio when he died,[2] the plate entered the collection of the Calcografia Nazionale in Rome as early as 1709. Although no record of the number of impressions pulled from the plate was recorded until this century, between 1905 and 1971—at which time further printing halted—185 were issued.[3]

1. E. Bruwaert, *La vie et les oeuvres de Philippe Thomassin*, Troyes, 1914, p. 77, no. 104.
2. Calzini, 1898, p. 107.
3. The information about the plate and its history were kindly supplied by Prof. Carlo Bertelli in a letter to the present writer dated Nov. 13, 1976.

77
76

one with all the lettering; the first lacked the identification of the artist, date, and city and the dedication to Cardinal Sabello; the signature appears for the first time only in the second state.[2]

The inscription in pencil in the lower margin of this impression may refer to an oval copy of the painting recorded in 1821 in the Grosvenor Gallery in London.[3]

1. Repr. in Olsen, 1962, fig. 122b.
2. J. C. J. Bierens de Haan, *L'oeuvre gravé de Cornelis Cort*, The Hague, 1948, no. 43.
3. Recorded by Olsen, 1962, p. 155, copy no. 5.

CORNELIS CORT

### 77 *Madonna del Gatto*

Engraving, 350 x 246 mm. (plate). Engraved in the plate above the margin at right: *Corneli Cort fec. 1577*; above the margin in center: *Di. Greg.P.P.xiii ex Privil. p. an. x.*; in the lower margin at center: *Federicus Barotius Urbinensis Inventor*; in margin, two verses of two lines each: *Ludit Joannes, tacitus miratur JESUS. /Utriusq' notat symbolu uterq' parens, /Ille refert hominem paradisj è limine pulsum, / Quam ferat hic pulso jam meditatur opem.*

London, Trustees of the British Museum.

Provenance: Richard Houlditch, London (Lugt 2214)

The engraving reproduces, in reverse, the design of Barocci's influential easel painting of the Holy Family in an interior with the infant St. John who uses a bird in his hand to attract a small cat. The artist executed only one autograph version of the subject, which he sent to Count Antonio Brancaleoni in Piobbico—the owner of the version of the *Return from Egypt* which Cort copied for his engraving published in 1575 (Cat. 76)—and which is now in the National Gallery in London. The date of Cort's engraving of the *Madonna del Gatto*, 1577, establishes a *terminus ante quem* for the completion of the picture. In the eighteenth century Mariette identified a red chalk drawing in Crozat's collection as Barocci's modello for the print.[1] The impression of the print exhibited here is the second and final state, after the addition of the lettering.[2]

1. Mariette, 1741, p. 71, possibly identifiable as Würzburg, Martin von Wagner-Museum, no. 7193 or London, National Gallery, no. 29A.
2. J. C. J. Bierens de Haan, *L'oeuvre gravé de Cornelis Cort*, The Hague, 1948, no. 44.

78

AGOSTINO CARRACCI (Bologna 1557–Parma
1602)

**78** *Madonna in the Clouds* (Bartsch
XVIII.57.32)

Engraving, 150 x 118 mm. (plate). Engraved in
plate at lower left: *Agu. fe. 1582.* Impression cut
down within platemark at bottom, inscription in
lower margin missing.

New York, The Metropolitan Museum of Art,
Harris Brisbane Dick Fund, no. 17.3.3434.

The graphic work of Agostino Carracci, the
older brother of Annibale and cousin of
Ludovico, includes over three hundred engravings.[1] When he made this print after
Barocci's etching of the same subject (Cat.
74), Agostino was only twenty-five and as a
printmaker relatively undeveloped. It was
subsequent to this print that he acquired his
own particular style of engraving which was
strongly modelled upon the example of Cornelis Cort. A comparison of Barocci's etching and Agostino's engraved copy reveals
a fundamental difference of approach. In
executing the copy the Bolognese artist was
prepared to sacrifice Barocci's characteristic
light effects for the sake of absolute clarity of
form. As a result, Barocci's vaporous clouds
seem to become in Agostino's copy as solid
and massive as chiseled stone, and the sense
of atmosphere and texture in the original
print gives way to sculptural definition.

1. See Pittaluga, 1930, pp. 337–342, p. 365 n. 1 and H.
Bödmer, "Die Entwicklung der Stechkunst des Agostino
Carracci," *Die Graphischen Künste,* IV, 1939, pp. 121–142;
V, pp. 41–71.

80

AGOSTINO CARRACCI

**79** *Aeneas' Flight from Troy* (Bartsch
XVIII.99.110)

Engraving, 415 x 526 mm. (page). Engraved in the
lower left corner: *Typis / Donati / Rasecottij;* in bottom margin at left: *Federicus / Barocius / Urbinas / in-
uen;* at right: *Augo. Car. / Fe. 1595;* in the center:
*Odoardo Farnesio / Cardinali Amplissimo /
Augustinus Carracci: s / Romuleus pietati, uirum vir-
tutiqe clarum / Vnus quem Vates cantat, et orbis amat/
Hic Odoarde vides Farnesj, certa propag / Heroum,
coetus purpureiqe iubat / Tu pietati illum praestas vir-
tuteqe totus / Te canit ecce Orbis, carus es et superis.* A
worn impression, cropped to borderline, center
fold; in ink at upper right on backing paper: *2.*

Cleveland, The Cleveland Museum of Art, Gift of
Mr. and Mrs. H. Austin Hauxhurst, no. 63.456

In the thirteen years between the execution
of the *Madonna in the Clouds* (Cat. 78) and
this print after Barocci's painting of *Aeneas*
(see Cat. 54), Agostino Carracci perfected his
own engraving system, which gave him a
claim to be regarded as the foremost engraver in Italy. According to the
seventeenth-century Bolognese writer Malvasia, Agostino was so pleased with his interpretation of Barocci's painting that he
sent the painter two proof impressions. In
reply Barocci sent a letter of censure which
in Malvasia's view demonstrated the painter's jealousy of Agostino's accomplish-
ments.[1] Whether there is any truth to this
story, a fundamental difference of approach
to both printmaking and to other areas of art
must have existed between the two artists,

as is amply illustrated by comparing the *Aeneas* copy to the *Perdono* or *Annunciation* etchings (Cats. 73, 75). An oil monochrome drawing at Windsor has been identified by Wittkower as Agostino's model for the engraving.[2]

1. C. Malvasia, *Felsina pittrice: Vite dei pittori bolognesi*, 1678 (ed. M. Brascaglia, Bologna, 1971), pp. 267–268.
2. R. Wittkower, *Carracci Drawings at Windsor Castle*, London, 1952, p. 113, no. 99.

ANONYMOUS, ITALIAN, Sixteenth Century

**80** *Rest on the Return from Egypt* (Bartsch XII.36.11)

Chiaroscuro woodcut printed from two blocks, 355 x 285 mm. Inscribed in tone block on stone at lower left: *F•B•V•I•*

New York, David Tunick, Inc.

In the inventory taken of Barocci's studio shortly after his death there appears a description of the plate for the *Annunciation* (Cat. 75) and of a chiaroscuro woodcut of the Flight into Egypt: *Un'altra stampa di legno di chiaro oscuro della Madonna di Egitto.*[1] In all likelihood this print can be identified with the anonymous chiaroscuro woodcut inscribed with the letters "F.B.V.I." which is exhibited here. The print reproduces, in reverse, the *Rest on the Return from Egypt* (see Cat. 76), a composition which the artist himself copied in two autograph works and which he allowed to be engraved by Raffaello Schiaminossi in 1612. It is conceivable that the artist provided the woodcutter a

finished drawing to serve as a guide—one of his *Dissegni . . . finiti che si possono mandar in stampa* also left in his studio—[2] and regarded the woodcut executed from it to be a reasonable facsimile. Except for the incident with Agostino Carracci's copy of the *Aeneas* (Cat. 79), this print provides the only testimony of Barocci's interest in the prints executed by others after his own works.

1. Calzini, 1898, p. 107.
2. *Ibid.*, p. 107. One possible candidate for Barocci's modello is the pen study in Würzburg, no. 7192, whose measurements and design agree with those of the chiaroscuro. Moreover, although dismissed as a copy by Olsen, the drawing would seem to be acceptable as an original as well.

# Bibliography

Albertina Catalogue: *Beschreibender Katalog der Handzeichnungen in der graphischen Sammlung Albertina*, 6 vols., Vienna, 1926–1941.

Amsterdam, 1970: *Italiaanse Tekeningen uit ein Amsterdamse Particuliere Verzameling*, Amsterdam, Rijkmuseum, 1970, intro. by K. Boon.

Andrews, 1968: K. Andrews, *National Gallery of Scotland: Catalogue of Italian Drawings*, 2 vols., Cambridge, 1968.

Andrews, 1976: K. Andrews, *Old Master Drawings from the David Laing Bequest*, Edinburgh, National Gallery of Scotland, 1976, p. 8, no. 5, fig. 9.

Bacou, 1967: R. Bacou, *et al*, *Le cabinet d'un grand amateur P.-J. Mariette*, Paris, Musée du Louvre, 1967.

Bacou, 1974: R. Bacou, *Cartons d'artistes du XVᵉ an XIXᵉ siècle*, Paris, Musée du Louvre, 1974, p. 19, no. 14, pl. IX.

Baglione, 1642: G. Baglione, *Le vite de' pittori, scultori et architetti*, Rome, 1642.

Baird, 1950: T. Baird, "Two Drawings related to Baroccio's 'Entombment,'" *Record of the Art Museum, Princeton University*, IX, no. 1, 1950, pp. 11–16.

Baldinucci-Barocchi: F. Baldinucci, *Notizie de' professori del disegno* (Florence, 1681–1728), ed. P. Barocchi, 7 vols., Florence, 1974–75.

Bartsch: A. Bartsch, *Le peintre graveur*, 21 vols., Vienna, 1808–21.

Baumeister, 1940: E. Baumeister, "Neu bestimmte italienische Meisterzeichnungen in der Graphischen Sammlung in München," *Die Graphischen Künste*, V, 1940, pp. 24–26, figs. 3–4.

Bellori, 1672: G. P. Bellori, *Le vite de' pittori, scultori et architetti moderni*, Rome, 1672.

Bertelà, 1975: G. Bertelà, *Disegni di Federico Barocci*, Florence, Gabinetto Disegni e Stampe degli Uffizi, 1975. (= Florence, 1975)

Bologna, 1975: Bologna, Museo Civico, *Mostra di Federico Barocci*, 1975, cat. by A. Emiliani (drawing entries by G. Bertelà). (= Emiliani, 1975)

Bianchi, 1959: L. Bianchi, *Cento disegni della Biblioteca Communale di Urbania*, Rome, Gabinetto Nazionale della Stampe, 1959, 2nd ed.

Bodmer, 1940: H. Bodmer, "Die Entwicklung der Stechkunst des Agostino Carracci," *Die Graphische Künste*, V, 1940, pp. 64–65.

Bombe, 1913: W. Bombe, "Unbekannte Zeichnungen Federico Baroccis," *Cicerone*, V, 1913, pp. 661–672.

Borea, 1976: E. Borea, "La mostra di Federico Barocci, a cura di Andrea Emiliani . . .," *Prospettiva*, no. 4, 1976, pp. 55–61.

Borghini, 1584: R. Borghini, *Il Riposo*, Florence, 1584.

Briquet: C. M. Briquet, *Les filigranes. Dictionnaire historique des marques du papier*, 4 vols., Paris, 1907.

Calzini, 1898: E. Calzini, "Per Federico Barocci (Documenti)," *Rassegna bibliografica dell' arte italiana*, I, 1898, pp. 103–108 (reprinted in *Studi e notizie*, 1913, pp. 73–85).

Cassirer, 1913–14: K. Cassirer, "Unbekannte Zeichnungen Fed. Baroccis im Berliner Kupferstichkabinett," *Amtliche Berichte aus den königlichen Kunstsammlungen*, XXXV, 1913–14, pp. 53–54.

Cassirer, 1922: K. Cassirer, "Die Handzeichnungssammlung Pacetti," *Jahrbuch der preuszischen Kunstsammlungen*, XLIII, 1922, pp. 63–96.

*Catalogo*, 1969: *Catalogo di disegni antichi provenienti da varie collezioni private* (sale catalogue, Sotheby's of London), Florence, Palazzo Capponi, 18 Oct. 1969, nos. D71–D77.

Colasanti, 1913: A. Colasanti, "Un palinsesto sconociuto di Federico Barocci," *Bolletino d'arte*, 1913, pp. 203–208.

Degenhart, 1937: B. Degenhart, "Zur Graphologie der Handzeichnung," in: *Kunstgeschichtlichen Jahrbuch der Biblioteca Hertziana*, I, 1937, pp. 233ff.

Disertori, 1922: B. Disertori, "La Regia Calcografia: II, Il primo secolo del incisione al acquaforte," *Emporium*, LV, no. 327, Mar. 1922, pp. 136–138.

Emiliani, 1975: A. Emiliani, *Mostra di Federico Barocci*, Bologna, Museo Civico, 1975. (= Bologna, 1975)

Fenyö, 1963: I. Fenyö, "Dessins italiens inconnus du XVᵉ an XVIIIᵉ siècle," *Bulletin du Musée Hongroise des Beaux-Arts*, no. 22, 1963, p. 98, fig. 55.

Ferri, 1890: P. N. Ferri, *Catalogo riassuntivo della raccolta di disegni antichi e moderni, posseduta dalla R. Galleria degli Uffizi di Firenze*, Rome, 1890, pp. 181–183.

Ferri, 1910: P. N. Ferri, "Un disegno del Barocci negli Uffizi già attribuito al Rembrandt," *Rivista d'arte*, VII, 1910, p. 29.

Florence, 1975: Florence, Gabinetto Disegni e Stampe degli Uffizi, *Disegni di Federico Barocci*, Florence, Leo S. Olschki Editore, cat. by G. Bertelà. (= Bertelà, 1975)

Forlani, 1975: A. Forlani Tempesti, "Una scheda per il Barocci," *Prospettiva*, no. 3, 1975, pp. 48–50.

Friedländer, 1908: W. Friedländer, "Barocci, Federico," in: *Allgemeines Lexikon der bildenden Künstler*, ed. U. Thieme and F. Becker, II, Leipzig, 1908, pp. 511–513.

Friedländer, 1912: W. Friedländer, *Das Kasino Pius des Vierten* (Kunstgeschichtliche Forschungen, III), Leipzig, 1912.

Frizzoni, 1886: G. Frizzoni, *Collezione di quaranta disegni scelti dalla raccolta del Senatore Giovanni Morelli*, Milan, 1886.

Fubini, 1955: G. Fubini, *Cento tavole del codice Resta* (Fontes Ambrosiani, XXIX), Milan, 1955.

Gandellini, 1771: G. G. Gandellini, *Notizie istoriche degli intagliatori*, I, Siena, 1771.

Gibbons, 1977: F. Gibbons, *Catalogue of Italian Drawings in the Art Museum, Princeton University*, Princeton, 1977, nos. 23–28, pp. 9–10.

Giglioli, 1937: O. Giglioli, "Nuove attribuzioni per alcuni disegni degli Uffizi," *Bolletino d'arte*, XXX, 1937, pp. 544–545.

Grassi, 1940–41: L. Grassi, "Intorno al Padre Resta e al suo codice di disegni all'Ambrosiana," *Rivista del R. Instituto d'Archeologia e Storia dell'Arte*, VIII, 1940–41, pp. 175–177.

Grassi, 1947: L. Grassi, *Storia del disegno: Svolgimento del pensiero critico e un catalogo*, Rome, 1947.

Gronau, 1936: G. Gronau, *Documenti artistici urbinati*, Florence, 1936.

Günther, 1969: H. Günther, "Uffizien 135A-Eine Studie Baroccis," *Mitteilungen des Kunsthistorischen Institutes in Florenz*, XIV, Heft 2, 1969, pp. 239–246.

Heineckin, 1788: K. H. von Heineckin, *Dictionnaire des artistes dont nous avons des estampes, avec une notice détaillée de leurs ouvrages gravés*, II, Leipzig, 1788, pp. 140–151.

Hermanin, 1913: F. Hermanin, "Federico Barocci incisore," in: *Studi e notizie*, 1913, pp. 127–133.

Hind, 1923: A. M. Hind, *A Short History of Engraving and Etching*, London, 1923, p. 113.

Hubala, 1975: E. Hubala, *Federico Barocci: Handzeichnungen*, Würzburg, Martin von Wagner Museum der Universität Würzburg, Galerie-Studio, 1975 (exhibition catalogue).

Huber, 1800: M. Huber, *Manuel des curieux et des amateurs de l'art*, III, Zurich, 1800.

Jaffé, 1977: M. Jaffé, *Rubens in Italy*, Oxford, 1977, pp. 52–53 and *passim*.

Kristeller, 1921: P. Kristeller, *Kupferstich und Holzschnitt in vier Jahrhunderten*, Berlin, 1921.

Krommes, 1912: R. Krommes, *Studien zu Federigo Barocci*, Leipzig, 1912.

Lanzi, 1795–96: L. Lanzi, *Storia pittorica della Italia*, I, Bassano, 1795–96, pp. 474–477.

Laran, 1959: J. Laran, *L'Estampe*, I, Paris, 1959.

M. Lavin, 1954–55: M. Aronberg Lavin, "A Late Work by Barocci," *Metropolitan Museum of Art Bulletin*, XIII, 1954–55, pp. 266–271.

M. Lavin, 1956: M. Aronberg Lavin, "Colour Study in Barocci's Drawing," *Burlington Magazine*, LXLVIII, 1956, pp. 435–439.

M. Lavin, 1964: M. Aronberg Lavin, "Barocci, Federico," in: *Dizionario biografico degli italiani*, VI, Rome, 1964, pp. 423–428.

LeBlanc: C. LeBlanc, *Manuel de l'amateur de'estampes*, I, Paris, 1854.

Linnenkamp, 1961: R. Linnenkamp, "Zwei unbekannte Selbstbildnisse von Federigo Barocci," *Pantheon*, XIX, 1961, pp. 46–50.

Lippmann, 1896: F. Lippmann, *Der Kupferstich*, Berlin, 1896, p. 178.

Lugt: F. Lugt, *Les marques de collections de dessins et d'estampes*, Amsterdam, 1921; *Supplément*, The Hague, 1956.

Malaguzzi Valeri, 1906: F. Malaguzzi Valeri, *I disegni della R. Pinacoteca di Brera*, Milan, 1906.

Malmstrom, 1969: R. Malmstrom, "A Note on the Architectural Setting of Federico Barocci's 'Aeneas' Flight from Troy,'" *Marsyas*, XIV, 1968–69, pp. 43–47.

Mariette, 1741: P. J. Mariette, *Description sommaire des dessins des grands maîtres . . . du Cabinet de Feu M. Crozat*, Paris, 1741.

Mariette, *Abecedario*, ca. 1750–54: P. J. Mariette, "Abecedario," ed. P. de Chennevières and A. de Montaiglon, in: *Archives de l'art francais*, I, 1851–53, pp. 68–73.

Mayor, 1947: A. Hyatt Mayor, "Visions and Visionary," *The Metropolitan Museum of Art Bulletin*, V, no. 6, 1947, pp. 157–163.

Meder, 1919: J. Meder, *Die Handezeichnung, Ihre Technik und Entwicklung*, Vienna, 1919.

Middeldorf, 1939: U. Middeldorf, "Three Italian Drawings in Chicago," *Art in America*, XXVII, 1939, pp. 11–14, fig. 1.

Molajoli, 1934: B. Molajoli, "Disegni di Federico Barocci," *Rassegna marchigiana*, XII, 1934, pp. 242–250.

Mongan, 1932: A. Mongan, "Federigo Baroccio (1526–1612)," *Old Master Drawings*, VII, 1932, pp. 5–6, pls. 12–13.

Morassi, 1937: A. Morassi, *Disegni antichi dalla Collezione Rasini in Milano*, Milan, 1937.

*Mostra, Florence, 1912–13*: R. Soprintendenza alle Gallerie e Musei della Toscana, *Mostra dei cartoni e disegni di Federigo Baroccio*, Florence, Gabinetto dei Disegni della R. Galleria degli Uffizi, 1912–13 (Bergamo, 1913), cat. by G. Poggi, P. N. Ferri, and F. di Pietro.

Muraro, 1965: M. Muraro, "Studiosi, collezionisti e opere d'arte veneta dalle lettere al Cardinale Leopoldo de'Medici," *Saggie e memorie di storia dell'arte*, no. 4, 1965, pp. 65–83.

Nagler: G. K. Nagler, *Die Monogrammisten . . .*, Munich, 1858–79.

Nagler, *Künstler-Lexicon*, 1835: G. K. Nagler, *Neues allgemeines Künstler-Lexicon*, I, Munich, 1835, pp. 278–280.

Nagler, *Künstler-Lexikon*, 1885: G. K. Nagler, *Allgemeines Künstler-Lexikon*, ed. by J. Meyer, H. Lücke, and H. v. Tschudi, III, Leipzig, 1885, pp. 27–30.

Noë, 1954: H. Noë, *Carel van Mander en Italie*, 's-Gravenhage, 1954, pp. 165–170, 265–269.

Oberhuber, 1966: K. Oberhuber, *Die Kunst der Graphik III: Renaissance in Italien 16. Jahrhundert*, Vienna, Graphische Sammlung Albertina, catalogue of exhibition, 1966, pp. 167–168.

Olsen, 1955: H. Olsen, "Federico Barocci: A Critical Study in Italian Cinquecento Painting," *Figura*, VI, 1955.

Olsen, 1962: H. Olsen, *Federico Barocci*, Copenhagen, 1962.

Olsen, *Artes*, 1965: "Some Drawings by Federico Barocci : 1. Drawings in East-Berlin; 2. Studies of Landscape," *Artes*, I, 1965, pp. 17–32.

Olsen, "Disegni anatomici," 1965: H. Olsen, "Disegni anatomici di Federico Barocci," *Atti della VI Biennale della Marca e dello Studio Firmano*, Fermo, 1965, pp. 256–264.

Olsen, 1966: H. Olsen, "A Drawing by Federico Barocci in the Louvre," *Artes*, II, 1966, pp. 72–74.

Olsen, 1969: H. Olsen, "Eine Kompositionsskizze von Federico Barocci," *Jahrbuch der Staatlichen Kunstsammlungen in Baden-Württemberg*, VI, 1969, pp. 49–54.

*Omaggio a Leopoldo*, 1976: A. Forlani Tempesti, A. M. Petrioli Tofani, P. Barocchi, and G. Chiarini di Anna, *Omaggio a Leopoldo: Parte 1, Designi*, Florence, Cabinetto Disegni e Stampe degli Uffizi, 1976.

Parker, 1956: K. T. Parker, *Catalogue of the Collection of Drawings in the Ashmolean Museum*, II, Italian Schools, Oxford, 1956.

Petrucci, 1943: A. Petrucci, "I 'fondi persi' del Barocci," *Primato*, IV, no. 7, 1943.

Petrucci, *Panorama*, 1964: A. Petrucci, *Panorama della incisione italiana: il cinquecento*, Rome, 1964, pp. 63–65.

Petrucci, *Dizionario*, 1964: A. Petrucci, "Barocci, Federico," in: *Dizionario biografico degli italiani*, VI, Rome, pp. 426–428.

di Pietro, 1909: F. di Pietro, "Un disegno del Barocci all'Albertina già attribuito al Domenichino," *Rivista d'arte*, VI, 1909, pp. 297–301.

di Pietro, 1913: F. di Pietro, *Disegni sconosciuti e disegni finora non identificati di Federico Barocci negli Uffizi*, Florence, 1913.

Pillsbury, *M.D.*, 1976: E. Pillsbury, "Barocci at Bologna and Florence," *Master Drawings*, XIV, no. 1, 1976, pp. 56–64, pls. 33–39.

Pillsbury, *Y.U.A.G. Bulletin*, 1976: E. Pillsbury, "Federico Barocci's 'Fossombrone Madonna': An Unknown Drawing," *Yale University Art Gallery Bulletin*, XXXVI, no. 1, Fall 1976, pp. 20–25.

Pittaluga, 1930: M. Pittaluga, *L'incisore italiana nel cinquecento*, Milan, 1930, pp. 313–317.

Popham-Wilde: A. E. Popham and J. Wilde, *The Italian Drawings of the XV and XVI Centuries in the Collection of His Majesty the King at Windsor Castle*, London, 1949.

Popham, 1966: A. E. Popham, "An Unnoticed Drawing by Federico Barocci," *Master Drawings*, IV, 1966, pp. 149–150, pl. 17.

Richards, 1961: L. Richards, "Federico Barocci: A Study for 'Aeneas' Flight from Troy,'" *Bulletin of the Cleveland Museum of Art*, XLVIII, 1961, pp. 63–65.

Rosenberg, 1963: J. Rosenberg, "St. Francis in the Chapel ('Il Perdono di S. Francesco d'Assisi') by Federico Barocci-Acquisitions," *Fogg Art Museum*, 1963, pp. 10–12.

Santarelli, 1870: E. Santarelli, et al, *Catalogo della raccolta di disegni autografi antichi e moderni donata dal Prof. Emilio Santarelli alla Reale Galleria di Firenze*, Florence, 1870.

Schlosser, 1913: J. von Schlosser, "Aus der Bildnerwerkstatt der Renaissance: Zur Rolle der Kleinmodelle im Studio des Künstlers und des Amateur," *Wiener Jahrbuch*, 1913, pp. 100–118.

Schmarsow, 1909: A. Schmarsow, "Federigo Barocci: Ein Begründer des Barockstils in der Malerei," *Abhandlungen der philologisch-historischen Klasse der Königl. Sächsischen Gesellschaft der Wissenschaften*, XXVI, 1909, no. 4, pp. 1–168.

Schmarsow, I–IIIB: A. Schmarsow, "Federigo Baroccis Zeichnungen: Eine kritische Studie. I. Die Zeichnungen in der Sammlung der Uffizien zu Florenz. II. Die Zeichnungen in den übrigen Sammlungen Italiens. III. Die Zeichnungen in den Sammlungen ausserhalb Italiens: A. Öffentliche Sammlungen im Westlichen Europa; B. Öffentliche Sammlungen in östlichen Europa," *Abhandlungen der philologisch-historischen Klasse der Konig. Sächsischen Gesellschaft der Wissenschaften*, XXVI, no. 5, 1909, pp. 1–40; XXVIII, no. 3, 1911, pp. 1–46; XXIX, no. 2, 1911, pp. 1–32; XXX, no. 1, 1914, pp. 1–44 respectively.

Shaw, 1969: J. Byam Shaw, "Two Drawings by Barocci," *Miscellanea J. Q. van Regteren Altena*, Amsterdam, 1969, pp. 88–89, pl. 296.

Shearman, 1976: J. Shearman, "Barocci at Bologna and Florence," *Burlington Magazine*, CXVIII, 1976, pp. 49–54.

B. Smith, 1970: B. Smith, "A Drawing by Barocci," *Bulletin of the Art Gallery of South Australia*, XXXII, no. 2, Oct. 1970, n.p., repr. in color.

Smith, 1970: G. Smith, "A Drawing for the Interior Decoration of the Casino of Pius IV," *Burlington Magazine*, CXII, 1970, pp. 108–110.

Smith, 1973: G. Smith, "Two Drawings by Federico Barocci," *Bulletin of the Detroit Institute of Arts*, LII, nos. 2–3, 1973, pp. 83–91.

Smith, 1977: G. Smith, *The Casino of Pius IV*, Princeton, 1977.

Stix, 1925: A. Stix, *Handzeichnungen aus der Albertina, begründet von J. Meder, N.F. II. Bd.: Italienische Meister des 14.–16. Jahrhunderts*, Vienna, 1925.

*Studi e notizie*, 1913: *Studi e notizie su Federico Barocci*, ed. by La Brigata Urbinate degli Amici dei Monumenti, Florence, 1913.

Tschudi Madsen, 1959: S. Tschudi Madsen, "Federico Barocci's 'Noli me tangere' and two Cartoons," *Burlington Magazine*, CI, 1959, pp. 273–277 (reprinted from "Barocci-tegninger i Norge," *Kunst og Kultur*, no. 41, 1958, pp. 1–16).

Van Mander, 1604: C. van Mander, *Het Schilderboek*, Haarlem, 1604, fol. 186b–187a.

Vasari-Milanesi: G. Vasari, *Le vite de' più eccellenti pittori, scultori ed architettori . . .* (1568), ed. G. Milanesi, 9 vols., Florence, 1878–85.

Venturi, 1934: A. Venturi, *Storia dell'arte italiana*, IX. 7, Milan, 1934, pp. 879–953.

Voss, 1920: H. Voss, *Die Malerei der Spätrenaissance in Rom und Florenz*, II, Berlin, 1920, pp. 472–498.

Watrous, 1957: J. Watrous, *The Craft of Old Master Drawings*, Madison, 1957.

Weihrauch, 1937–38: H. R. Weihrauch, "Einige unbekannte italienische Handzeichnungen in der Graphischen Sammlung zu München," *Münchener Jahrbuch der bildenden Kunst*, XII, 1937–38, pp. XXXI–XXXII.

Wickhoff, 1892: F. Wickhoff, "Die italienischen Handzeichnungen der Albertina," *Jahrbuch der Kunsthistorischen Sammlungen des allerhöchsten Kaiserhauses*, XIII, 1892, pp. CCXXIII–CCXXIV.

Winner, 1964: M. Winner, *Entwurf und Ausführung, Italienische Druckgraphik und ihre Vorzeichnungen von Barocci bis Piranesi*, Berlin, Staatliche Museen, Kupferstichkabinett, exhibition catalogue, no. 2, pp. 8–10.

# Lenders to the Exhibition

(Numbers refer to catalogue entries)

BACK COVER ILLUSTRATION
Federico Barocci,
*Madonna in the Clouds,*
etching and engraving.
(Cat. 74)

Typesetting: Connecticut Printers and Typographic Art Inc.

Printing: The Meriden Gravure Company

Design and production supervision: The Yale University Printing Service